PLEASE
BE WITH
ME

A SONG FOR MY FATHER,
DUANE ALLMAN

Galadrielle Allman

SPIEGEL & GRAU NEW YORK

Please Be with Me is a work of nonfiction.
Some names and identifying details have been changed.

Published in the United States by Spiegel & Grau, an imprint of Random House,
a division of Random House LLC, a Penguin Random House Company, New York.

SPIEGEL & GRAU and the HOUSE colophon are registered trademarks of
Random House LLC.

Grateful acknowledgment is made to the following for permission to
reprint previously published material:

Tim Buckley Music: Excerpt from "Once I Was" by Tim Buckley and Larry Beckett,
copyright © 1968 and copyright renewed 1996 by Tim Buckley Music (ASCAP) & BMG
Platinum Songs o/b/o Third Story Music (BMI). All rights reserved. Used by permission.

Elijah Blue Music, Alfred Music Publishing Co., Inc.: Excerpt from "Melissa" written by
Gregg Allman and Steve Alaimo, copyright © 1972 by Elijah Blue Music/Unichappell
Music Inc./EMI Longitude Music. All rights reserved. Used by permission.

Linda Miller: Three letters written by Berry Oakley. Used by permission.

All credits for reproduction of photographs can be found on pages 371–72.

Library of Congress Cataloging-in-Publication Data
Allman, Galadrielle, author.
Please be with me: a song for my father, Duane Allman / Galadrielle Allman.
pages cm
ISBN 978-1-4000-6894-4
eBook ISBN 978-1-58836-960-4
1. Allman, Duane, 1946–1971. 2. Allman, Galadrielle. 3. Rock musicians—United
States—Biography. 4. Allman Brothers Band. I. Title.
ML419.A565A45 2014
787.87'166092—dc23
[B] 2013046247

Printed in the United States of America on acid-free paper

www.spiegelandgrau.com

2 4 6 8 9 7 5 3 1

First Edition

Book design by Liz Cosgrove

*This story is for the rambling men, the lovely children,
and every hungry woman who's been in my place before.*

Where the myth fails, human love begins. Then we love a human being, not our dream, but a human being with flaws.

—Anaïs Nin

Contents

Introduction

Beyond the circles of light cast over the band's waiting instruments, I felt the vast, moving crowd in the darkness. My mother stood at the edge of the stage, holding me on her hip, my head resting on her shoulder. I was four years old. My uncle Gregg walked up to us, his long blond hair tucked behind one ear, smiling at me with heavy-lidded eyes. He wore a white suit, rings on his fingers, and a silver ankh around his neck. He smelled of warm cologne and cigarettes, and looked as clean and pretty as a doll. He lifted me out of my mother's arms and walked a few steps into the white light. I remember the whistling cheer that washed over the stage like a wave when the audience saw him. Little flames from lighters, raised in outstretched hands, shone like distant boats on a night sea. Gregg spoke into a microphone at center stage, holding me curled against him, my face hidden in his neck. His low whisky voice called out, "This is my brother's little girl, and he lives on through her."

He lifted me out into the darkness and the whistles turned into a roar.

. . .

My father is killed in the first paragraph of every article ever written about him. His life story is told backward, always beginning at the end: in the road, his motorcycle down, his body broken. People linger over the wreckage as if it says something meaningful about his life. Duane is most often described as a rock star, although he did not live long enough to know how famous he would become. His brief, brilliant life has become mythic, a cautionary tale and a cliché: Live fast, die young.

Duane Allman's story is more than a tragedy; it is a true romance. He fell in love with his guitar and gave his heart away. At fifteen years old, he often stayed up all night, bent over on the couch, his fingers wandering the frets of his guitar in the dark. His mother would come home late from the restaurant where she worked and find him playing with reddened fingertips and a crick in his neck, deaf to the sound of the front door. She'd go to sleep and wake in the morning to find him in the exact posture he had been in the night before, still playing. When she asked him what he was doing, pushing himself so hard, he said, "Mama, I'm searching for my sound. I'd go hungry to play this guitar."

The sound he found helped change the way the world perceived the South. White southern boys were most known for backward thinking and racist cruelty. My father's guitar sang out idealistic, astounding music that tipped that notion over. The Allman Brothers Band made every southerner with a radio proud of himself. Their music described a world of tough towns and darkened woods, men laughing down the length of beer-soaked bars or sitting alone in their rooms, waiting by their telephones. You can hear them yearning in their songs, and growling out their defiance, refusing to be chained. The Allman Brothers took the blues, the root of all American music, and electrified it in a way no American band ever had with an integrated band in the segregated South. It was revolutionary.

Duane played guitar so beautifully the world came to him. Eric Clapton, Aretha Franklin, Wilson Pickett, King Curtis, Boz

Scaggs. Famous recording artists sought out this young man to record at FAME Studios and Muscle Shoals Sound in Muscle Shoals, Alabama; Atlantic Records in New York; and Criteria Studios in Miami. His remarkable talent brought him the opportunity to build a band of his own, and he formed a group of players that matched his skill and his commitment to playing, note for note. They raised the bar for one another, each honing his skill against the other, blade against stone. The powerful chemistry between the Brothers came together so fast it seemed magical and destined.

The Allman Brothers Band became known for their epic live performances, six men synched up and improvising in the jazz style. No two shows were the same. Success came to them very quickly. Inside of three years, a private jet replaced their tour bus, which had replaced the Winnebago and their first Econoline van. Dive bars and public parks where they played for free overflowed into beautiful old theaters, until stadiums were packed with thousands of fans. They built their following, playing hundreds of shows from the Fillmore in San Francisco to the Fillmore East in New York City. They called traveling from one coast to the other their commute, no joke. Drugs, decadence, and a growing darkness came along, tucked into their pockets. The Allman Brothers Band was the number-one band in America in 1972, and by then my father was already gone.

According to *Rolling Stone* magazine, Duane Allman is remembered as one of the greatest rock guitarists of all time, second only to Jimi Hendrix. Just a few short years into his remarkable career, after creating several of the best-loved rock-and-roll albums ever recorded, he was killed in a motorcycle accident at the intersection of Hillcrest Avenue and Bartlett Street in Macon, Georgia, on October 29, 1971. He was twenty-four years old and I was two. We never had the chance to know each other.

The band continued on without my father, and my mom took me to Allman Brothers concerts every year when I was a kid. We went with groups of women and children, all related in some way to the band. Our mothers made the annual pilgrimage to return us to our nomadic tribe, the band of men we had long since parted from, through death, divorce, or distance.

The Brothers played stadiums in the seventies, massive domes of concrete rising like dark castles on the outskirts of town. My mother carried me through the back doors, which were guarded like a fortress by burly guards in satin tour jackets, their arms crossed in front of their chests. She would stick her backstage pass to her blue-jeaned thigh and sail through the gauntlet with a mention of our names. In every city, backstage was the same—a rabbit warren of hallways leading to small gray rooms glowing with fluorescent light. Mom switched me from one hip to the other, then sat my squirming self on a metal folding chair. We waited for what seemed like hours for the band to arrive, picking at trays of cold cuts and digging our hands into iced buckets full of drinks. We kids gobbled handfuls of M&M's and chased each other around the tight passageways until someone settled us down. Clusters of people dressed in wild finery waited in the hallways: young blondes in hot pants, grizzled guys in leather vests, and moguls in three-piece suits. You could feel how much everyone wanted into the rooms where we waited alone.

The band would finally arrive, gliding out of their limousines after being driven a few short blocks from their hotel. They were protected from their shouting fans by sawhorse barricades while their road manager steered them quickly through the back door with a hand on their backs. Sometimes the musicians greeted us with kisses and called out our names. Other times they gazed watery-eyed over our heads and disappeared quickly behind closed doors. We never knew which way it would be, warm or cold. I came to accept either possibility, and learned to look for Red Dog, the legendary roadie, who lit up like a firecracker whenever he saw me. He carried me with one wiry arm while he strutted from one side of the stage to the other, taking care of business with a joint dangling from his lip. He kissed my cheeks and called me princess. He told me I looked just like my daddy, and got tears in his eyes.

I loved his wild red curls and gruff, scratchy drawl. He may have been a badass, but he was also a prince.

Once the music started, we were told not to cross the lines of white gaff tape dividing the black floor of the stage from the wings, and never to walk behind the drums. The first note played changed the very air into a charged blast of electric love. A wave of joy came over the bodies pressed against the stage; you could feel it, like heat. I danced beside the dusty black curtains, twirling my skirt and galloping in place like a pony.

The amps were so loud that after a few songs my limbs grew heavy and all I wanted was sleep. The complex cry of guitars and rumbling drums spread a fever through my little body. I'd crawl behind a road case to hide, or reach up for any known adult and beg to be held. On rare occasions I was carried into the crowd, a flood of undulating bodies flashing smiles in the multicolored light, the sweet and sour stink of weed and sweat nearly suffocating me. The band loomed high above us, a new and surprising perspective.

There is no time in my memory before I knew their songs by heart: the clapping crescendo of "Revival," the thumping bass intro to "Whipping Post," "Jessica" swelling with delighted piano runs. I knew every note before knowing their names: the familiar rise and fall of chorus and verse, a bridge to my world of dreams.

After the final encore, while the crowd stomped and screamed for more, the remaining members of my father's band walked into the wings—Gregg and Dickey, Jaimoe and Butch—and as they passed, I knew not to reach for them. I could see their fatigue and relief, the sweat soaking through their shirts. They climbed directly into their chauffeured cars and were gone before the stadium seats were half empty.

Sometimes we met them back at their hotels and visited. I watched TV in icy air-conditioned rooms while Mom talked to her old friends. We kids ate ice cream and french fries, delivered by room service, then raced in the hallways and pushed every button in the elevator. I would finally fall asleep tucked under a coat on top of a carefully made bed, only to wake up the next morning in my own room, a world away, remembering nothing of the long ride home, crushed with disappointment that they were gone. Or worse, the night would end immediately with the music, my mother leading whiny me away by my tightly held hand directly from the stage. She'd carry me through the endless, trash-strewn parking lot to our red Chevy Impala and drive us home.

Like every circus, they folded their tent and left town before daylight.

This grand excursion happened every year the band toured, and represented the most tangible connection I had to my father. Seeing the band play was never balanced by more traditional family time spent with the people who knew my father best. They lived on the road during those years. They were gypsy troubadours who were most at home onstage. I was raised in a world of women and children, and the main things we had in common with the band were our shared losses and our love of the music, which was always a force of good in all of our lives.

No one believed in the power of the music and the Brotherhood more than my father had. His spark set their fire. He was their driving wheel. Losing him irrevocably changed everyone who knew him, and literally changed the way the world felt to all of us. It seemed impossible that someone who lived so fiercely, and with such hunger for all that life could offer, could be taken so suddenly.

The void he left can never be filled. It is that simple.

I wanted to fill that space with knowledge of him, but I did not know how and the confusion that created was constant. The force of my longing for my father was a defining part of me from the beginning, and nothing could touch it.

My mother took very few things with us when we left Macon in 1971, after she and Duane separated. Duane gave me his stuffed toy Eeyore, the worried donkey from Winnie the Pooh, for safekeeping. Donna took back the elaborate valentine she had made him from their bedroom wall and tucked her small bundle of letters from him into her suitcase along with the tab of LSD and the Seconal he gave her as an odd and uncharacteristic parting gift into her purse. The beautiful Mexican silver bracelet he had given her was lost and they never wore wedding rings.

There was not a single photograph of the three of us together.

Precious little evidence of Duane made its way into our successive homes. Most of our pictures of him were the same publicity stills reprinted in the press. I didn't have his clothing or trinkets to treasure and cling to. But his music was everywhere, and it became an increasingly important source of comfort and connection as I grew up. My mother would say, "Listen to him play. His music is the best of him."

Duane's story can only end one way. It ends with goodbye. But you can live forever inside a goodbye. I have, all my life so far. What better way to live in longing than with a song, repeated endlessly? How many daughters can lift the needle of a record player and trace backward to the first groove in an album and hear their fathers, young, strong, and alive? I count myself lucky for this, the luckiest of the unlucky. I have no memories of my father, but even as a young child I understood he was not lost completely. I could find him in my own pale face and red hair. He is in my walk, with shoulders held high; his good friend Johnny Sandlin told me that. My mother tells me I am his when I twist my mouth into his half grin or roll my eyes at her. His brother says I look just like him when I cry. I know his friends are seeing him in me when something passes through their faces that looks a little like fear. It's troubling to feel like I have disappeared for a moment, eclipsed behind a memory of him, but I have grown to like it. When I see people startle, I feel linked to my father in an undeniable way.

My mother didn't talk about my father easily. I wasn't raised with stories of Duane's adventures or tales of their love. My father's world was a perilous one, especially for women and children, and she felt we were lucky to have left it when we did. His story was not child-safe. She says I was a sunny little girl who woke up happy every day. I was her lifeline in the wake of his death, and moment to moment, I helped her heal. If I sometimes bit other children or flew into tiny fits of rage, those things didn't seem dire or unusual. She didn't see my bad behavior as an expression of loss. Mom believed I was protected from mourning by my ignorance and my age. She sincerely hoped I would never really know all we had lost. How could I miss a father I had not known?

In turn, I saw her sorrow and it frightened me. Donna sometimes withdrew into a part of herself I couldn't reach, and I watched her very closely, looking for a way in. Her fragility and vulnerability were barely masked by her fierce defensiveness and silence. Asking about my dad would only hurt her, and my longing to know him wasn't worth causing her more pain. That was my belief.

We were both wrong, and it took decades for me to tell her so.

I was forced to look out into the wider world for more public sources of information about Duane. I found him playing on my radio and saw his picture on album covers in the "A" bin of every record store. In this digital age when every current Allman Brothers show is recorded and filmed in high definition and immediately launched on YouTube, it is still very rare to find ephemera from "the Duane Era," as fans call the years 1969–71. Still, even after all this time, new artifacts emerge and make their way to me, creating an unsettling counterpoint between my curiosity and the passion of his fans.

When I was sixteen, I slipped into a head shop on Polk Street in San Francisco to buy a pack of cigarettes, only to be confronted by a giant tapestry printed with the same photograph of my father that I had framed on my bedroom wall. His eyes upon me, I slunk away, ashamed, knowing I was too young to smoke.

Going through stacks of old magazines in a junk store in Athens, Georgia, when I was eighteen, I came across a yellowed copy of *Rolling Stone* from 1971 with a tribute to my father on the cover. The proprietor, a man in a top hat and cape, swooped down and grabbed the carefully bagged newsprint out of my hands and barked, "That is not for sale! You have no idea the value of that! Do you even know who Duane Allman is?"

He turned his back on me and marched away with his treasure, muttering to himself.

I didn't know what to say. Would it feel worse if he believed me or if he didn't? I thought about showing him my high school ID card. Would he embrace me and pour out his story of an Allman Brothers concert that changed his life? Would I suddenly be a celebrity guest instead of an annoying girl pawing at his prized possessions? Why did I deserve that glory? What could I tell him about Duane that he didn't already know? Oddly, both options made me feel like a con, so I said nothing and ducked back out into the street, anonymously.

When I turned twenty-one, I inherited the only objects my father ever really loved: two Gibson Les Paul guitars carved out of flaming hardwood. Twiggs Lyndon, the Brothers' tour manager and Duane's close friend, traded his beloved 1939 Ford Opera Coupe to Gregg for Duane's most treasured guitar and kept it safe for me. Donna lent the other to Joey Marshall, the man who introduced her to Duane. Joey and Twiggs's three brothers—John, A.J., and Skoots—returned the guitars to me in remarkable acts of generosity, considering their escalating value. The Lyndon brothers told me they knew if they had kept the guitar, Twiggs's ghost would have visited each of them, shaking a lit Kool cigarette and yelling, "I told you to give that guitar to Galadrielle, damn it!"

After hiding the guitar under my mother's bed for years, I loaned both instruments to the Rock and Roll Hall of Fame in Cleveland, Ohio. Before I shipped them away, I touched them, but only very lightly. The guitars lay encased in their worn lilac-velvet-lined traveling cases, as solid and silky as coffins. I pressed my fingertips gently to their steel strings, but I didn't pick up either of them. I didn't want to disturb the sense that my father had held them. Now they are just beautiful pieces of sculpture, alone in the museum's dim light.

There are people who hungrily research my father's gear, to learn the gauge and action of his strings, their necks' precise widths. They look for serial numbers on the headstocks to find out the year the instruments were built. They can name the color of the stains rubbed into the guitars' bodies and they know when Duane traded one instrument for another, and why. They must hope to learn the mystery of how he made his sounds. While I treasure his instruments, they seem abandoned to me, silenced by his absence in an irrevocable way, and I know his secrets are not in them. Like breath leaving a body, the music went with him and is gone.

When I was in my early thirties, the cuff of a fancy silk shirt Eric Clapton gave my father during the *Layla* sessions appeared in my mailbox, sent by a stranger who said she once dated my uncle Gregg. The fragile purple silk shirt, decorated with batik peacocks, had been washed in a machine and was all but destroyed. The cuff was frayed and threadbare, with one small button barely hanging on. She wrote that she had auctioned the rest of the shirt on eBay, and the back panel alone had sold for fifteen thousand dollars. She planned to use the money to pay her way through school. Her letter continued for pages, with intimate details of her life. She told me not to be angry with my father for leaving me, but to be proud of his accomplishments.

I marveled at the faded scrap of cloth in my hand, amazed that it had found its way to me, thirty years after it was his. I kept it in a box on my desk for several years, then loaned it to the museum that was built inside the home where I learned to walk: the Allman Brothers Museum at the Big House. The cuff is locked in a glass case in the room where the band once practiced. It rests beside Duane's award from the Rock and Roll Hall of Fame. Later, another fan showed me a necklace made from a few threads from the same shirt, suspended in a tiny glass vial hanging from a string. There are apparently several like it floating around out there.

A group of friends pooled a ridiculously large sum of money to buy me a pair of very eccentric orange and black suede bowling shoes that belonged to my dad. Duane had left them behind in a girlfriend's apartment in 1971, and the landlord had held them for ransom for decades. I sat with my hands tucked inside them for a long time.

Clues about my father are scattered everywhere and I have learned to make a feast of scraps. A postcard Duane sent to a childhood friend, decorated with peace signs; lyrics to a song written on motel stationery; a little lock of his hair wrapped in velvet; glass pill bottles he used to play slide guitar; intricately tooled guitar straps; and a golden mushroom medallion he never got the chance to pick up from the jeweler. Ticket stubs, concert posters, and, most horribly, the hospital records from the day he died. The detritus of my father's life is bought and sold. Everything he touched has turned to gold. The fragments of his life belong to strangers—strangers who do not consider themselves strangers.

Last year, for the first time in my life, I saw a photograph of my parents together. In it, my mother is still wearing the hospital ID bracelet from my birth and my father is holding a baby rattle. They look young and fairly terrified. I stumbled on it while looking at a woman's blog under the heading "Wail on, Skydog!" She had made it her mission to post a different photograph of Duane every Wednesday for several years. She is one of the many thousands of Allman Brothers fans connected by the lore of the band's beginnings and the intensity of their music. All I could think when I saw it was how much it would have meant to me to see it before, when I was younger.

Grown men have challenged me, saying they have seen more Allman Brothers Band concerts than I have. Cashiers have seen my last name on my credit card and held up long lines to tell me their concert memories. I have found myself in a tiny backstage elevator surrounded by four people, all wearing Duane Allman T-shirts. None of them knew who I was, and I wasn't about to tell. I have met more than one man with my father's face tattooed on his arm.

I have thrown loose change into the hats of street musicians in New York, New Orleans, and San Francisco while they randomly played "Midnight Rider" as I walked by. I envy the simple comfort and pleasure that fans take from my father's music, and the happy extended family they feel they share. It confounds me that I am not alone in loving and missing him.

I have listened intently to every song Duane ever recorded. I have hunted through magazine articles and newspaper clippings found in cardboard boxes in my granny's garage. I have trolled the Internet for hundreds of hours, lost in the deep recesses of chat rooms and digitized archives. Somehow, it all made me feel like I knew less instead of more. The spotlight rendered Duane too simple and too perfect to know. The public stories were like Zen koans or fairy tales, recalling moments of kindness, wisdom, and genius. Lists of concert dates and long discussions of his influences and gear left me wanting something I could not name. The higher Duane ascended into the ether of fame and adulation, the more he felt lost to me in every meaningful way.

I wanted something more personal. I wanted a way in to the beautiful beaded, bell-bottomed, patchouli-scented world captured in my mother's sparse photo albums. There's a picture of her wearing Duane's striped pants, reclining on their bed in the Big House looking like a nymph. Duane holds me in his arms in another, my favorite, taken in their Bond Street apartment, standing in front of an Egyptian wall hanging from the 1904 World's Fair in St. Louis. He's wearing a red T-shirt that says "City Slicker" and grinning through his orange muttonchop mustache. I have treasured these images as fragile proof of our love. I have tried to build a lasting and resilient sense of where I come from.

My mother's silence and the transient nature of my connection to the men in the band conspired to make me feel like a bit of an outsider in my own family. Privacy and secrecy seemed to be twin values held by all, and my curiosity about my father seemed to run counter to them. My wires were crossed. I was confused about what was public and what was private, and which side of the line my desire to know about Duane fell on.

I dreaded pursuing his story as a reporter would, by asking uncomfortable questions and following every lead. I couldn't imagine interviewing my family, but I knew that if I didn't I would never be satisfied. At concerts, I had learned how to contain myself and wait for the proper time to talk. Now I read the silence of my father's friends as a signal to back off, don't ask. Wouldn't they have told me about him by now if they wanted to? I couldn't risk losing my place in our family by asking them to revisit the pain of losing Duane. Wasn't asking my uncle for his memories very like a stranger asking him for his autograph? Wanting to know made me feel like everyone else who wants to know; it put me on the outside looking in. I was afraid to be another person with my hand out to the band, longing to feel special and acknowledged.

One of the rare stories my mother did tell me was particularly haunting. She went to see the Brothers play a concert in Love Valley, North Carolina, and my father didn't expect her to be there. When she and Linda Oakley, wife of Brothers bassist Berry Oakley, showed up, he asked her what she was doing there. He wanted her to be home with me. He was uptight and exhausted and said he was dreading an interview with someone important from the press. That night, he got very drunk, and instead of going into the bathroom, he threw off the covers of their hotel room bed and peed on the radiator. The next morning, Donna didn't say a word about it, but before he left, Duane fixed her with a glare and said, "Don't go airing our dirty laundry and putting our business in the street."

That single story really slowed me down. I dimly imagined crossing that line, invading the privacy of the people I love. I wasn't sure what would happen, but I knew it would isolate me even more. I didn't feel entitled to ask, and I certainly didn't feel entitled to write about what I learned for public consumption, and writing our story was at least part of what I wanted. I told myself that kind of public exposure would be the ultimate betrayal. But I wanted to be an artist in my own right, and books were my love. Writing was the only thing I ever wanted to do, and I was born into an incredible story: an epic tale starring a hero for the ages. How could I resist?

The Allman Brothers Band has a particularly juicy backstory: bikers and booze, heroin and teenage groupies, even murder and prison. My mother moved us away from the band's increasingly dangerous world when I was still a toddler, but I was aware of the darkness very early. My curiosity was stronger than my fear and my eyes were always open. There is a lot of dirty laundry in the extended Allman Brothers family and I came to realize that most if not all of it has been strung up and left flapping in the breeze for decades. I told myself I had nothing to fear.

I let myself feel entitled to know where I came from, very gradually. I was especially curious about the stories that the women around me had to tell. Their lives were nowhere in evidence in magazines or books. The men's life on the road was fairly well documented, but I knew it wasn't the whole story. For the family, the music was not everything. The band was only one aspect of who the men were and who they could have been. The road took them farther away from who we needed them to be. They came home less connected to the people they left behind.

Their music is beautiful and blameless, and now it is all we have. Allman Brothers songs capture and express the essence of an ideal family none of us got to have. The music doubled back and returned to us, even after it carried the men we loved and needed away. The world the brothers and sisters made together didn't last, but it is forever immortalized in music, and the songs will not fade away.

I was finally brave enough to ask for their memories—my mother and grandmother, the wives and children of our extended tribe, Duane's cousin and friends. I added them to the memories of the band and their crew and greatly enriched my picture of Duane, as a man and a musician.

My father did something most of us are desperate to do—he found his perfect mode of expression and he used it to move people. Playing guitar was his passion. It was all he ever wanted to do, and he did it with determination and joy. He became a conduit, creating music that seemed to come through him from a higher source. He hadn't even begun to reach his full potential as a player or as a person. Duane was fearless and he was never satisfied.

Learning about him changed my life completely. Finding the courage to ask questions and write about him has helped me begin to heal. I feel more deeply integrated into my family, and my father is integrated into my life. A missing piece that I thought could only be had by knowing him has been returned to me, assembled from all the gathered fragments, word by word. This story is my song of love, built around the lost chord.

 **1**

The growling voice and speed of the motorcycle thrilled her. It was a pretty thing, a Harley-Davidson with glossy curves and gleaming spokes, and big enough to feel secure. In helmet and goggles, Geraldine took flight down the river road behind her mother's house, past stands of sugar maple and hickory trees and neat rows of tobacco plants lining the fields of Rocky Mount, North Carolina. She wheeled downtown by the railroad tracks that divided Main Street, past the brick façades of shops shaded by fancy awnings, the wind on her pink cheeks. She had ridden her bicycle down the same roads in her childhood to visit neighbors, leaving her farm chores undone, forgetting to stoke the smokehouse fire or weed the kitchen garden. Her motorcycle gave her that same floating feeling of freedom for a while.

Then Bill wrote home from the front in France during World War II: "That motorcycle better be gone by the time I get home, or you can choose: it or me." Jerry thought, *That decision won't be as easy to make as he thinks.* He didn't realize that when she wanted to do something, she did it. She didn't care how it looked or what other people thought. Like when she cut her long hair into a short crop—it was the new fashion and it felt light and easy, but her mother was so shocked she'd cried. And no one approved of the way she kept working, even after the babies came; she refused to give that up.

Jerry needed a vehicle while Bill was away and the motorcycle was cheaper than a car and used far less gasoline. She was smart with money. During the Depression, she saw how no one could afford gas for their cars, so they disconnected the wheels from their chassis, hooked them up to mules, and called them Hoover carts. She even brought her sister Janie's baby girl, Jo Jane, her first birthday cake on her motorcycle, strapped behind her in a box. She drove it all the way to Fort Bragg, where Janie's husband, Joe Pitt, was stationed. The Harley was practical and it was a pleasure to be able to go wherever she liked.

Bill wouldn't have liked it if he had known how she learned to ride. Jerry saw an ad in the newspaper for the Harley, and decided to go and get it; then she had to walk it home. It was heavy to push, but she had no idea how to ride it. While she was rolling that metal beast beside her, a man drove by in a truck, slowly circled around the block, and passed her again. On the third pass he finally called out to her, "Hey! You know how to ride that thing? You want me to carry you home with it?" She ignored him. "Miss, I ride a motorcycle, too, and if you'd like to learn, a bunch of us meet on Saturdays and we'd be happy to show you how." She climbed into his truck and they became friends. Now she spent her free days learning to ride with a new group, and she wasn't the only woman there. She didn't see anything wrong with it. With a little help, she learned to trust her instincts, steering with her body before her mind could get in the way. She leaned into turns, powering the engine with a twist of her wrist on the throttle, braking with her feet and hands; it all became second nature.

But Bill got his way in the end. She decided the motorcycle

wasn't worth the fight it would have taken to keep it. When Bill came home from the war, all that was left of the bike was a great photo of Jerry riding it. That picture came in handy later, when she was raising their two sons. The sight of her on that motorcycle was instant cool to Duane and Gregg. They teased her that she was *one hot mama*, and later they asked her if they could put the picture on an album cover, but she said no.

The first rebel on a Harley the brothers ever knew was their mother. Now that picture sits on my desk.

My grandparents, Willis Allman and Geraldine Robbins, called Bill and Jerry by their friends, met in a local tavern in Jerry's hometown of Rocky Mount. Bill and a fellow serviceman joined Jerry and her girlfriends, sliding in beside them in a circular booth. Bill joked easily and looked smart in his khaki uniform; his eyes kept meeting hers. It wasn't love at first sight, but she had to admit they had chemistry. Soon he was challenging her to have another drink, then one more, and when he swore she couldn't have another, she drank it in a single gulp. She outdrank him with her head held high. The taste of whisky burning down her throat, the low, glowing light of the bar, and Bill's smile, none of it could bowl her over. Later, he told her that was the moment he decided she was the girl for him. With her blond Betty Grable curls piled neatly on her head and high-heeled shoes with straps around her ankles, Jerry was a beauty with a sparkle in her blue eyes. More than all that, she had a quick mind. She had an answer for everything and she was funny—Good Lord she could make him laugh. Within a week, walking home from the movies, passing through pools of light under streetlamps into darkness, Bill said, "Geraldine, I'm going to marry you." She told him he was crazy and quipped, "I hope you don't ask every girl you meet. One of them might say yes."

Jerry had been married before. Memories of her first love got in the way of giving Bill an answer for a time. She didn't let herself think of Roy very often. She didn't much like to form her first husband's name in her mind; it still hurt that much. They were sweethearts and jitterbug partners, and married right out of high school in 1935, when they were both eighteen. Her first two years with Roy were wonderful. They set up house and took romantic trips to Daytona Beach, Florida, where they stayed in a motel with little separate cottages by the sea. He was sweet and daring, and she was completely in love. He also liked to drink, just like her daddy.

Jerry's daddy, Simon, was what they used to call a garage drinker, secretive and solitary, not fun-loving like Roy. Her daddy sipped gin from a hidden jar while walking in the woods with his rifle, hunting at dawn while he drank. Simon Robbins brought his kills home and skinned them on the porch, bent over the body of a rabbit or a squirrel with his big knife. Her mama cooked the little animals for his dinner, and he ate alone after his children went to sleep. He thought his kids didn't see his drinking, until they became teenagers. Then he noticed how they avoided his eyes when he said he was going out. He pulled away from all of them then, even his eldest son, fearing their judgment. He had his share of disappointments. Simon was forced to close his garage and filling station and go back to working leased land after the market crashed. At harvest time, his three children had to work in the neighbors' cotton fields, weighed down by canvas bags as long as they were tall, picking bolls for hours in the sun. Jerry hated it. She hated the work and she hated how her father gave up. He flat refused to help them, and her older brother Robbie took his place, doing the work of a man even as a young boy. And then their mother, Lizzie, had a fourth child, a baby boy named Erskine, after all her other children were almost grown. They loved and doted on the baby, but it wasn't easy to add another need to their own.

Jerry's mama never spoke of hard things. Lizzie was a saint, the way she understood each of her children and showed them her love. She was sixteen years old when she met the handsome suitor who became this surly sinner, her husband. Simon gave her a gold bracelet as a promise of his intent to marry. She was the daughter of a Primitive Baptist preacher, and her family believed she was too young to wear an engagement ring. Even though she was proper, Lizzie wasn't above a good joke, saying, "When I first met that man, I loved him so much I could have eaten him alive. After we were married, I wished I had."

Jerry understood that. The real trouble in her first marriage to Roy started when she realized she wasn't the only one who appreciated her husband's looks and charm. Women loved Roy and he let them. He took Jerry to parties, and before long a girl would come sit on his lap and say, "Why is *she* here?" gesturing to Jerry. She would answer the tramp herself: "You better get off of his lap or I'll show you why I'm here."

Roy would laugh and reassure her, but she could see through him. He couldn't help himself when it came to drink or women. It took Jerry three more years to leave him, after the first two good years were over. She had to be sure he would never change. She cried her tears before she got in front of a judge and asked for a divorce. She wasn't going to wail in a public courtroom and make a fool of herself.

By the time she met Bill in 1943, Jerry had learned how to hold on to herself and her liquor. She wasn't looking to marry again, but Bill was tenacious. He was handsome and tall with sandy hair—a country boy from a town fifty miles west of Nashville, Tennessee, called Vanleer. You almost couldn't call Vanleer a town, just a place with a post office, a church, and a dry goods store. A few hundred people lived in small homes nested in the dense green hills, eating what they could grow. His parents' place had a dirt floor, tamped down and swept clean. Their kitchen was outside under a little roof and their water came from a well. Bill's father was another hard drinker, and his mother wanted more out of life but couldn't figure out how to get it.

Bill knew from a young age the army was his best way out. He got his younger brother, Sam, to come with him, and they both worked as recruiters, convincing other seventeen-year-old boys to join up. Eventually, they were able to move their mama into a comfortable home in Nashville. Their daddy stayed behind, and lived out the rest of his life alone in the country. Bill and Jerry shared common ground: They both watched their parents work hard and end up with very few comforts. They were determined to live better lives for themselves.

While Bill was courting Jerry, he brought little gifts of scarce and rationed treasures: a pair of silk stockings, red roses, and an enormous box of Whitman's chocolates. Jerry and her sister Janie, who was pregnant with her daughter, sat knee to knee balancing the big candy box between them and ate every perfect piece.

Bill said, "Geraldine, to know you is to love you, but you won't let anyone in close enough to know you!" That was true. She was cautious with herself now, but the idea of getting away from North Carolina, away from her family's opinions and advice, that was a notion strong enough to pull her toward Bill. She was close with her brothers and sister, but she was cut from a different cloth. They seemed as rooted to home as the oak tree planted in their mother's front yard. Jerry wanted to live out in the world. She wasn't satisfied to nest in North Carolina forever. Bill was career military. He was strong, and confident, moving from town to town with ease. He didn't know where his next assignment would take him and she liked that idea. She thought he could be a good father to the children she dreamed of having, and she wasn't getting any younger. She had planned to have a family long before she turned thirty, but here she was, twenty-five and divorced. She was ready to begin again. She better be, she told herself. It was clear Bill wasn't going to stop asking until she said yes. After a short ceremony at the justice of the peace on the army base, Jerry told Bill, "This marriage is the result of a smooth snow job!"

They were married only a short time before the war called Bill away. Jerry waited for letters from him, rode her motorcycle, and worked for her brother-in-law, Joe, managing his restaurant out by the airport. She stayed with Joe and Janie, and spent time with her friends. As much as she missed her new husband, she was also comfortable in her independence. It was her nature.

When Bill came home from Europe, he was a changed man. He had landed in Normandy on D-Day and survived. He was volatile and moody, what they used to call *shell-shocked*. Jerry knew he had horrible stories to tell, but he only talked about the war at the Officers' Club, with other men who had been there.

Bill was continuously reassigned once he was home. If something didn't have wheels or fit in a box, they didn't own it. They moved around North Carolina, on to South Carolina, then to Tennessee, sometimes living on army bases, sometimes in houses near small storefront recruitment centers. They settled for the longest stretch of time in Nashville, where they bought a beautiful clapboard house on Westbrook Avenue in 1947. That is where they lived when their first son, Howard Duane Allman, was born.

Bill's brother Sam lived with them, and it was a happy time. Jerry cooked big dinners to share with their friends. They played cards in the kitchen, and Bill seemed better than he had in a long time. Bill carried Duane proudly around the house and took him to Vanleer to show him off to his father. He took him to the Officers' Club and set his little bottom up on the bar beside his glass of beer. But the happy time did not last for long.

Bill soon got word he was once again going to be reassigned, and they packed up and sold their house.

Jerry hated to give up their first real home, and then, when it was too late to get it back, they found out Bill's reassignment was only across town, in another part of Nashville.

Instead of settling in again, Bill found a couple of rooms to rent in a large house, shared with an officer and his wife and a traveling candy salesman. Their second son, Gregory LeNoir, was born just a year and eighteen days after Duane, into a far different home.

Duane had a little tuft of ginger hair and skin as pale as cream. He never seemed to tire, and if you held him, he wiggled and grabbed your hair. If you set him down, he reached for the nearest thing to pull himself up with, or cried in frustration if he couldn't reach anything. Gregg looked like an angel or a baby in a magazine: white-blond and round-eyed, calm and watchful. He was easy to handle, and the officer's wife who shared their house doted on him. She carried Gregg in her arms and sang him little snatches of songs from the radio. She couldn't handle Duane. He screamed if she tried to touch him.

Duane didn't adjust well to his new baby brother, and Gregg soon had tiny scars on this hands and feet from Duane's teeth. Any little part of Gregg that dangled out of his crib was liable to get chomped, and how he screamed!

Jerry had never loved anything like she loved her babies, freshly powdered and dressed in white. Bill wasn't a great help when it came to parenting. When one of the boys would cry, Bill would say, "Your son needs something." And Jerry would answer, "You mean our son?" The pressure between them grew by the day. Bill was distracted by work, that's what he said. He had been promoted to first lieutenant and had to adjust to new responsibilities. He wore a haunted look and struggled to sleep. He angered easily and would rage for hours about little things, and Jerry wasn't the type to back down. When their battles were over, she cleaned up the broken glasses and plates they had smashed on the floor in the dawn light, before her toddlers woke up and risked cutting their little feet. Then Bill would wake and go to work again, and her day would begin. You can adjust to almost anything, she found.

Granny told me she had a babysitter in Nashville who left the boys sitting in wet diapers, but she did not have the time or money to replace her. Instead, Jerry taught Duane and Gregg to change their own training pants. She had a low shelf built in the bathroom, and stacked the pants within the boys' reach. She put a little wastebasket beneath it and explained to her sons that whenever they felt wet, they should go into the bathroom and change themselves. She told them not to bother the woman watching them, just go and take care of themselves. They learned, and she never found them in wet clothes again.

"Really, Granny?" I asked. "How old were they?"

"They were babies. They were just toddling, still in those tinkle pants."

Gregg was napping on a couch beside us while we talked. He woke up in time to hear her say "tinkle pants" and bellowed, "What are you telling her? Good God, Ma, tinkle pants? Come on, now!"

Bill was assigned to Fort Story, Virginia, and Jerry struggled with leaving Nashville. She would miss the green trees shading the Craftsman houses on the hill overlooking the neon lights of the clubs downtown. Nashville was home. Moving felt different now with her boys to think about, but Virginia was beautiful, and best of all—they would be living by the sea.

Their duplex on the base at Fort Story wasn't anything fancy—it was built of cinder blocks—but it was steps away from white sand dunes, and salty breezes blew into their windows in the evening. Jerry worked as a shopgirl downtown to keep her mind sharp and help with money. Working allowed her to buy little luxuries like new shoes when she wanted to. On warm days off, she took Duane and Gregg down to the beach with tin pails and shovels and watched them dig and splash in tide pools. A lighthouse stood proudly on the shore, the ocean a vast blue backdrop, and the marshland behind her, encased in low clouds, caught the ever-changing light like a painting come to life. Jerry could feel her life expanding out across the open horizon as she watched Duane tossing handfuls of sand into Gregg's lap. She was a mother, and they were so beautiful.

I have a stack of baby pictures of Duane and Gregg now, something I never had as a child, when I really ached for them. A few of the best photos came from Janie's daughter, Jo Jane. I finally went to visit her in North Carolina after more than thirty years of silence. She enveloped me in a flood of warmth as soon as I arrived. She had covered her mother's bed with photo albums in preparation for my visit. The baby pictures overwhelmed me. Looking at his dimpled knees and fluffy baby hair, I could imagine the powdery smell of Duane and the feel of his skin. As he grows into a toddler, Duane stands taller and bigger than Gregg and he often has his arm around him in a proprietary grip. Duane stares into the camera, his expression a little unnerving. His powerful presence is the first thing people who knew him try to describe; he was really seeing you when his eyes met yours. He was born with that intensity. Gregg smiles and sometimes looks a little worried, his pale brows knitted and watchful. Their essential natures are so close to the surface, captured in every frame.

My favorite picture of the boys as babies was taken on the beach in Virginia: soft limbs, tender heads turned away, and sun in their downy hair. Even with their faces hidden from the camera, the image holds all the intimacy and constancy that was always between them. I could cry for the perfection of that moment.

The Allman brothers, I think. Here they are.

They lived on the base in Fort Story through the winter of 1949, when Duane turned three years old and Gregg turned two. Both boys were active and Duane was already a precocious talker, repeating words he heard his parents say. His birthday was November 20 and Gregg's was December 8, so Jerry picked a day to celebrate both at once. She bought two little cakes and the boys chose the color of their icing. Gregg asked for blue and Duane green. "Green icing?" she said. "Who ever thought of anything so ugly?" But that's what he wanted and that's what he got. The boys were given matching cowboy outfits with felt hats and real leather holsters to hang from their belts. The fancy black shirts had pearly snaps and the pants were trimmed in silver. Best of all, they each received a shiny silver cap gun and real smoke rose from the barrels when they were fired. An extra length of string had to be tied around Gregg's waist to keep the weight of the gun from pulling down his pants. Duane and Gregg chased each other from room to room, galloping on invisible horses.

Bill drew an unpopular rotation and had to stay on base for Christmas Day that year, so Jerry drove the boys to Rocky Mount to visit her family for a couple of days. Duane begged to be suited up in his cowboy clothes, and loudly refused to wear anything else for the long drive to North Carolina. Gregg put on his cowboy hat and wouldn't take it off. She said, "Suit yourselves," and hustled her two little Hopalong Cassidys down the driveway.

On the way out of town, Jerry stopped at a roadside stand and bought fireworks. Duane and Gregg could barely sit still just knowing there was a bag of sparklers, bottle rockets, and Buck-a-Roo flashlight crackers in the car.

At dusk, Jerry took the boys and their cousins, Jo Jane and Ervin, into the backyard of their grandparents' house to light the fireworks. She wore a little fur jacket over a red party dress, her curls piled high with combs, and when she lit the fuses and sent those paper rockets screaming into the sky, Jo Jane told her she had never seen anything so wonderful. The kids ran in the grass painting hot white circles in the air with their sparklers, until they bent and fizzled, and Jerry took the molten wires away.

The grown-ups settled around the kitchen table, Jerry and Joe sipping shooters of whisky, poured from a bottle kept in a paper bag under the kitchen sink, while Janie watched them gravely. Duane, Jo Jane, and Ervin lay on the living room rug listening to the radio while Gregg wandered alone into his granny's bedroom and crawled under the bed to hide. Lying on his belly, he kicked his legs out like a frog and hit something with his ankle. It was too heavy to scoot with his foot, so he wiggled back out and grabbed the little package with both hands. In the light, he could see that it was a hard leather holster, a bigger version of the one he wore, and inside, a familiar shape resting beneath a snapped flap.

Gregg rushed into the living room with the long black pistol unsteady in his hands, the weight of it pulling him forward, the barrel weaving wildly, and exclaimed, "Gee! A real gun!" Duane jumped to his feet and Jo Jane followed. Ervin stayed frozen on the floor and watched openmouthed while Gregg pulled the trigger.

The bullet struck the brick mouth of the fireplace with a force that sucked the air out of Gregg's lungs and knocked him into a sit. The sound was so loud, it left a hum that rang through his ears for a long time. That shocking crack became his earliest memory, the blast and the weight of the gun against his lap. Jerry descended on him, a fluttering flock of bodies behind her, yelling and whooping. The gun was taken away and Gregg was in her arms, squeezed and held and rocked, his soft little body folded into her, her warm breath on his forehead.

The next night, the boys slept slumped against each other in the backseat on the long drive home, Jerry navigating carefully through the darkness, her mind still clutching the moment she heard the gunshot and didn't know where the bullet had gone. It made her dizzy and she turned the radio up and rolled her window open a crack to feel the cold air on her face. She was so tired, only wanting to lay the boys down in their beds, change into her nightgown, and settle in to wait for Bill. It was just after ten o'clock. She imagined he had gone out for drinks with his friend Bucky, as he often did. She wanted to tell him about the gun. She needed to get the sound of that shot out of her head, and stop thinking of what could have happened so easily if it had pointed any other way. Her heart was in her throat as she drove as fast as she safely could.

She was startled to see the post commander and his wife sitting grimly in her living room when she opened her door. She could see they were shaken. The feeling in her stomach tightened. Bill was hurt. She turned from them and rushed to change out of her traveling clothes. Whatever had happened, she would go to Bill now. The commander called out to her, stopped her, and stammered, "He's been shot, Jerry. Bill is dead."

Jerry ran into their bedroom, shook off her slacks, and changed into stockings, dress, and coat, pushing every thought away. The commander's wife stayed behind to watch Duane and Gregg. The commander guided Jerry to his car, then into the hospital, and down the corridor to the waiting room. She felt half blind; her eyes and her mind seemed disconnected. She was asked to wait.

The hospital was horribly cheerful, with a little evergreen tree covered in tinsel and greeting cards arranged on the nurse's desk. She didn't want to look at any of it. Behind closed eyes, her mind began spooling out her life with Bill. The horrible sound of the gun was still pounding in her ears. Bill must have heard an explosion just like it, the last sound he would ever hear. The thought made her ache. She felt the memory of the shot's sound cut through her chair and into her back. She bent forward and pressed her folded arms against her lap. Then someone rested a hand on her shoulder and asked her to come identify her husband's body.

The Oriental Gardens was a bit of a dive, with multicolored Christmas lights flashing over a long greasy bar, and a shuffleboard table in the back. When their shift on base was over, Bill and Bucky went for a beer and a game, just in time for happy hour. Bill sprinkled sand across the long wooden shuffleboard table and sent his red puck gliding down the edge without tipping off the far end. He twisted his wrist with a flick, saying, "Bucky, you've got to put a little English on it!" The disk spun back toward him just in time and Bucky laughed at the easy perfection of the maneuver. He was an easygoing guy, not long back from Europe, and Bill liked how calm he was and how he never tried to talk about the war, even though they both felt the experience between them, like a numbed wound. Bucky rushed through his own turn, his black puck bounding off the side in a blur. Bill smirked and patted Bucky's shoulder.

A man walked up and asked to join in, and they welcomed him. A few people had gathered around a tuneless piano by the back door and began to sing. After a few rounds of play, the man walked away before his turn was done, then came back after a half hour or so and asked for a lift to a bar down the road. Bill and Bucky finished their pints and agreed. No one should have to walk alone from bar to bar. The man had been in the service; you could tell by the proud way he walked squared-off and tall. He didn't say much, just that he could use another drink and maybe another chance to redeem himself at shuffleboard, so on they drove him to the C&C Bar and Grill. They played two quick games and said their good-byes. It was getting on to nine o'clock, but the man asked again to be taken to one more place, Jimmie's Drive-In Grill, just a little farther down the road.

Bill nodded and they walked into the parking lot. Bucky opened the passenger door to the man, but he insisted on riding in the backseat of the car.

Just as the pink glow of Jimmie's neon sign came into view, the man leaned between Bucky and Bill and asked a little loudly to be taken home, to a little lane off Sewell's Point Road, a name he pronounced *souls point*. As Bucky made the final turn, the man pushed a gun into his ribs and said, "This is a holdup."

He ordered them to stop, get out of the car, and remove their shoes. As they slowly raised their arms and edged out into the road, twin beams of light rushed over them, a car approaching from the other end of the lane. The man yelled at them, "Get back in the car!" They crouched quickly back into the front seat for a moment, exchanging a quick glance before the man was leaning between their seats again. He ordered Bucky to roll the car back into the adjacent lane until they faced Sewell's Point Road again. He shook the gun in a frantic wave and said, "Get out of the car! One at a time!" and they did. By the little light mounted over the license plate, the man looked through their billfolds and took most of their loose change, letting a few coins fall in the dirt. He shoved the four dollars they had together into his pocket with his fist. He made them remove their shoes and marched them along the road's edge toward a grove of trees. He ordered them to lie facedown on the black ground, at a distance from each other.

Bucky begged, "Don't shoot us, buddy."

He said, "You know my name, so here is where you get yours."

Bill lunged for the man. A loud popping sound made Bucky jerk his head to the side to look behind him. Then he heard a second shot and saw Bill running into the trees. He was calling Bucky's proper name, "Robert!" and he yelled back to Bill, "Run!"

The man had disappeared in the darkness, and Bucky leaped to his feet and ran toward a farmhouse at the head of the lane. A light in a single window, a golden bounding square in front of his eyes, led him as he ran. At Bucky's pounding, an old man opened his front door a crack and said quickly, in a strange, formal way, "I am sorry. I am unable to help."

In deepening shock, Bucky ran back to the road, a sick metallic taste in his throat, until he saw his car and called out again, "Bill!" He heard the car door slam and called again, "Bill!" There was no answer but he could hear the car door open again and footsteps moved toward him. He stepped back from the gravel road as silently as he could and saw the silhouette of the man turn and get back in his car. The door slammed and the car sped away, leaving Bucky alone in silence.

Bucky had no memory of it later, but he must have run down the lane to another house and used a telephone to call the police. He did remember sitting in a kitchen by a blackened oil stove and looking at his watch: It was only nine-thirty. It seemed impossibly early.

Several policemen searched for a long time, walking close together in the furrowed field. They parted at the trees, stepping carefully and sweeping the grove with flashlight beams. They found the body of Lieutenant Allman facedown with a bullet in his back.

Later that night, the police found Bucky's car parked outside a silent wood-frame house three miles from the crime scene. An elderly couple led the officers to their son's bedroom, where they found the man asleep in bed, his warm gun under the pillow.

Robert described the whole scene in an official statement. A copy was given to Jerry, typed on onionskin paper and signed. He told her as much as she could stand to hear before the funeral, and most of the story ended up in the newspaper. Jerry read that Bill wasn't the only man who carried the war home inside him. His killer was a fellow serviceman, still fighting invisible battles in his mind. He shot Bill without a thought.

In his confusion and sickness, he took Bill away from his family forever.

Jerry didn't have any interest in his trial or punishment, although she attended the proceedings with a soldier appointed to sit by her side in the courtroom. She heard Bill's killer sentenced to life in prison, but it didn't matter what happened to that man. Nothing would bring back Bill.

Sixty years later, Duane's cousin Brenda gave me an original copy of Robert's signed police statement. She mailed me the fragile, yellowed pages that describe the day my grandfather was killed. I try to imagine what it felt like for my granny to read the words. The statement gives just enough haunting detail of the crime scene to fire one's imagination, but my granny doesn't think that way. She protects herself by staying in the present now, defiant of memory. "I've got better things to think about," she says when I ask her about Bill. "That was a hole I fell in. And my son was another hole, but you can't live in a hole. You have to heal." She likes to think of riding her motorcycle, the wind clearing all the ghosts from her mind. She says riding was the joy of her life. She speeds away from the patch of dirt where Bill no longer lies; her body leaning into the curves in the road, she leaves it behind her.

She is stronger than I am.

Bill and Jerry had made it safely through the worst danger they would ever face; that was what she had thought when he made it home from World War II. Bill was a survivor and her fears for him were long over. In Normandy, Bill marched through waist-deep water with one hundred pounds of gear on his back and a steel helmet on his head. He crawled through sand with machine-gun fire whistling by him, and saw his friends killed where they stood. He saw ships blanketing the English Channel and fighter planes filling the sky. Sirens screaming, huge engines grinding and howling while thousands of shots deafened him. And then he made it home. But he let his guard down in Virginia, on the night after Christmas. He didn't see the bullet coming for him.

Bill's coffin was draped with the American flag. Soldiers stood in full dress uniform, faces wooden and expressionless. Jerry recognized many of them from the base, from picnics with their families and children's birthdays on the beach. She had never seen them look so stern. Her sister Janie sat beside her. Bill's mother and father stood at a distance wrapped around each other in a rare moment of tenderness, their sons beside them—Sam in his uniform and young David in his first suit.

Duane and Gregg: This was the first time in hours she had let herself think of the boys. The weight of them was resting on her chest like a stone. "Where are the boys?" Jerry asked Janie.

"Safe with your housekeeper, remember?"

A trumpet played taps, ceremonial shots were fired, and the flag from his casket was folded and presented to his mother, who pressed it to her chest. Soldiers marched in formation and Janie rubbed Jerry's back in quieting circles. Now Bill's body would be sent to Tennessee on a train, and buried at the Nashville National Cemetery in a silent sea of identical white headstones.

Duane's cousin, Jo Jane, wrote a short story about where she, Duane, and Gregg were while their parents were at Bill's funeral. Duane was wiggling in his seat wedged between Jo Jane's little body and the familiar curves of their housekeeper. They'd been in this car forever, circling downtown, winding through the empty streets under garlands of holly, passing the same store window with a mechanical Santa nodding and waving.

"Where's Mama?" Duane asked again. Every time he asked, he was told he'd see her soon, but soon wasn't coming and he was getting mad. "Where's Mama?" he said a little louder.

Jo Jane put her arm around him and told him to hush and they would get ice cream. Gregg was in the front seat on a strange woman's lap, his white blond head resting on her dark brown shoulder.

Gregg furrowed his brow and whispered, "Where's Mama?" in his lispy baby way. Duane didn't know who that skinny lady was, holding his baby brother, or who the man next to Jo Jane was, either. That man had dark skin and black hair plastered flat against his head. One shiny gold tooth peeked out from his mouth and Duane couldn't stop staring at it. He wanted to ask how he got it, but he didn't.

Their housekeeper's husband was driving all over town, even though it was cold and crowded in the car. Duane knew him all right. He had watched him help his daddy change a tire on their car. He was a soldier like daddy, even though he was colored. There were colored soldiers, too, his daddy said. Duane kicked the back of the front seat as hard as he could and Gregg's eyes opened so wide they looked like they might pop out.

"Take me home!"

"Duane, you been told, now. We are going to get ice cream, baby."

She squeezed him against her bosom and rested her warm hand on his head and he settled for a minute. No one would really talk to him, or look him in the eye. No one but Jo Jane, but she was just a kid, too. She treated him like a baby, but he wasn't a baby. He wrapped his finger around one of Jo Jane's long brown ringlets and watched it tunnel into the shining softness. She turned her pretty face toward him, her blue eyes serious.

"Your mama's at the funeral," Jo Jane said. "For your daddy, remember?"

"Look at that Santa, baby! Isn't he pretty?" the woman he didn't know in the front seat shouted out.

"I ain't no baby!" Duane yelled back.

Duane felt the horrible thing that happened in the night lingering into the day. People he didn't recognize came and filled up his house and now he wasn't supposed to go home, and his daddy was gone. His mama had told him. His daddy had gone to heaven to sing with the angels. Nothing made any sense.

The car stopped in front of a small whitewashed building with a hand-painted sign over a sliding window and a few picnic tables tilting in the sand. They were far away from home, on the other side of town.

"This ain't the ice cream place," Duane said.

"Baby, this is where we get ice cream, and it's just the same."

"I want vanilla!" Gregg shouted.

"I don't want any," Duane said.

"Oh, come on now, honey. Don't be that way."

"Just get him chocolate," Jo Jane said. "He'll eat it. Can I have a Coke instead of ice cream?"

By the time they got back to the base, night had fallen on Jerry like a heavy thing and she couldn't keep her eyes open. She lay in her wide bed and turned away from the space beside her. She couldn't feel him here. Shouldn't she still be able to feel Bill close to her? She couldn't stay with the thought of Bill, or his spirit and where it resided now. The emptiness beside her yawned and sank in like a hole. She grabbed on to the one golden image in her mind—their boys. Her boys. They belonged to her alone now. Their sturdy little bodies, their pale and perfect skin, and sweet smells: She would think only of Duane and Gregg and all it would take to protect them. They would be her strength tonight and every night to come.

The next evening, Jerry dressed her sons in matching corduroy coats and brim hats with earflaps snapped under their chins. She kissed their fat cheeks and didn't let herself cry. They would return to Rocky Mount with Joe and Janie until Jerry could get her mind straight and decide what was next. She had been told she would have to leave the base in less than a week. When she saw Duane and Gregg again, somehow they would have a new home in a new town, the three of them alone.

On the night drive back to North Carolina, a ripple of panic passed through the children. Gregg began to cry that he was thirsty. The sodas and bottle of milk Janie had brought for the ride were finished and they were at least an hour away from any town. Duane and Jo Jane sat in grim silence listening to Gregg's steady

22

whining. By the light of the moon, Janie spotted water flowing over rock, a small waterfall by the road. Joe pulled over onto the soft shoulder and took three empty soda bottles and Gregg's baby bottle to fill them with the icy runoff. The kids wiggled out of the car and into the night, Janie yelling after them to get back in the car, or at least button their coats. They lined up like three little frogs squatting next to Joe, and watched him dip the mouths of the bottles into the flow. They huddled together in the total darkness and tasted the sweet water, colder than the winter air, each holding their bottles for themselves. "You see?" Janie said. "The Lord will provide. Now get back in this car."

I was a teenager when my mother first told me about Bill. She told me a hitchhiker had killed Duane's father. That is how she described him: Duane's father. She did not say "your grandfather." I was well into my thirties before I saw my first photograph of Bill. I was clearing a box of magazines out of Granny's garage when I found an old folder of photographs. One of them was a formal portrait of a soldier in a baggy uniform and lace-up boots, sitting with his legs crossed. I knew who he was without asking. He had my father's eyes, and mine. I saw in an instant that Duane and I shared something far deeper than our features. I knew something true, something no one else could ever tell me. Duane and I both knew, from the most fragile age, that death is real and sudden and the loss never ends.

When you lose your father, everything he could have given you is lost. With Bill's picture in my hand, standing in the dusty garage of my father's childhood home, I knew what my father had felt; the pain I had always suffered and hidden, he'd shared. The deepest hole I ever fell in, he had fallen in, too. We were together in all the things we could never know about one of the people we could have loved the most. I felt my father close to me, looking over my shoulder at Bill's face.

3

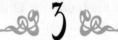

After Bill's death, Jerry's first husband, Roy, showed up in Janie's living room and asked Jerry to marry him again. He said he would help her raise the boys. Roy was still handsome but his forehead was creased with worry. Without hesitating for a moment, Jerry said no. There may have been a time when she had wanted nothing more than to hear Roy admit he missed her, but those days were gone. She knew she would never let another man raise her sons. If she ever saw any man raise a hand to her children in anger, he'd better never fall asleep near her again, or he'd wake up without that hand.

Jerry decided to return to Nashville and stayed with Bill's mother, Myrtle, while she looked for a job. She found a bookkeeping position at a NAPA auto parts warehouse and, after two long months apart, brought the boys home from Janie and Joe's to join her. They lived together under Grandma Myrtle's watchful eye for a couple of difficult years. It seemed there weren't many things she and Myrtle could agree on. Myrtle was a country music fan and Jerry preferred big-band dance music and crooners like Perry Como. Myrtle was critical of Jerry going out for drinks. Myrtle thought Jerry spoiled the boys. She dressed them up in suits and ties and took them to the symphony, shaking them awake when the swelling music subdued them into sleep. She bought them a record player with a lid like a little suitcase and a pile of picture books with 45 records included. She wanted Duane and Gregg to get used to having nice things. She told Myrtle, "If I put them in silk sheets now, they'll figure out how to get themselves silk sheets later."

When she was finally able, Jerry moved to her own home on Scotland Place, in a neighborhood that bordered the sprawling Belle Meade Plantation. Most of the green land had been transformed into rolling golf courses, but abandoned slave quarters still stocked with iron cooking pots and wooden beds nested in the trees behind fancy horse stables where wealthy whites learned to ride. The boys were forbidden to play there, but of course they did. Carrying their fishing poles, they scooted under the fence and found a pond that was stocked with tiny fish. They rolled their blue jeans over their ankles and rolled the sleeves of their T-shirts above their shoulders like the greasers they saw hanging out at the drugstore. They spent whole afternoons sitting on the trim turf in the sun, their sunken hooks baited with bacon. The little fish were full of bones, but they picked around them and ate their catches for dinner proudly.

Their new house was on a corner lot with a big backyard, across the road from Parmer Elementary School, where Duane could start first grade in the fall. Jerry found a housekeeper they all came to love. Duane and Gregg would watch in the mornings as Betty walked up the hill from the city bus stop with her pocketbook in the crook of her arm, chatting with the other black ladies coming to work in the white suburbs. She was a patient person and a wonderful cook—best of all, she didn't miss a trick. When Betty called the boys in to wash their hands before lunch, she'd watch Duane running the faucet without putting his hands underwater, trying to fool her. "You think I can't see what you're up to, Duaney?" Jerry was gone all day, but she told herself the boys really wanted for nothing as long as she had Betty.

A troop of little children lived on their street: girls with runny noses and messy hair, loud boys with pockets full of marbles. The brothers fell in easily with the crowd. Duane, with his flattop haircut, crooked teeth, and a gleam in his eye, rose in the neighborhood ranks quickly; he was the swaggering gangster, the crack-shot archer, and the redheaded stranger on a wild painted pony. He was soon the leader in every game and Gregg followed in his wake, running to keep up.

Beyond the school yard fence, a few trees shaded a shallow brook where patches of wild mint grew and a field of red dirt stretched the length of a city block. It was the perfect spot for cowboy games. Duane surveyed the wild territory with an invisible rifle on his back, watched by silent braves lying on their bellies in the brush. Hours were spent re-creating scenes from movies the neighborhood kids watched at the Tennessean Theater downtown. But fight scenes could easily turn into real fights. Duane was moody. He'd suddenly cross his arms, cut his eyes at an offending friend, and stalk home in a rage, where he'd kick walls and slam doors until he cooled off on his own. It wasn't easy to calm him down.

When Gregg first told me that Duane kicked his ass every day of his childhood, I thought he was joking; it was so at odds with my romantic notions about their brotherly bond. Then he filled in the details: knuckles to the skull, punches in the ear, constant shoves and kicks, how Duane pounded his fists into Gregg's back while he curled himself tightly into a ball, and I knew it was true. Gregg was often on the receiving end of Duane's anger, which is not to say that they were not close. Part of the reason Duane felt he could hit him and push him was that he felt Gregg belonged to him. The brothers had an absolute pecking order, with Duane dominating his little brother at every turn, unchallenged. But when other boys tried to join in roughing up Gregg, or even when girls pinched him because he was so cute, Duane defended his baby brother ferociously. Protecting Gregg was Duane's most serious job; they were united against everyone.

Gregg completely idolized him, even when he was hurting. He and his brother were two halves of a whole, two sides of a coin, and they were never apart for long. Gregg says he never learned how to be completely alone. He never had to, because his big brother was always there.

Jerry was struggling. She needed to learn a skill that would pay if they were going to be able to survive. Her first real job out of high school had been at Montgomery Ward, and when the bookkeeper quit suddenly, she talked her way into his job. She was confident with numbers and she learned quickly, so she decided to study bookkeeping at night school. The boys adjusted to eating supper in their pajamas at ten o'clock, after she had completed her endless day.

Duane and Gregg had beds arranged toe to toe in the corner of their shared bedroom. Duane fell asleep deeply and quickly every night, worn out by the day. Gregg wandered back to his mother, asking for one more glass of water, one more trip to the bathroom.

Jerry stayed up late writing letters to Janie in Rocky Mount, and sipping from her glass, listening to "April in Paris." As tired as she was, it was the only time she had to herself. She read romance novels, listened to crooners on the radio, and balanced her checkbook. She would soon have to admit she couldn't continue to juggle everything, even with Betty's help. Finding a boarding school for the boys was her solution. Because of Bill's service, the boys qualified for reduced tuition at Castle Heights Military Academy. It was in Lebanon, Tennessee, about an hour from Nashville.

Gregg was eight years old and Duane was nine when she sent them away.

Jerry drove with Janie beside her in the front seat and the boys and Jo Jane in the backseat for the drive to Castle Heights. Trees filtered the late summer light and the car was quiet. She had been up half the night packing the boys' clothes, pressing their pants and moving a button a quarter inch over on the neck of Gregg's white dress shirt. They were growing faster than she could clothe them. She told them they could wear these things when they came home for a visit soon. She was tired and nervous, grateful for her sister's steady company. The boys were dressed in their new uniforms, complete with stiff hats and shiny black shoes. No one spoke for long stretches of road.

At the school, they wandered under tall trees and around immaculate flower beds and posed for pictures by a giant cannon. The scale of the brick building was awe-inspiring. Jo Jane ventured that she guessed it sort of looked like a castle. Duane said, "More like a prison." After putting off the moment for an hour or more, taking the official tour and leaving their trunks in their shared room, she hugged her boys goodbye. As their mother's car pulled from the curb and rolled down the long drive, Gregg started to cry. He ran after the car as fast as he could, chasing his mama out of the school gate. Duane stood watching him, then sat on the dorm's stone steps with his arms crossed tight in front of his chest. He twisted his mouth into an angry scowl and if he felt tears rise, he swallowed them. When the car turned out into the road, Gregg walked back with his shoulders shaking and his face red and wet. Duane rose and put his arm around him. If Duane was afraid, Gregg couldn't see any sign of it, and that made him feel a little better. "We're in this together, Baybro," calling Gregg by the endearment he always used, slurring together the words *baby brother*.

Jerry wept in the car and insisted she was doing what she knew was best. They would learn strength and discipline, things she couldn't teach them herself. They would be home for vacations. They would adjust. Janie nodded her agreement and sniffed into her handkerchief. Jo Jane was trembling in fury. Twisting around and looking out the back window, she watched Gregg running, his arms reaching toward his mama, his hat flying off into the gravel road. She couldn't believe what she had just seen. It was a terrible betrayal.

28

Duane and Gregg were marched through strictly organized days at Castle Heights. The clothes they loved were packed away and their hair was cropped close to their scalps. They were expected to wear their summer uniforms every day: gray cotton pants with a black stripe down the side and gray shirts so full of starch they could have stopped bullets. During their first year, Duane and Gregg shared a small room for a short time, sleeping in bunks that folded away into boxes during the day, like Murphy beds. Then they were separated into their grades. It took a while to get used to the strange sounds of coughs and whispers floating down the halls at night. It was never completely quiet. They woke up to the sound of a bugle playing in the yard as the sun rose and marched in formation to the dining hall for a breakfast of mush. They had separate classes all day, where they were expected to sit in silence. Along with math, English, and ancient history, the boys learned to assemble, clean, and fire real weapons. They carried M1s without the firing pins, and practiced shooting at targets with .22-caliber rifles on a range. They had drills in the afternoon and were confined to quarters after lunch to study. Rebellion and disobedience were not tolerated; punishments were given by a complicated system of demerits and restrictions. The school had all the structure and gravity of the military. There were rules for everything: how to shine your brass belt buckle on both sides, how to make your bed tightly, and how to tie your shoelaces. They checked to see if your fingernails were clean. Compared to life in their mama's house, this was surely hell on earth.

The rigors of the day wore Gregory out. He found it easy to be obedient; he sat quietly in class and did all of his work well, but he couldn't shake the feeling that he had been abandoned. It seemed like life would never be easy or happy again. Duane saw their new school as a challenge. He didn't like it, but it wasn't going to break him.

Castle Heights had its share of troubled boys sent there for disciplinary reasons, mixed in with the well-bred sons of military families. Duane could talk to anyone. He had the swagger and intelligence to befriend older boys who taught him when it was safest to steal away into the dense woods behind the school, or sneak cigarettes in a secret spot called the Butt Hole. There were late-night gab sessions in boys' rooms in Hooker Hall, where Duane learned new cuss words and how to throw a real punch. But he saw how brutal school was for Gregg and how he retreated into himself. He kept his eye on his little brother and helped him when he could. He showed Gregg the best way to organize his footlocker before inspections, and stayed in his room with him when he saw he was down. On Wednesdays, they were allowed to go into town to see a movie or go to the drugstore for a soda. It was amazing how special something like that could feel when you couldn't do it all the time.

Duane and Gregg were encouraged to join the marching band. Jerry splurged and bought them identical trumpets, no small investment, but their interest didn't last for long. The band room had a piano and Duane was drawn to it. He began taking lessons and his teacher found him so promising, she gave him permission to play during any free class period he had. He didn't like her much. She came on with an intensity he found embarrassing. She sat too close on the piano bench and told him he had beautiful hands. Sometimes she put her palms against the back of his hands to keep them arched correctly. She made strange sighing sounds and smelled of powdery perfume. His friends heard her encourage him and teased him about it: "Off to tinkle those keys, Allman?" That did it. Getting out of study hall and playing music alone in the afternoons whenever he liked was great, but he wasn't going to take shit for it. On the eve of his first piano recital, Duane told his teacher he didn't want to play anymore. She knew he had practiced for it; he knew every piece by heart, but he could not be moved. He told her he didn't see the point of playing music. His teacher was so upset she called Jerry in tears. She told her Duane was excelling, but wouldn't perform. He had a rare, natural gift, she said, and she didn't want to give up on him. Jerry told her that once Duane had set his mind on something, no one could change it—just forget it. He never took another music lesson.

After two years at Castle Heights, while home for a rare weekend, Gregg told Jerry he felt like she had fallen off the face of the world. It shook her to her core. She knew she had to make a new plan. She had finished her degree in bookkeeping and had befriended the two men who ran the NAPA franchise where she worked. She hosted cocktail parties and cookouts for their families, grilling steaks in her big backyard while dressed to the nines, and charmed everyone. Her boss, Mr. Hicks, said his wife had inherited a small hotel in Daytona Beach, Florida. He and his partner were relocating their families, and planned to run an Amoco gas station there while they renovated the hotel. Jerry told them that she wanted to come along.

In February 1957, at the age of forty, Jerry took Duane and Gregg out of school and moved to Daytona Beach, the vacation spot she had visited with her first husband, Roy, more than twenty years before. It was a place of happy memories, and damn, she could use a little happy.

4

When my mom was four years old, she made it out of her house
alone. She paused at the end of the driveway and looked back at the
front window, hoping her mother would see her go and feel sorry
for shouting at her for giggling with her sister during their nap.

She wandered along the edge of the freshly paved street, finding it easy to keep walking. She walked for a long time, carrying
her cardboard suitcase. It wasn't heavy; it held only a blue plastic
comb, a pair of white socks rimmed in lace, and a doll with golden
hair and tiny shoes. Her brother's small red cowboy hat hung down
her back. She had never taken anything from her big brother before. The hat's white string pressed into her neck. She did not turn
around to look back. She would never go back.

She made a gunslinger's shadow in the street, turning her knees
out bow-legged and pulling the hat onto her head. There were no
sidewalks in the neighborhood and the street was a danger in itself,
she knew. After a while, houses grew taller and yards widened and

her heartbeat sounded in her ears. This was the feeling she was looking for, a little ripple of fear and thrill. She had always wanted to walk until she crossed the invisible line beyond which nothing looked familiar, but she usually got caught before she could.

She sat on a grass plot for a moment and pushed the toe of her sandal into a bubble of warm tar at the road's edge. It didn't pop, only squished silently. She rested awhile, and then walked on until she passed a white house with gray shutters and a green lawn full of trees and shadows. A stranger stood in her doorway waving her hand. Donna waved back and walked up the path to meet her on the covered porch. The woman bent down and asked her if she wanted a cookie. She wore bright red lipstick. Donna nodded silently and followed the woman inside. She asked Donna how old she was, and Donna held up four fingers. She asked her name and where she lived and she said, "Iveland Drive." "Where is your mother now, dear?" she asked. Donna answered, "Home." "Well, you made it pretty far on your own, didn't you?" she asked. After two cookies, the woman told her she would walk with her back to the corner of Iveland Drive. Donna decided that was all right. She could run away again tomorrow.

She made it home just before the porch lights came on in the darkening street. The woman waved her inside, then disappeared. The house was cool and she could hear her mother's radio crooning through the closed kitchen door. Donna smelled the dizzy lacquer smell of her mother's nail polish. Her father was still at work; otherwise he would have whistled for her, a shrill single note that shot down the block like a bullet made of sound. Donna climbed up the small staircase to the hall of bedroom doors. She rested her brother's hat on the floor in front of his door, then went silently into the room she shared with her little sister. Joanie was still napping under a pink blanket, breathing deeply with her mouth open. Donna lay down on her bed's slick satin spread, a bit of saved cookie still curled in her hand. She passed it into her other hand and licked the melted chocolate from her salty palm and closed her eyes.

Riding to the grocery store with her mother the following week, they passed the woman's house, a half mile or so down the road. Donna pointed and said, "That's where the cookie lady lives." Her mom didn't know what she was talking about.

The next time she tried to run away, her mother saw her slip through the gate and was behind her instantly, swinging a switch torn from their tree, landing stinging licks on the backs of Donna's legs. "Where do you think you're going, young lady?"

I recognize my mother in miniature in this memory of hers. She was always a gypsy and a rebel. But most of her childhood stories play out in a strict home I don't recognize at all. Her descriptions of her parents in no way resemble the kind people I knew as Grandma and Grandpa.

I have watched the Roosmann family home movies with fascination. Pastel-pink birthday parties, Christmas mornings around the tree, and trips to the zoo—each scene is orderly and formal. Donna is a tall, painfully thin girl, her knees poking out from under layers of petticoats, her teeth covered by braces that push her lips into a pout. She and Joanie wear matching perfectly starched white pinafores even while playing jump rope and hopscotch in their driveway.

Their mother, Tommie Jean, made all of their clothes, the curtains and throw pillows, everything in their home. She is gorgeous in printed day dresses protected by crisp aprons, her auburn hair set in elaborate swirls. She has the bearing of a celebrity, waving off the camera, peering over sunglasses. In several scenes, the kids are lined up on their concrete porch, dressed for church: the girls in buttoned coats and sculpted felt hats, their brother Gil Jr. in a suit and fedora, a miniature replica of their father. Laura, their baby sister, is held in Tommie Jean's arms, her pale curls tucked under a white bonnet. They are groomed and still, like children imagined by Hollywood. I don't entirely believe this lost world ever existed; it is completely foreign to me.

Donna traveled a long way from her origins before she had me, and brought very little discernible baggage with her. Mom raised me in a different world, one she built for herself. The more I learned about her childhood, the clearer that became.

Donna's father, Gilbert Roosmann, worked for a trucking company as a rate clerk and her mother, Tommie Jean, stayed home with their four children. In the early fifties, they lived in a St. Louis suburb called Overland, one of many neighborhoods sprouted from seeds planted by the GI Bill for soldiers returning from World War II. Their little gray house on Iveland Drive was one of many identical homes built in a grid.

Tommie Jean kept her home quiet and spotless. Their dinner table was silent, without talk of school or sports. Their days followed a steady routine, from Mass in the morning until bedtime prayers.

Six days a week at 8 A.M., Donna went to Mass at All Souls Church. She was awakened in darkness and sent to clean up in the bathroom, where she crouched over the heating vent and let the warm air fill her nightgown like a balloon. She smoothed her navy jumper over a freshly starched white blouse. She liked wearing her school uniform; she felt it disguised her secret self like a costume. She was a dreamer, a ballerina, and a painter hidden in a schoolgirl's garb. In winter, she wore a wool beanie secured to the crown of her head with a felt-tipped hatpin. In spring, a white lace chapel veil covered the curls made by the perms her mother gave her. Every few months, starting at six years old, Tommie set Donna's head in tight rows of metal curlers, arranged according to the charts in her hairdo magazines. The chemicals burned her scalp and stank.

Donna rode the school bus to church, and her class entered the pews ordered by age, youngest in front, eldest at the rear. All Souls Church was the most beautiful and exotic place in Donna's life. The grand stone walls danced with transient stained-glass colors and the air smelled of spicy sweet incense. The Mass was chanted in Latin, a low humming drone that washed over her like a magical incantation. They sang hymns and memorized catechisms. Who made you? God made me. Who is God? God is the creator of all things. Why did God make you and all things? For his own glory. How can you glorify God? By loving him and doing what he commands. A carved Christ hung on a cross high above them, a remarkable presence: a mostly naked man, beautiful, long-haired, and bleeding. The girls took in his transmogrified body in the form of the sacramental wafer, dusty and bland on their tongues. Donna loved the way it made her feel to share in the rituals, like secrets unspoken but witnessed and kept.

After morning Mass, a long day at All Souls School began. The Sisters of Notre Dame, in starched bibs and wimples, shepherded the girls through their lessons in mathematics, history, and religion. The nuns' bodies were hidden under layers of black wool, and long rosary beads swayed from their belts as they walked between rows of desks.

After school, Donna retreated to the bedroom she shared with her little sister Joanie. She played her parents' copy of the Warsaw Concerto on her child's record player and choreographed elaborate dances to the swelling, serious music. Time fell away; she was so engrossed in her body's ecstatic movements. Her room became a castle in the air. Her body was a ship adrift on the wind, her hair a spinning halo of light. She could stretch out, guided by the music, finally released from the confines of the day.

One afternoon, Donna sat at her dressing table and wrote a story describing what it might feel like to kiss a boy. She dipped her fountain pen in peacock-blue ink and imagined her lips touching the mouth of a boy she knew. Warmth spread through her like she was stepping into a bath. She pictured the boy's pale cheeks and dark eyelashes and her heart began to pound. She realized that what she was doing was wrong; she was having impure thoughts. So she tipped her bottle of ink over the whole page until a deep wet stain eclipsed her words, and put the ink bottle away. The lid on the bottle was loose and ink soaked the bottom of the drawer, the blot a reminder of her sin.

Her daddy was a calm and quiet man, tall and handsome with bright blue eyes. He was raised on a farm but held his body with the upright posture of a gentleman. He wanted nothing more after a long day at work than to read the newspaper undisturbed, reclining in his chair. But before he settled in for the evening, he had to address his wife's long list of daily grievances. She described the girls' noisy fights, the disrespectful, mouthy answers they gave her, and the messes left behind by their hands. He would walk heavily upstairs, unhooking his belt, and call out his daughters' names. Discipline was his duty as a father. Donna would hide in her closet and watch him spank Joanie through the slats of the door. Watching her little sister's red crying face was worse than knowing her own spanking was coming next.

Other times, a spanking would come from nowhere, a terrible reminder of the price of breaking a rule. One night, behind the closed door of her room, Donna taught herself to braid her doll's hair. After struggling for what seemed like hours, she had a breakthrough and her hands just seemed to know the right rhythm. After dozens of feeble tries, the code was cracked. She held the slippery golden ends of three twists and tried to keep them from unraveling. She distantly heard her mother calling her down to dinner, but she ignored her. She knew that if she stopped now, she would forget how to braid. She had to keep going so she would always remember. Her father came stomping upstairs and threw her door open. Before she knew what was happening, he was jerking her up by her arm and striking her. He bent her over his lap and spanked her until she couldn't breathe.

At the dinner table, she gasped and shook while her brother and sisters stared at their plates in silence. Her mother told her she didn't need to help with the dishes, which was as close to a comforting word as she was going to get. Once safely back in her room with her blanket over her face, Donna cried in rage. She tried to think of Mother Mary laying a comforting hand on her head, but she couldn't help it: She hated her father, and her mother, and everyone. Then her daddy came to her and put his big hand on her head. She couldn't help but love him, a wide warm feeling of forgiveness and repair spreading through her.

5

The taxi ride from the airport in Jacksonville to the Mayo Clinic should have been familiar. We were nearly retracing the route my school bus took thirty years ago, but freeways and strip malls had taken root where trees and swampland had once thrived. The curve of the waterway under the concrete bridge and the smell of pine and saltwater were the only hints of the seaside hippie town of my childhood.

I arrived at the massive medical complex during the hottest part of a June afternoon, after flying all night from California. The land around the hospital was as painfully landscaped as the neighboring golf courses, and the grand foyer, visible through enormous windows, was very like the fancy hotels where I usually visited my uncle.

Gregg and I had rarely spent time alone and never under such difficult circumstances. I was slow to learn that waiting for an invitation to visit him didn't work, and if he didn't call, it didn't mean he didn't want to see me. I was in my thirties before I started reaching out to him, and I was surprised by how he welcomed me. Soon we were closer than we had ever been. Still, when I offered to help him after his liver transplant, it was his turn to be surprised. I told him I was grateful for the chance to show him my love. Being near Gregg made me feel closer to my father, and I hoped it did the same for him. He had waited for a liver for six months, and when it finally came, I got on a plane.

I found him asleep in a dark room, surrounded by blinking machines. He looked impossibly healthy and handsome given all he had just gone through. I settled on a stiff couch under the shaded window. A fishing show was playing mutely on TV, glowing with gloomy underwater light. I was half watching a group of men grappling with a small shark when Gregg suddenly spoke.

"My brother and I used to watch them catch sharks from the pier at night. They used a chain and a big hook."

I felt the zinging thrill of hearing his low, familiar voice.

"Hi!" I said, but he kept looking at the screen. I watched his face and waited for him to say more. After a while, I asked, "How old were you?"

He turned his dreamy eyes to me and said, "I don't know. Nine or ten."

"You must have just moved to Daytona, if you were nine," I said, but he closed his eyes. I watched the TV with new interest. A large pink-skinned man in a green vest leaned over the edge of his boat, searching the water for another flash of silver skin.

As Gregg floated away on a cloud of morphine, I could see him as a child walking with his big brother across Atlantic Avenue, both in rolled-up jeans, hands in their pockets, their white T-shirts glowing in the darkness.

The dim moonlight rode the endless ocean and lit the beach with an eerie gleam that seemed to come from everywhere at once. Duane and Gregg climbed the steps to the wooden pier that stretched out into slowly churning water. They walked until they were near the dock's end, and saw two men heave a baited hook at the end of a chain into the water. Another man scooped chum from a bucket and tossed it over the edge of the dock.

A cooler sat behind the fishermen, and Duane called to them once they were close enough to be heard. "Hey, sir! Can we have a beer?" Gregg watched, amazed, as the man with the bucket glanced up, smiled, and tossed Duane a can without a word. Duane pulled a church key out of his pocket and pushed two small triangular holes into the lid with a quick turn of his wrist and handed Gregg the open can like a dare. "Drink up, Baybro." They passed the can between them, sipping the cold and sour brew until their bodies felt heavy and odd. Suddenly three men jerked forward, clutching the chain that thumped against the dock's edge. They tugged hand over hand, pulling up a writhing shadow until it slapped heavily against the boards. The boys leaned in and watched the little sand shark twist desperately, skin luminous and jaw bleeding. Duane smiled and stepped a little closer.

As Jerry drove down A1A beyond St. Augustine, the oaks that shaded the road thinned then disappeared completely as the terrain became low-rolling and sandy. Little dunes and curtains of saw grass parted for quick glimpses of blue water. At Flagler Beach, rough wooden steps bleached gray in the salt air led down from the road to the sand, and the sun drifted higher in the sky with every mile. Duane shoved Gregg away from his window, laughing, trying to block him from their first view of the Atlantic. The interminable drive from Nashville was almost over.

Daytona Beach shimmered ahead of them like a mirage. Shingled houses and cinder-block bungalows gave way to a steady stream of motels with names from lazy daydreams: the Kasbah, the Sahara, the Tangier, and the Miramar Motel. The Sandpiper, the Sea Horse, the Thunderbird, Blue Heaven. The Nomad, the Castaway, and Memory Lane Motel. Motor inns wrapped their futuristic curves around asphalt parking lots, and stucco cabanas with red tiled roofs nested in the dunes. Thousands of little bedrooms faced the sea, waiting to be filled.

Daytona was one of the few places in the world where driving on a beach was legal, and cars cruised slowly ocean-side, night and day. The hard-packed sand was ideal for the speed trials and stock car races held there since the turn of the century, long before the sprawling speedway was built. The boys whooped when Jerry pointed their car down a concrete ramp and drove onto the sand. Motorcycles and curvy Chevrolets rolled by them and fishermen stood hip-deep, casting out their lines. Surfers paddled out to the break. It was February when the Allmans arrived, and the Ferris wheel stood still above a silent, shuttered arcade. Bumper cars sat parked in a clump beneath a painted canopy. The Sky Lift's bright gondolas hung empty on cables a hundred feet above the Main Street Pier. The boys begged to stop, but Jerry told them to sit still and calm down. There would be plenty of time to explore. Just you wait, she said. When summer came, their new home would be a holiday paradise: the Land of 2,000 Cottages on the World's Most Famous Beach.

They lived for a while in a first-floor rental on the beach in the center of the tourist district. It was furnished and shabby, but the view of the water made up for everything. Jerry watched the sun rise from a screened porch and dipped in the ocean every morning before the boys woke up. She swam until the icy water felt hot against her skin. It was almost enough to shock the sad right out of her body.

Within a few short weeks of their arrival, she was as busy as she had ever been, keeping books for Mr. Hicks's Amoco station and for a real estate agent in a nearby storefront. She started to plan her future. She figured she would be able to buy a house of her own in a year or less, if she planned well. *Let me live in a house by the side of the road and be a friend to man.* She had always loved the line of that poem, and if she needed a motto, that would be it. She wanted a place no one could take from her, a place to raise her boys without interference. Her traveling days were done.

In the summertime, they moved to another rented house, a few miles south in a sparsely developed neighborhood called the Shores. Dense patches of primordial woods surrounded their little concrete bungalow on Cardinal Boulevard, but rows of identical homes were being raised fast in spaces cleared by a local developer. Still, it had a wild feeling, and her boss asked her why she was moving "way out there."

The boys were old enough to mind themselves as far as Jerry was concerned, and after Castle Heights, their sudden freedom shocked them. It wasn't as much fun as they thought it would be. They missed their friends in Nashville, their cousins and uncles, and there wasn't a lot to keep them busy. Their house was across Atlantic Avenue from the beach, but you could only spend so long staring at the sea. It was lonely. At night the buzzing cicadas and the thrum of waves lulled them to sleep in blackness so thick Duane could close his eyes, then open them and see no difference in the dark. They woke up alone, left to dress and pour cereal for themselves, and the days were long and hard to fill. They walked the beach and dug deep holes in the sand. They listened to the radio and waited for Mama to come home at lunch and again at dinner.

It was a great relief when cousin Jo Jane came to visit for the summer, in her dual role of playmate and babysitter. She was fifteen years old now. Duane and Gregg were eleven and ten. Jerry had empowered her to rule the roost, but she also told her firmly never to challenge Duane. If he got mad or refused to do something, Jo Jane should just leave him be. There was no sense fighting with him—she would never win, and his temper was explosive. Jo Jane understood. She had terrible fights with her mom herself, which she always regretted and apologized for. It was one of the reasons she loved escaping to her aunt's home. Aunt Jerry was more relaxed and open than her sister Janie, not to say Jerry couldn't flare up. She was so tired most of the time, her fuse could be pretty short, but she treated Jo Jane like a friend and it made her feel very grown-up.

Jo Jane made tuna salad sandwiches for their lunch. She ironed the long-sleeved cotton shirts Duane wore every day, buttoned at his wrists and tucked into belted jeans. He was fussy about wrinkles. Gregg was usually stripped to the waist in cutoff shorts and ready for the beach, but Duane had to be careful of his fair skin. Gregg had to carry him home swept up in his arms like Scarlett O'Hara once, after the bottoms of Duane's feet scalded while he napped on the sand.

The three cousins rode bikes up and down the beach, speeding past old ladies in cat-eye glasses sunning themselves on lawn chairs. Gregg bodysurfed while Jo Jane and Duane sat and talked, their backs resting against the little dunes that blocked the wind. Teenage girls with bouffant hairdos covered by gauzy scarves wandered slowly past the lifeguards. Jo Jane had her own, mostly make-believe romance with a lifeguard farther down the beach, but Duane and Gregg would frown fiercely at her if she stopped to talk to him while they were around. They'd start shoving each other to create a distraction, which would often turn into a real fight. She'd have to drag Duane off Gregg's curled-up body and separate them until Jerry came home. They didn't like sharing Jo Jane with anybody.

They took a city bus to the boardwalk, where the beach was crowded with bright towels and striped umbrellas stuck in the sand, teenagers thick on the ground. It was heaven. Jo Jane found "Yakety Yak" on the jukebox at the arcade and they played Skee-Ball. Duane hustled the boy who worked the concessions to help Jo Jane win a stuffed lion. She never figured out what he said to the kid, but Duane came sauntering back to her with a wink and a long ribbon of extra cardboard tickets.

In the hottest part of the afternoon, they'd stop in Metz's Drugstore and pick through racks of comics and *MAD* magazines, sitting cross-legged on the cold floor and basking in the air-conditioning. Finally home, they listened to Top 40 radio and sang, miming "Twilight Time" by the Platters and "Little Star" by the Elegants. Duane always got to be Elvis Presley and Gregg was Ricky Nelson. Jo Jane was every girl singer, but she loved being Patti Page best.

When Jerry came home, she'd change into her swimsuit and short shorts right away. The kids would beg for burgers, and she'd drive them back to the strip in her yellow convertible with the top down. "Come with me to the Kasbah and we'll make *beautiful* music together!" the kids shouted in goofy accents just like the radio announcer did each time they cruised by the Kasbah Hotel on their way to Steak 'n Shake or Krystal for hamburgers.

One evening on their way home from dinner, Jerry told them she needed to stop by Amoco. While they sat out by the pumps in the backseat, Mr. Hicks strolled over. He leaned in and said, "You boys better mind your mama. She can send you right back to military school just as easy as she pulled you out, and don't you forget it." It took everything Duane had not to push his face in. He balled his hands into fists in the pockets of his windbreaker and mumbled, "Yes sir," along with Gregg. Jo Jane scowled after Mr. Hicks and stretched her arms around the boys, pulling them toward her in a protective clutch. The threat of being sent back never completely went away.

On one of the last mornings of Jo Jane's Daytona visit, Jerry woke them before dawn for a sunrise breakfast on the beach. She said summer would be over soon and they had to seize the day. They loaded the car with a charcoal grill and grocery bag and drove across the road to the sand. Jerry scrambled eggs over dim coals while the darkness slowly lightened, but the sky stayed an ominous shade of gray and it started to drizzle. Jerry laughed at the sky with her wet palms raised and told the three shivering kids to hang in there. They sat wrapped in damp beach towels with their teeth chattering, mostly miserable, while she made milky coffee for them, but then the rain came down hard and the wind started gusting. Jerry laughed about rain getting in the scrambled eggs.

The boys began the school year at R. J. Longstreet Elementary School, a few miles down Peninsula Avenue. They needed new clothes before classes started. Nice clothes were a real point of pride for them. Jerry didn't have time to take the boys shopping for school clothes, so she called their neighbor Mr. Torme. He worked in the boys' department at Doby's Clothing Store on Beach Street. Jerry gave Torme her shopping list over the phone and told him when to expect Duane and Gregg. She said, "Call me if they don't make it," and gave the boys cab fare and instructions. She told them they had damn well better mind Mr. Torme. Once Duane and Gregg had all the socks and underwear on their mama's list, they took their time, slowly sifting through piles of folded slacks and racks of dress shirts. In dressing rooms behind swinging saloon doors, they tried on stiff blue jeans and plaid shirts, T-shirts with stripes, and windbreakers. Back home, Duane came out of their bedroom wearing a new burgundy smoking jacket made out of satin with a shawl collar and deep pockets, belted around his waist. He sauntered into the living room pretending to smoke an invisible pipe. His mama sure yelled her head off, but he got to keep it anyway.

By their second year in Daytona Beach Shores, a house was being built for them in a grid of modern ranch-style homes. Their plot was on a dirt road spanning three blocks from the ocean to the river. Jerry modified the builders' plans. She liked the slanted roof and walls of windows, but she asked for the main living space to be left open. The builder had planned walls where windows should be, never considering the morning light. She wanted her kitchen rearranged so her sink and counter would face the backyard and imagined watching her boys play outside the window while she cooked. Their backyard was deep and shaded by a big tree and she wanted to see it.

The new house felt tropical, with cool, speckled terrazzo floors. The boys would still share a bedroom, but they'd have their own bathroom tiled in blue. She bought new beds and dressers, and three tall stools for the kitchen's built-in breakfast bar. A couch was beyond her budget, so she made big floor cushions and arranged them in front of a television cart. A wall sculpture of the Three Musketeers with plumed hats, knee britches, and swords raised in mutual salute hung in the living room. Duane pried the blades out of the carved hands and fenced with Gregg, clanking and jabbing, until one sword broke. They carefully folded a piece of gold paper to replace it and you could hardly tell.

Jerry found a new job at an upscale restaurant called the Bali. She kept the books, redesigned menus, and ordered all the produce and supplies, cutting their costs significantly. The owner came to depend on her completely. Her days lasted ten hours or more, and she worked seven days a week. Most nights, the boys were unsupervised and they learned to heat frozen pizzas and graze on snacks from the cupboards. Duane had a phone number where Jerry could always be reached. When she did find time to make late suppers long after dark, she unwound with whisky while she cooked. No one could argue with that; she had earned it.

My granny still lives in the house she had built in 1959. When I was a baby, I sat up for the first time in her big backyard, pulling myself up with a handful of grass while she watched from the kitchen window. I napped on the twin bed where my father used to sleep and sat on the sofa where he did homework and taught himself to play guitar. In the bedroom, two large windows let in pale light. On a recent visit, while falling asleep in their childhood bedroom, I realized that my father stared out these windows as he fell asleep every night. He heard the same suggestion of the ocean's pulse when the wind shifted and stared at the cracks in this ceiling. He was everywhere I looked. The faint hum of my thoughts became a stronger buzz that shot forward with a loud and sudden growl. A motorcycle gunned its engine down the street outside as if driven straight from my mind and headed east over the waterway, and into the night.

Daytona was full of distractions, and Duane found it hard to care about school. He was sassy in class and cracked jokes. He pulled pranks like gluing down rulers and protractors to the table in shop class, and even once locked his teacher in the tool cage. He brought

46

in comics and read them in the bathroom, counting down to three o'clock. At the sound of the final bell, he and some neighborhood boys would ride bikes back to Duane and Gregg's house to watch TV, propped on pillows scattered on the woven grass rug. The boys called themselves a gang and buried a secret time capsule in McElroy Park. They carved their names in wet cement around the base of the new basketball hoop and played football on the lawn of an empty house nearby. Duane was a ferocious fullback, shoving the defensive line out of his way, always unafraid and quick on his feet.

The gang chased one another on their bikes to hotel pools, and walked casually through the fences, impersonating tourists from Tennessee with their towels around their necks, and went swimming. They spent whole afternoons at the Castaway, the only local hotel with an Olympic-sized pool with a real high dive, and Duane's new friend Larry Beck was the best diver around. He leaped off the platform headfirst and twisted his body before straightening out perfectly and barely breaking the water's surface on impact with a little splash. It was a beautiful sight to see. Duane didn't have Larry's technique. He would throw his arms up over his head in a silent cheer, then jump in after him, feetfirst. Duane was skinny and awkward next to Larry, but he was proud of his friend's skill and he'd slap his back and tell Larry he was the best.

A couple of blocks down the road, another neighbor's house was right beside the Neptune Drive-In movie theater. They'd run an extra-long line for a speaker into his yard; the kids, sprawled on blankets, all turned toward the movie screen that glowed like a giant floating postcard in the sky.

Duane was unfailingly confident, always the leader of the pack, but as he got a bit older, he began to disappear for stretches of time. He felt so restless sometimes he walked as far as he could on the beach just to wear himself out, or he'd head to his favorite quiet spot on the river where their street ended. A dirt path led through trees to the water's edge, a perfect place to sit and think. He'd pull off his shoes and dangle his bare feet in the water. Pelicans would dip down to fish, so close you could catch a whiff of how badly they smelled. The sky was huge above the low bridge, and scant homes lined the river. Sometimes he took a book and read until daylight gave out. Sometimes he just watched the world go by, trying to keep his mind as still as he could.

In the summer of 1960, their uncles Sam and David came to visit. It was a great thrill to see them, Sam a strapping, handsome man and David a slightly awkward teenager with wavy hair and glasses. They took the boys on fast car rides on the hard-packed sand, went to the boardwalk and rode every ride, and then ate steaks in a nice restaurant with their mama, all of them dressed to the nines. After a week or so, they carried Duane and Gregg back to Nashville, to visit Grandma Myrtle and give Jerry a break.

Summer days in Nashville were long and hard to fill. One lazy afternoon at Myrtle's house, Gregg wandered across the street to look in on her neighbor, Jimmy Banes. Myrtle didn't approve of Jimmy; she said he wasn't quite right. He was harmless, but surely slow. Jimmy was painting his car with black house paint and a brush—headlights, chrome trim, and all. Gregg thought, *Maybe he likes the way the wet paint shines*. He walked quietly across the road to get a closer look and sat on the edge of Jimmy's porch. He noticed an acoustic guitar leaning against the house.

"Hey, Jimmy, can you play that guitar?"

Jimmy smiled and nodded. He put down his brush and took up a seat beside Gregg and played a simple song. He wasn't bad. Gregg thought, *I could learn to do that if Jimmy can*. Jimmy passed the guitar to Gregg and that was it: Gregg caught the fever.

This story is the answer to the question Gregg Allman has been asked hundreds of times: "When did you first know you wanted to play music?" I have read Gregg's answer many times and I've heard him tell it. He sits back in his chair and laughs, his eyes skimming the floor, one hand smoothing his blond hair back into a ponytail. His accent grows a touch stronger as he describes the heat of the summer day, the paintbrush in Jimmy's hand dripping black paint.

The story has the symmetry and perfection of a creation myth, and it has been repeated and embellished by every reporter who ever greeted Gregg with a tape recorder. Sometimes, he describes Jimmy painting his car, and other times, Jimmy's car is old and dusty, like it was once painted with house paint. Sometimes, Jimmy plays "She'll Be Comin' Round the Mountain" on a Silvertone and sometimes "Long Black Veil" on a Beltone, a real finger-bleeder with strings set high above the neck, and hard to play. Gregg is a great storyteller, funny and warm, and even if the details shift and change over time, when he describes Jimmy patiently showing him his first song, it's magical to imagine that he can locate the exact moment he found his path.

And Duane's moment? Gregg tells that story, too. The brothers went to see a rhythm-and-blues review at the Nashville Municipal Auditorium that same summer: Otis Redding, Jackie Wilson, and B. B. King all in one show. The crowd was segregated, with the black teens seated high above the stage on wooden benches in the balconies and white kids below in red velvet seats. Jackie Wilson, smiling and smooth, swayed and clapped in his sharp suit. Hot lights blazed above the stage and everyone rocked in their seats, all except Duane. Gregg says his big brother sat forward on the edge of his seat perfectly still, transfixed.

Otis's band would glide through love songs, then build to a foot-stomping frenzy, horns synched together so tight and fine you had to shout back at them. Pulsing with the backbeat of the drums, Otis scatted out notes lightning-fast, jumping up and down on his toes, and when the whole band stopped on a dime and suddenly bowed in thanks, a whoop rose up from every mouth in the room.

Then B. B. King took the stage, his gleaming guitar high around his neck. His band swung into action, taking off like a train building a rhythm. The perfect, clear tone of his electric guitar rose out above them all. B.B. sang with his eyes closed and his eyebrows raised in curved surprise, trading verses with his own guitar, singing for him with a voice pure, clean, and so cool. His hand, flashing a big gold ring, wrapped around the guitar's neck and danced there, shivering and gliding over the strings, effortless, almost involuntarily. B.B. rocked from one foot to the other, nodding his head, sweat pouring over his face, punching the notes with precision, the space between each held like a breath. What he didn't play was as important as what he did, and the way he made you wait almost hurt.

Gregg watched Duane staring at B. B. King's hands with complete focus and astonishment. Gregg says he could almost see a decision forming on his brother's face.

Duane leaned in to Gregg and said, "Bro, we got to get into this."

Out with their young uncle David one afternoon, they noticed the greasers that were part of the local music scene that was in evidence everywhere they went. They had swooping hairstyles combed up and back in defiance of gravity and wore their combs in their back pockets in case of emergency. They dressed with every bit as much care as their girls, matching their pressed shirts to the cuffs of their socks. The boys watched how they walked and stood, with their shoulders square, but relaxed, too. They even saw the Everly Brothers shooting pool downtown once. The Everlys had a song on the charts, but when they were home in Nashville they still hung out like regular guys. They wore custom-made jeans with only one pocket in back and the legs pegged tight; real slick. Kids surrounded their pool table, standing at a respectful distance to watch them play. Cool just flowed from them. Duane and Gregg were impressed.

When the brothers went back to Daytona, they brought home a little Nashville style and swagger. They put metal taps on the toes of their shoes so you could hear them coming, click click click. They pegged their black pants tight from knee to ankle and wore them with white dress shirts and white socks. They swept their hair back from their foreheads and carried combs. They sure stood out at Longstreet School, slinking down the hallway like a couple of toughs. No one dressed like that at the beach, especially not kids so young. Everybody took notice.

Gregg followed through on the idea planted by Jimmy's guitar and the thrill of the Nashville show. He decided that when he returned to Daytona, he would get a job and earn enough money to buy himself a guitar. He did it, too. Within a week he found an early morning paper route and was out riding through the neighborhood on his bicycle, tossing folded papers overhand onto porches while Duane slept.

On September 10, 1960, Gregg rode his bike across the bridge to the mainland to Sears on Beach Street and bought his first guitar. He would always remember that date. A new Silvertone acoustic guitar cost twenty-one dollars, and Gregg had earned exactly that and then quit his job. The salesman at Sears counted Gregg's money and turned him away because he didn't have change for sales tax. His mama had to drive him all the way back downtown to give that man his handful of coins.

That guitar was the best thing Gregg had ever owned and he'd bought it on his own, which made it even better. Duane heard Gregg make his way through a few real songs and asked, "What do we have here, Baybro?" with all the menace of the Big Bad Wolf. Gregg could see it was going to be hard to keep Duane's hands off his new prize, so he showed him the few chords he knew and seethed in frustration when Duane wouldn't pass the guitar back. Duane took it from Gregg as much to piss him off as to play it at first, but soon he couldn't put it down. Gregg stayed by his side and listened, showing him things and learning from him, wondering how Duane took to it so fast. They passed Gregg's guitar back and forth, playing and listening, their radio playing low on the nightstand between their beds. Music soon filled the space that had held games and friends the year before.

6

Duane rounded the tight turn into adolescence on a blue Harley-Davidson 135 given to him by his mother for his fourteenth birthday. It was freedom and power, as she well knew, and she hoped it would help him burn off some of the intensity that smoldered behind his perpetually pissed-off expression. She gave him his own acoustic guitar for Christmas a month later, in an effort to keep him away from the guitar Gregg had worked so hard to earn. Not only had Gregg remained committed to playing; he had also stepped out alone and played for an audience for the first time.

The Longstreet School cafeteria smelled like boiled hot dogs and dust. Gregg was onstage and his eighth-grade class was waiting for him to play. The two guys who promised to accompany him didn't show up and he was so nervous to play alone, he almost backed out. Then a teacher offered to join him on drums, so Gregg decided to go ahead with it. He picked his way carefully through a few surf tunes, never looking up from his hands. Once he got going, he managed to forget his butterflies and focused on the shapes his fingers needed to make, and he thought it sounded pretty good. Everyone clapped and smiled when he finished and relief and pride washed over him. It felt great. Kids he didn't even know came up to him and asked when he was going to play again.

When he got home from school, he told a kid who lived around the corner that he was going to be a star. The boy laughed at him, but Gregg wasn't kidding. He didn't want to let that good feeling go.

Duane didn't go to school that day, so he missed the whole thing. He was ducking class all the time now. He'd take the school bus with Gregg in the mornings and then part ways with him to head to his "office"—Frank's Pool Hall on Main Street. He walked past the magazine racks and front counter with a swagger. In the back room, he ran the tables like a pro, squaring his shoulders and leaning his hip against the felt bumpers, steady as a judge. He could seem arrogant and stubborn to some, the way he dominated a room, but kids followed him around and waited for him to say something worth repeating. Things seemed to happen around Duane, and if they weren't happening, he made them happen. He told stories while shooting pool about getting pulled over for speeding and talking back to cops, and he claimed he drank booze right at the dinner table in front of his ma. The kids that gathered there late in the afternoon would just stare. When they lingered too long, hungry for his attention, he'd yell, "Get out of my face!" and stalk off to walk the beach.

When the sun got too hot to stand, he'd go home to drink the beer out of the fridge and cool off. There was plenty of time to chase the smell of his cigarettes out the back door before Mama and Gregg came home. Soon he wanted to drink more than she would buy, and he started boosting beer from the liquor store. One night he and his new buddy, an older kid named Jim Shepley, took a hacksaw to the locks on the coolers that sat outside the store and made off with almost twenty cases of beer. They buried a trash can full of ice in the backyard to store it all, their private stash. They never did get caught and it didn't last as long as you'd think.

Duane rode his Harley-Davidson, the pride of his life, beside the ocean on the quiet end of the beach near home. He'd push the engine and really open it up and take off wailing into the wind. He felt the edge of fear as he picked up speed, but it never came any closer than the horizon line. The only thing that scared him was how little it all mattered: speed up or slow down, walk around, talk to folks, play some pool, meet a girl, lie in the dunes with a can or a bag, go home, sleep it off; just keep rolling.

He was trying new ways to get high. He drew in the icy chemical breeze that came up from the Testors glue at the bottom of a paper bag crumpled hard against his nose and mouth, and stopped his mind cold. Dumb stillness—a moment of pure emptiness overtook him, and Duane wanted it back as soon as it started to fill up again with the sound of his buddy's laugh and the edges of every shitty thought that had been there before—how late it was and how his mama was going to be waiting, how his girl was waiting, too, and how hard it was just to steal a little time. So inhale again as deep as you can, kid, and here it comes again, the big buzzing nothing, the echo at the bottom of a well.

Gregg couldn't understand the changes he saw in his brother. Duane seemed compelled to cause trouble and push up against authority wherever he found it. Duane rolled in at dawn and got into his bed just as Gregg was waking up. Sometimes he'd tell Gregg about a party he'd been to, but mostly he told him to mind his business. Duane knew that Jerry could always get Gregg to tell her where he was. Sometimes Gregg went along and he could sort of keep up with the drinking and all, but Duane usually wanted to be with older kids, and it hurt Gregg to be left out even while they were in the same room.

One night, Duane went riding in a borrowed car with four boys from the neighborhood, speeding down the straight stretches of Peninsula Avenue, windows rolled down to the hot night and loud engine. They'd been drinking beer for hours and his head was spinning, his stomach was seizing up in the worst way, and he wanted out. They were headed to Tomoka State Park, but Duane didn't want to go all the way out there. They were going to the middle of nowhere to look for the ghostly lights.

Since the turn of the century there had been mysterious sightings in the dense forest beside the river, a phenomenon called the Tomoka Lights. On the two-lane park road, thick branches of oak trees draped with Spanish moss blocked the light of the moon and darkness reigned. It was difficult to see the road ahead and drivers were left to navigate by instinct and guts. The road itself was humped like an animal's back and fell off into shallow ditches on either side. Driving fast with your headlights out gave you the best chance to spot the inexplicable orbs glowing in blackness. Some saw small groups of lights dancing together among the trees, drifting above the ground and moving beside their cars as they drove. Others said a single menacing ball of light as bright as fire sped through their windshields like a living thing protecting its territory. The light blinded drivers in a flash that forced some of them off the road. Skeptics guessed the lights were reflections from distant headlights magnified by the long, straight stretch of road. Others said natural phosphorescence caused by swamp gas was the source, but witnesses said the lights were clearly supernatural—spectral and strange.

Leaning against the car door, Duane knew he had to get out or get sick, and when their car came to his street corner, he asked to be dropped off. His friend Tom got out with him, but Ronnie Rainnie and two other boys from Father Lopez Catholic High School sped off without looking back.

The next day, it was on the news: three boys killed in a car crash in Tomoka Park. Ronnie's car had veered off the road in a swinging second and flipped over, crushing everyone inside. While Duane was on his knees in his bathroom, drunk and sick, his friends lay dead in the road, just after leaving him behind.

Reckless races and fascination with speed were a major part of local culture in Daytona. On the primal overgrown back roads, a night world of thrill rides and risk taking thrived in stark contrast to the happy beach scenes that played out by day, but this story carried a more ominous personal suggestion about Duane. Several people told me versions and while no one spelled it out explicitly, it was clear what they all believed: Death was stalking Duane, and it was only a matter of time before it claimed him. The car crash in Tomoka was a bitter taste of what was to come. It foreshadowed the accident that would take Duane's life.

The number of foreboding stories told about Duane mounted. Friends recalled him speeding away on his motorcycle, visibly drunk or drugged. They witnessed fights and daredevil maneuvers, all building to a sense that Duane was driven to risk himself in ways big and small. I was surprised at first by the turns our conversations took, then I realized I was hearing answers to a question I had never asked, but which was somehow implicit in the dramatic velocity of Duane's short life. The people who loved my father were still looking for a coherent narrative to lead from the way Duane lived to the way he died. This dark path kept emerging, whether real or imagined, and I couldn't ignore it. Loss and trauma dogged him, and he ran from it as if something chased him, pushing toward something better. By Duane's freshman year of high school, layers of experience covered him like armor. He lived with energy and intensity, wily intelligence, and a defiant nature, and the seeds of his creativity were germinating in his restlessness and discomfort.

Jerry had to step over her boys' sleeping friends sprawled all over the living room floor many mornings on her way to work. She didn't mind. She had an open-door policy when it came to the boys' friends. She'd rather have them drinking at her house than running wild in the streets. As young as they still were, her boys were full-fledged teenagers and the evidence was everywhere. Food disappeared the moment she put it away, and Duane and Gregg were changing. Their hair had grown down over their ears and past their collars and Jerry started calling them her girls, until Duane asked her to stop. She told them she was sick of finding strands of their hair in her food, but she never tried to force them back to the barber. She had cut her hair off when she was their age. What was the difference? Her sons wanted to have a little control over themselves and the way they looked. Besides, they were the ones who were going to take all the heat for it. She thought hell would be a place where they passed her one more huge pile of laundry to press. Her boys would fly by her ironing board, then rush out the door in shirts still hot as fire. There was never enough time.

Girls clearly liked the way they looked. They were coming around her house, and that was harder for Jerry to accept. Every girl they passed in the market or on the beach seemed to know one son or the other, and she could barely stand to see them smiling and staring at them. Those little girls would be nothing but trouble; that was clear.

Duane noticed a pretty girl named Penny on the school bus. She had blond hair and was about as tall as him. He sat beside her and asked about the book in her hand. It's just for English, she answered, but he seemed really interested. He walked her to class and stayed in school that day hoping to see her again. The whole time she knew him, she never realized how seldom he went to class; he seemed very smart to her. He was always reading adventures like *Treasure Island,* or science fiction novels she'd never heard of, when she hung out at his house after school. They would lie side by side and read with their feet tangled at the bottom of his little bed. His mother was never really home, so Penny stayed for hours without interruption, which was a rare experience for her. She and Duane were very innocent together. Maybe they kissed a little, but mostly they talked. They walked on the beach at night and sat together in tall red lifeguard chairs high above the sand. She suspected he had other girls even though she never saw them, but that didn't matter so much. She could tell he liked her. When Duane wanted to call Penny, he pulled the long coiled cord from the phone on the kitchen wall out the back door and sat crouched against the back of the house, smiling into the receiver out of Jerry's view. He and Penny stayed friends for a long time.

Duane did have another girl, and he kept her to himself. Her name was Patti and they were getting in pretty deep. She was a cute little girl, with short brown hair, dark eyes, and a sweet smile. Her family was more well-off than his, but she liked to drink and kiss, and well, she was down for just about anything. Gregg tried to ask him for details but he'd just wink and walk away. He was private about her; she was his alone. Gregg could see Duane had experience; he could just tell. While Gregg wasn't so interested in the risky thrills consuming Duane, girls were another thing altogether. That was an interest that more than any other would come to fascinate Gregg.

"So, I hear you have a girlfriend now."

Jo Jane couldn't believe Gregg was fourteen and in love. Walking on the beach during a visit, they had their first real talk in years.

"Yeah. Her name is Vicki."

"What does she look like? What color is her hair?"

"At night it's black, and in the daytime when the sun shines on it there's red in it. It's beautiful."

"What color are her eyes?"

"Oh, they're different. They're green, and as they get close to the pupil, they're yellow. They're beautiful." He walked a while, looking over her head to the water and said, "Why don't you write a story about me and let me be the first one to read it?"

"What kind of story?" Jo Jane asked.

"Write about how I've got this sickness and I'm dying."

"Of what?"

"Love."

They walked closer to a shallow tidal pool and Gregg stopped to roll up the cuffs of his jeans.

"Is this your first love?"

"I hope it's my only one. It hurts."

"Yep," Jo Jane said. She watched her cousin walk ahead a little, pick up a shell, and toss it into the pool with a flick. He had grown so tall and his hair was almost white from the sun. He was the beautiful one.

When they got home, Duane was reading a novel, *Catch-22*, with total concentration, curled in the brown vinyl reclining chair in the living room. Jo Jane asked Duane how he was doing. He said, "All right," and kept reading. She let him be and sat facing him on the daybed with the corduroy cover, writing in her notebook. She wrote down her conversation with Gregg so she wouldn't forget this first sign of romance in her young cousin. She and Duane settled into companionable silence and stayed that way for hours.

Later, they leaned against the recently painted dark gray walls of the boys' bedroom. Duane and Gregg had wanted to paint them black, but this was as close as Jerry let them get. Jo Jane sat on Duane's twin bed and Duane sat on Gregg's, both neatly made up with matching blue bedspreads.

"Can I tell you something?" Duane asked.

"Anything, you know," Jo Jane answered.

"You won't like it."

"That's okay."

"Sometimes I do crazy shit. Like last night, me and a friend went down to a bar and sat inside people's parked cars in the parking lot for a while."

"Why'd you do that?"

"Well, he had this linoleum cutter, see? And we tore up the seats. We kicked a couple windows out, too."

"Duane, why would you do something like that?"

"Sometimes we just have to."

Jo Jane wasn't sure what to say.

"Don't you understand?" he asked.

"Not really."

"I guess it's because we're mad at society," Duane said, looking at her with fierce eyes. "I mean it, Jo Jane."

"You were born pissed-off," Jo Jane said. "Society's got nothing to do with it."

"You were, too," Duane said, and smiled a sideways smile she could feel mirrored on her face.

"You're right about that," she said, and they laughed.

She was happy he trusted her, but she was worried about him. She identified with Duane. They shared a similar rebellious and creative nature, and a similar story. Jo Jane lost her father Joe to cancer when she was nine years old, then watched her mother Janie struggle to raise her alone. Jerry and Janie were very different, but they both fussed and pried into their kids' business, then finally succumbed to yelling. Jo Jane and Duane learned to retreat into their books and their private thoughts. They both wanted to be artists, to travel and have adventures; they couldn't wait to be free. Duane turned his moods and frustrations toward the outside world, while Jo Jane felt weighed down by her feelings.

"Why don't you play me something?" she said. She passed him the acoustic guitar that was resting beside her on his bed, and he took it with a little smile and played to her until night came and it was too dark to see.

Duane's long, truant afternoons were consumed by teaching himself simple songs guided by his ear. Gregg says Duane's playing passed his own like he was standing still. Duane had a fluent confidence that Gregg couldn't believe and it seemed to develop so fast. Duane's guitar took the intensity inside him and focused it like a sun ray through a magnifying glass.

I'd be that good, too, if all I did all day was cut school and play, Gregg thought. But if he stayed home, he'd get caught and punished. Duane could do whatever he wanted and it never seemed to matter.

Duane started seeking out other guys who played. He was hungry to know what other players knew and was keen to share what he was figuring out on his own. Duane's friendship with Jim Shepley, which had begun at Frank's Pool Hall, was built on their shared love of playing. His parents were separated and his mother lived pretty close to Duane's house. His father was an editor at *Time* magazine and lived in Connecticut. Jim would come back from visits up north loaded down with new records by Bo Diddley and Jimmy Reed, whose fingerpicking style he was determined to master. He and Duane listened to records for hours with their guitars in their hands. Jim also turned Duane on to WLAC, a Nashville radio station.

WLAC was broadcast out of Nashville on a weak signal Duane could pick up only at night, as if the music were carried by the darkness itself. DJ John R. (John Richbourg) played an intoxicating blend of songs that paid no mind to genre. Ballads and true blues followed rocking dance tunes and country crooners. Duane played while he listened until he could see the shapes his fingers took behind his closed eyes. Listening to Big John R.'s show was like throwing open a window and letting the wind blow through. Suddenly everything seemed possible and music was all that mattered.

The stronger his hands became, the easier it was to pull complex sounds out of the guitar and the sounds began to mirror the way he was feeling. His touch was getting more sensitive and accurate. He could put his skills into the service of his emotions, and he didn't have to struggle so hard to bring everything together. He tried to toughen up the tips of his fingers by soaking them in turpentine and he washed his hands less than he should. He thought water would soften his new calluses. Playing became a maze with high walls and turns in which Duane could get lost for hours at a stretch.

This is the quiet time I picture most when I try to place my father in the world. I see him sitting on the edge of his narrow bed, the blazing heat of the afternoon buzzing with cicadas on the other side of his bedroom window. The curved body of his guitar rests comfortably against his thigh like a piece of a puzzle returned to its proper place. Duane's golden head bends over the guitar's neck, and he watches his fingers stretch and flex, pressing strings. He tenses his jaw with the effort to move faster, his cheeks rising up in a squint. His mouth forms the round sounds he's reaching for: oh, oh, oh. His thumb strikes the uppermost string, sending a harsh buzz through his body, and he blunts it suddenly with an open palm and tries again.

Playing helped him cope with the things happening around him, things he couldn't control or understand—like what happened to his friend Larry Beck. When Larry was fifteen, and he and Duane had both moved up to Seabreeze High School, he brought his daring from the diving board to the trampoline. In gym class, Larry could do masterful flips by bounding off a mini-tramp onto a padded mat. He gained height with each bounce and executed perfect twists in the air, then landed upright on his feet like magic. Then one afternoon, Larry overshot the mat's edge and fell onto the hard gym floor. It was just a moment, a slight variation on all the other jumps he had completed effortlessly. He was knocked unconscious, and lay twisted in an awkward position while his classmates stood around him with their hands cupped over their mouths, their eyes tearing. He had shattered several vertebrae in his back.

Larry didn't realize how badly he was hurt right away. When he was brought to the hospital, he could still move his arms but not his hands or his legs. He was transferred to the Harry-Anna Children's Hospital in Umatilla, where he spent an entire year in rehab. Larry was paralyzed and he used a wheelchair for the rest of his life. Duane was one of the few friends who made the effort to visit Larry, and when he and Gregg went to Nashville for the summer, Duane sent Larry letters.

....

July 1961

Dear Larry,
Hi! How are you doing? Fine I hope. Me and Gregg are in Nashville now spending our vacation. It's pretty dull but I know its not as dull as it is for you. Are they giving you them

daily workouts still? Hope so. Sure will be good to see you again. We'll be going back to Daytona about August 17th, and we will probably stop in there to see you. Here's the latest:

1. Ernie got a motor. It's a 165.
2. Bob, Gregg and I have started a band, we played a Y-Teens for money.
3. I got a guitar a red Gibson electric.
4. I had a job for a while. Three whole days.
5. Things are really dead around Daytona, or so I hear.
6. Teddy Petruccianna got in a big fight with some kid from the Mainland, and the guy cut him straight down his arm.
7. There are really some good looking girls in Nashville. We had a party the other night, and there wasn't a homely one there.

Everyone asks me about how you're getting along, so get a letter off and tell me so I can tell them. Milcie hasn't changed a bit. Peggy is looking better all the time.

No kidding! She changed her hair and everything. At that party we had some guy brought "juice" and really got loaded and started messing with another guys girl, and he busted a coke bottle over his head! No foolin! Well, I gotta run. You take it easy and do what they tell you and you'll be outa that hole real soon.

See ya in August,
Duane

He drove his motorcycle an hour to Umatilla to see Larry. He used to take Larry on motorcycle rides to the Neptune Drive-In, speeding over the bumps used to prop up the front end of cars facing the screen. He'd whip around in a wide circle, then gun it over the bump and just fly, Larry whooping and holding on to Duane's

63

waist. It was hard to accept that those days were gone. Larry's accident traumatized Duane. Life was blowing by and anything could happen at any time; that was clear.

When Larry returned home, Duane visited him with his guitar and blew his mind with all the songs he had learned. Larry knew that success was in Duane's near future, and he told him so. Duane was more than just another kid picking for fun; he was going to make it. It meant a lot to Duane that Larry believed in him.

Soon Larry got a van with special levers he could drive himself, and he'd head over to the Allman house to watch Duane and Gregg rehearse. The brothers were beginning to put their first band together.

"Allman Joys"
DAYTONA BEACH, FLORIDA
CL3-1355

7

Duane drove his Harley into the ground, then sold it for spare parts. He used the money to buy his first electric guitar: a Gibson Les Paul Junior. The little red solid body was a simple instrument with strength of purpose and a pleasing weight in his hands. Filling up his room with that electrified sound sent a thrill through him every bit as exciting as any other high. He communed with that guitar, bending notes to his will, learning to rely on his ear by mimicking and repeating licks in popular songs.

Duane and Gregg's first band, the Uniques, performed at the dances held at their local YMCA. The brothers both played guitar and took turns singing, but Duane did all of the talking between songs.

If it was her day off, Jerry would drive them to the Y and stay to watch, even though they said she made them nervous. She thought that was just ridiculous.

Jerry was genuinely surprised by what she saw. Her gangly,

awkward boys were all polished up with their hair brushed and their shirts pressed, and the music sounded more impressive in the high-ceilinged room full of kids than it did blasting through her closed garage door, driving her neighbors crazy.

Her sons were having a real effect on those kids. She watched a fourteen-year-old girl in Bermuda shorts, her hair in a ponytail, stand in front of Gregg, then dreamily drift back to Duane, then right back to Gregg as if she were in a trance. For a moment Jerry could see her boys through that girl's eyes. They were handsome boys, lit with a glow from within. They were remarkable, and she was so proud.

Soon Duane and Gregg moved on from the Y and started playing house parties. They went through a series of band names: the Uniques, the Shufflers, and finally, the Escorts. It was hard to find guys who played well and owned their own gear, and harder still to find guys who took playing as seriously as Duane did. Each new incarnation of the band became a little more professional. On weekends the Escorts traveled as far as Gainesville, home of the University of Florida, to play fraternity parties and proms, bringing home travel stories and pocket money. The measure of freedom the brothers had was rare and impressive to their friends.

Duane and Gregg started haunting the nightclubs down by the Daytona shore. Duane was quick to introduce himself to owners and managers. He met other young musicians, black and white, wherever he found them. He wanted to learn everything he could. That's how he and Gregg met Floyd Miles. Floyd was a young black kid with the voice and presence of an older, seasoned performer. He fronted a vocal group called the Untils, who were backed by a white band called the Houserockers. They could tear through "Twist and Shout" and "Land of a Thousand Dances," then smooth out with a tune like "Daddy's Home." They had a standing gig at a club on the ocean pier, and kids would roll in off the beach and get mesmerized. Floyd had style and a strong set of pipes. At sixteen years old, he already had a wealth of experience and had lived on his own for a year. Duane and Gregg took turns sitting in on guitar with the Houserockers and they invited Floyd to come hang out at their house. He hesitated at first, but he did come.

It was an unusual thing for white kids and black kids to become friends. Beaches, schools, restaurants, and clubs were all segregated in Florida, and a nightly curfew was strictly enforced. If a black person went out on the white side of Daytona after dark, the police would be called. But music was an exception; young black musicians had talent that even bigoted white people wanted to enjoy, so rules were bent when it came to performers. Music was a force of change in the lives of young people.

Gregg didn't seem to entirely realize what he had. However, Duane heard something developing in his baby brother that he didn't have himself: a voice. Duane told Jo Jane, "If I had that voice, I could rule the world."

Even though he was still shy about it, Gregg had great pitch and natural control over his voice, and emotion just poured out of him when he sang a song he really liked. Duane had the passion and confidence, but singing wasn't his gift. He asked Floyd to show Gregg the ropes.

Soon Floyd was teaching Gregg how to sing from his diaphragm, and how to protect his throat. Duane and Gregg snuck Floyd into parties to see their new band play, and sometimes hid him in the kitchen to watch from the doorway of white clubs. Floyd took the brothers to his neighborhood record store and eventually to George's Place, a nightclub where white kids were not often seen. Jerry said Duane looked like a marshmallow in a cup of hot chocolate, the only white face there.

Duane would pick up his guitar case and head out the front door, his cigarette in the corner of his mouth, and drive his mother's car over the high bridge, to the other side of the river, the neighborhood whites had ugly names for: Darktown, Niggertown.

The trees were taller there, the roads narrow and lined with churches and bars, little cinder-block houses, people sitting on concrete porches in metal folding chairs in the dark. He went to George's Place and sat by the small stage with Floyd. He was happy to be there and he was never afraid. Why would he be? He had friends and he made more, just by playing and being smooth. He was young and strange, with his long hair and pegged pants, but he was always kind and respectful.

He'd ask to sit in with a band, usually an R&B cover act of guys not much older than him, and he'd catch on quick. He shared the stage well, knowing how to stand back and support with rhythm until the other player looked him in the eye and nodded ever so slightly, just tipping his head to the floor, and Duane would step into the empty space carved for him in the song and fill it with a hot lick. The sound of his guitar whipped through the room, funky and changeable, then he'd drop down into the rhythm and the other player would laugh with his eyes. Damn! Where did you come from? Duane would nod and smile back, thinking, *What is better than this? Playing your way into a world that doesn't belong to you? A world your mama can't follow you into?* Music filled up the space between people, moving their hips. Songs about love and longing, bald-faced and fearless. It felt good to play so sweet and earnest, then rock the room and forget where you were altogether. You forgot the walls, the floor, the bridge over the dark water that divided the town. You moved and found your body in the music. It was everything, and he was making it.

Jerry wasn't keen at first on her boy's friendship with Floyd, a fact that is hard to imagine now that she and Floyd have been friends for more than forty years. She was a white woman of a generation in the South raised in racism, and back then she saw black people as belonging to a separate and lower class. But her boys were not deterred when she loudly tossed out slanderous names and washed the glasses they had used—twice.

"He's a musician, Ma" was all the explanation they felt was needed.

Floyd stayed and Jerry grew to know him and love him. Jerry grew, period.

Eventually the Escorts moved up to playing in nightclubs they were too young to enter legally as patrons. Jerry would go down and introduce herself to the owners, so they'd know the boys weren't on their own and couldn't be taken advantage of. She made Duane and Gregg join the local union and pay their dues out of their earnings. If they were going to do this thing, they were going to learn to be professionals, as far as she was concerned. Duane insisted that they buy matching suits to wear onstage. They took publicity photos at a local studio, and made calling cards to give to club owners. They looked like clean-cut young men with a slight bohemian edge, their carefully combed hair touching their mandarin collars.

Duane was making up his mind to leave school. The more he played, the more he wanted to play, and school was feeling like a waste of precious time. He wasn't getting away with anything. Jerry knew he was skipping class and no amount of yelling was getting through to him. Duane would say what he always said. "I will never use anything they're teaching at that school. I can read. I can write. What more do I need?" If she really started screaming at him, he'd just leave the house and stay away for a day or two.

The dynamic of their family of three was a complicated balancing act. Duane and Jerry were both strong-willed and fiery, and Gregory was left to retreat into himself, or step up and become the peacemaker. When his mama questioned him about Duane, he would tell her just enough to keep her satisfied. She kept a closer eye on Gregg because she knew he was more likely to listen to her. He was gentle and easygoing. Duane did what he wanted, regardless. The best she could hope for was that he would do what he wanted to do while staying under her roof. Myrtle and even Janie wondered whether Jerry working so hard was the real issue with the boys; they suggested she had taken on too much at the restaurant. They didn't understand her ambition or her desire to give her sons nice things. She had raised them to take care of themselves. They had the right to make choices of their own. They were young men. She even understood and respected their rebelliousness, up to a point.

Daytona was a small community, and the drinking and smoking, the beer heists from the local liquor store and the speeding through town, were not going unnoticed. Patti's father would yell at Jerry over the phone, telling her to keep that wild boy away from his daughter. Mr. Hicks gave her pitying looks. Gregg's grades started to dip down, too. All he thought about was his little girlfriend. Jerry was getting sick and tired of her neighbors' talk. She wasn't going to let her sons become juvenile delinquents and something had to be done to rein them in.

In 1962, when Gregg was a sophomore and Duane should have been a junior, she decided to send them both back to Castle Heights Military Academy. Duane had missed so much school that Jerry hired a special tutor so he could pass the entrance exam, but he was still held back and enrolled as a sophomore, a further indignity. The upper school was even more rigid than the lower school had been. Their hair was clipped close to their scalps, their uniforms were heavy, and classes, drills, and inspections accounted for almost every waking moment. Defiance and broken rules were met with swift corporal punishment and total loss of freedom.

Duane took his guitar, his record collection, and a portable record player off to school. Music remained his focus. He holed up in his dorm room, practicing guitar while listening to records. He held records still with his big toe while he figured out riffs, controlling the flow of music. He and Gregg formed a band called the Misfits and performed at school parties, but it wasn't enough to divert Duane or keep him there for very long.

Within the year, Duane left Castle Heights with his guitar case in hand and hitchhiked to Nashville, where he boarded a bus home to Daytona without telling anyone but Gregg—AWOL.

After being home alone with his furious mother for a couple of weeks, he couldn't take the heat and went back to school and hid out in Gregg's dorm room. Jo Jane later teased him that he was the only guy who ever ran away *to* boarding school. He didn't stay very long, and when he returned home again he refused to return to Seabreeze High School, no matter what Jerry said. He was finished with high school for good.

"Wait, Granny. When did Duane drop out of high school?" I asked.

"Which time? He was in and out of school."

"Was he just a sophomore? Like, fifteen or sixteen years old? Didn't you try and stop him?" I asked.

My granny reared up in her chair and seemed to grow a few inches taller, her voice hard and loud, her eyes blazing.

"Galadrielle, I'd like to see you try and tell a boy taller than you and stronger than you what to do! I couldn't stop Duane from doing anything he wanted to do!"

I was glimpsing her as she must have been fifty years ago—strong enough to handle two young men on her own through sheer force of will. Whether she could control them or not, she was clearly a force to be reckoned with. I had never seen this side of her before, but I was certain my father had.

She said, "I'll tell you what I did. I told him: 'You sure as hell aren't going to lie around my house or walk the beach like you've been doing.' I said, 'If you don't work, I won't work, either, and we will both sit right here all day, staring at each other and starving!'" She was quiet for a moment, and then Granny said, "Duane would have become a killer if he hadn't found that guitar."

Duane did go to work. He found a job playing music in a strip joint. Jerry saw it for what it was—an opportunity to be a paid musician—and she didn't stand in his way. In fact, she let Duane borrow her car, as long as it was sitting safely in the driveway when she woke up to go to work. He didn't have his driver's license yet, but he was a workingman now.

Bucky Walter's Five O'Clock Club was on the opposite side of the river. The live trio that played for the dancers was looking for

71

a bass player and Duane went to check it out. He took a job washing dishes in the kitchen and chatted up the players during their breaks. He talked them into letting him sit in with them.

Duane took to the nightlife without skipping a beat. There was a world going on out there, bodies moving, cars screeching, girls shaking, and bands swinging. Duane was headed that way, and why walk when you can run? He smoked cigarettes and let his hair grow back down over his collar. He pressed his long-sleeve shirts and shined up his dress shoes. He didn't look like a kid of sixteen; he carried himself like a man. He brought home money and lived his own life. Music was everywhere, in everything, a light shining brighter than every other. Duane's ears and mind were wide open now. He saw the beauty and promise in it, and it called to him. He slept with his radio in his ear, and turned it up loud in his mama's car coming home from playing at work.

Duane played bass, because that's what the band needed; he'd stand in front of a piano player who played only the black keys. It was an after-hours joint that would often get busted for selling cheap liquor in top-shelf bottles. When the police came by, the rest of the band would hide Duane away in the girls' dressing room or make him hunch down in a car in the parking lot.

Duane looked into the little crowd of men seated at small round tables with glazed eyes. They were only hearing the backbeat, the one-two coming off the hips of the girl's slow shimmy. The music was just the water she was swimming in, this sweat-shiny mermaid gliding in place through waves of smoke. Duane didn't care. He wasn't playing for the men anyhow. He was following the song through its changes and keeping pace with the beat, he was learning every minute, and it felt good to forget what he was trying to do, and just do it, like breathing. It was happening. The life in this dark club was a mysterious brew served in a chipped cup—his first taste of another world. He was on the inside now, building this thick atmosphere brick by brick, part of a rhythm section, no longer a spectator. Even on this little stage, he could feel it was where he belonged. This was his classroom; these cats laying down this sleazy groove were his teachers and he was going for a gold star.

Gregg hated Castle Heights, too, but he managed to stay for almost two years. The work was never a problem, but he was heartsick over being separated from Vicki. She told him she would wait for him, but he learned on a home visit that she was dating a football player. He decided to drop out, too, and when he finally stirred up his courage to leave, he was determined to go with dignity. He put on his full dress uniform and walked into the headmaster's office. He said, "If you see me getting smaller, it's because I'm leaving."

Once Gregg was home, music took up its rightful place in their lives again, and it remained the most powerful thing he and Duane shared. Duane wanted Gregg to quit high school so they could really hit the road. Jerry backed him off quick, saying, "You do what you want with your life, but you leave your brother alone."

Jerry enrolled Gregg in Seabreeze High and he stayed until he graduated in the summer of 1965.

In their room Duane and Gregg listened to everything: corny crooners and perky pop stars, blues criers and rhythm kings, and the Beatles, oh God, the Beatles. Their heads were just swimming with Beatles harmonies and the brilliant simplicity of their melodies. How could so much power and feeling hide in so few chords?

Their garage smelled of cool, dusty concrete. The walls were lined with metal shelves of gardening supplies and cardboard boxes. Duane and Gregg set up little amps and played out there for hours, woodshedding with the door raised up for air when it got too hot, standing facing the road, and whole afternoons passed within a Beatles song like "This Boy." Neighborhood kids were drawn to the sound and sat in their driveway to listen to them practice. The brothers ran through the same song over and over until they got it down, perfect, and then moved on to another. They played every day for months. Then at night, Duane and Gregg would lie in their beds in the dark and sing the harmonies until they were just right. What was left to do as a young band that the Beatles hadn't already done better? Duane was determined to learn from them and keep going.

Their biggest break came in the spring of 1965, when the Escorts were offered a chance to open up for the Beach Boys at the City Island Ball Park. The only trouble was, they had to share the limelight with their local rivals, the Nightcrawlers, who always seemed to be a step ahead of them. They had recorded a song that became a regional hit on the radio called "Little Black Egg." The envy and frustration of hearing their rivals' song played around town lit a fire under Duane. They practiced constantly for that gig, and when the time came, they knew they had to blow the Nightcrawlers out of the water.

The Nightcrawlers and the Escorts were told to set up side by side on the big stage, and trade off tunes, one band and then the other. If they hadn't felt like rivals before, this gig would have done it. The Escorts had worked so hard and it showed. Their tones were better, their energy higher, and at the end of the night, they felt great.

Duane couldn't stop talking about everything that was to come. They were going to hit the road and be a real professional outfit! It just wasn't happening fast enough. The rest of the guys sat quietly listening, thinking about all the other things they wanted to do more than take off and play. No one had the drive or focus that Duane did, and even if they had, their folks would have killed them. They had to admit they were not ready to make a career out of their high school band; they wanted to go to college, even Gregg.

Gregg had a taste for playing, of course, but he had a fallback plan. He wanted go to dental school and get himself a stable career, but he learned to keep quiet about it around his brother. He didn't want to disappoint Duane, and he never had his brother's blind faith that they could succeed as musicians. Gregg imagined a house on the water, a wife, money in his pocket, cars, and nice clothes. Duane didn't care about any of that; he just wanted to keep playing. Gregg would slip off with his girl and miss practice, and Duane would ignore him as punishment, disappearing for a few days and never saying where he'd been.

Granny says, "Duane could see Gregg's talent long before he saw it in himself."

When Gregory told me about this notion of becoming an oral surgeon, I searched his face to see if he was kidding, but no joke—that was his teenage plan for the future. I tried to imagine him with a Pat Boone haircut and a white coat, smiling over open mouths all day, pulling teeth. It is impossible to picture.

When I asked Gregory how he and Duane got along in their early bands, especially in the moments when Gregg considered moving on, he said, "Well, let me see." He paused.

"My brother beat the shit out of me just about every day of my life. I mean, he could just make you feel about this small," he said, pinching his fingers together on a half inch of air. "Then, I got to be bigger than him and I fought back. One time, I was hanging out at this apartment that was owned by a club owner in town, just across the road from the club where we were set to play later that night, and here comes Duane. Drunk and pissed-off, cuz I have this beautiful honey sitting on my lap, a girl he liked, too. He walks up and says, 'Baybro, did you go to the doctor and get that rash on your dick looked at?' and I mean that did it. I was so pissed-off. I told him to get the fuck out, and he leaned in to punch me and I shoved him away. He was not expecting that, and we ended up out in the middle of the street, just brawling. We were just beating on each other, until finally, I clocked him in the ear and he was just laid out flat. The police came and everything, and I had to carry Duane home. Blood was coming out of his ear, and I was terrified, but that was the end of it. He never hit me again."

Gregg looked into my eyes for a moment, proud and strong, and I didn't know what to say. Then he softened a little, mumbling something about how playing music together helped smooth things out between them, too.

In the end, it didn't matter what Gregg wanted. Duane never left any room for doubt about the plan. Giving up was not an option. Music was the only way forward. He wouldn't let his baby brother walk away.

When Gregg graduated from Seabreeze, they renamed their band the Allman Joys and hit the road hard. Their sets were so slick. They were a real pro club act, with long vamps between every song, and Duane talking in the low, melodic voice of an emcee: "Thank you, thank you very much . . . Bless your hearts. This next one is by James Brown, and he'll be in town . . . soon." They were so sharp in their matching suits, singing harmonies, and Duane was commanding, flinging out licks and leads like it was the easiest thing in the world.

But before Gregg graduated from high school, before he and Duane hit the road as the Allman Joys, before their lives became completely devoted to playing, something happened in Duane's life that was kept secret from everyone around him.

In September 1964, when Duane was seventeen and his girlfriend Patti was sixteen, they had a baby girl.

Learning that I am not my father's only child was a confusing shock, and I chose to focus my outrage on how I found out. A woman armed with a tape recorder had traveled to Berkeley, California, in 1989 to interview my mother. She was a serious Allman Brothers fan who edited a photocopied newsletter called "Les Brers." She and her boyfriend wanted to write a book about the band, and they had already spoken to Linda Oakley, Granny, and even Gregg. My mom was assured that this would be the first authorized telling of the band's story, including the families' perspectives, and she didn't want to be left out. Although she had been approached many times, Donna had never given an interview about Duane before and she was nervous.

76

On the tape, you can hear Donna's hesitation and discomfort at first, but after an hour or so, she opens up and offers the woman a choice of wine, red or white, and completely lets down her guard. She describes meeting Duane, my birth, their breakup, and his death in great detail. Mom told her stories that were secret, stories I thought she would only ever tell me. Worse, she described things with a candor and openness I did not recognize at all, and listening to the tape, I felt jealous.

Several weeks after the interview was done, the woman sent my mother a letter to ask her one more question: "Have you ever met the child Duane had with his first wife, Patti?"

Donna called Gregg. "That baby died," he said.

Then she called Jerry, who said she had met Duane's daughter. The woman writing the book about the band had brought her by her house. Jerry said the young woman did not look like Duane to her. She said she thought Duane believed the child had died at birth. Frankly she was not sure what he thought happened. Patti had given the baby up for adoption at birth, and when Duane and Patti later tried to find out about the baby, they could have been told anything.

Donna called Jaimoe, but he said Duane had never mentioned a baby other than me. No one could tell Donna what she really wanted to know: Why hadn't Duane told her?

My mom flew to New York, where I was in college at the time, and told me while we rode a city bus to the Whitney Museum of American Art. She was sitting, and I swayed over her holding the chrome bar above my head. I don't remember the words she used, or how I received them, only my anger slowly rising while I looked out the window at the crowded sidewalk. My next memory is of standing in front of the Calder circus inside a glass box in the museum's lobby. I could hardly see it. My fury found its target in the woman with the tape recorder, this stranger who knew more about my family than I did.

Patti's parents hated Duane, and Jerry would barely tolerate the mention of Patti's name. Patti's father yelled into the phone, "If I see your son put his foot on my lawn, I'll shoot his ass with rock salt!"

Jerry screamed right back, "If you touch one hair on my son's head, you better start looking for the red lights of the police car, coming to toss you in jail!" She would defend Duane with her life, which didn't mean she wasn't also absolutely furious. Duane wasn't the one she blamed. She had always known these little girls traipsing in and out of her home were looking to trap her sons and make meal tickets out of them; Patti just confirmed her worst fears.

Patti was sent to a home for unwed mothers in Jacksonville. While she was pregnant, she contracted rubella, and the baby was born deaf, with heart complications. The baby girl spent the early years of her life in an orphanage and then foster homes, until she was adopted by a couple at age five. Her new parents had a deaf relative and understood her needs. She was raised in Jacksonville, the same city I lived in until I was eleven.

Later in life, Patti and her daughter found each other and formed a relationship.

They visited my granny and gave her a school picture: a pale girl with brown eyes and dark brown curly hair with a sweet smile, a stranger.

Twenty years after learning of her, I still cannot untangle how I feel. She makes me see that I built my identity on being Duane's only child. The thing that I felt most special in me feels threatened by her existence, in a childish way.

Stranger still, all I have of him, which never felt like enough to satisfy my need for him—the stories I have gathered, the relationships with our extended family, and even my name—suddenly feels like a great wealth of riches that she does not share, and I feel ashamed of that. Most of all, I am wounded by the thought that she cannot hear his music.

The woman with the tape recorder got in touch with me just a short time ago and informed me that my sister wanted contact with me. I took her phone number and we began talking through emails and texts, brief polite notes, telling about our lives in the simplest terms. It's hard to know what to say. She sends me pictures of herself and her son and daughter, and she even has a granddaughter. I can't help but search all of their faces for some trace of my father. I cannot see him in them, and I have no way of knowing what that means.

My mother reminds me that we have no way of knowing the truth of her paternity, but it seems unkind to ask her, after all this time, to take a test. There seems little harm in letting things stay where they have always been, in the mysterious gray area where my father kept his most personal moments. I wrote to Patti but she didn't answer my letter. Her silence doesn't surprise me, even though I remain disappointed and curious about her relationship with my father. Duane's constant determination to keep his private life private seems to be holding fast. His will is still at work, and I accept it.

When Gregg graduated from Seabreeze High School in 1965, the Allman Joys were freed up to spend their first summer as a traveling band. Jerry watched her boys packing the Chevy station wagon and trailer she had helped them buy to haul their gear. Her sons were grown and would wheel in and out of her life from now on. Duane was loose-limbed and relaxed; he'd rest his big hands on his hips, narrow his eyes in thought. He'd be watchful and a little wary until a smile broke through. She tried to memorize him. Gregg had grown from cute to handsome in a season. His skin browned up like a biscuit and the summer sun made his blue eyes startling. They were a study in contrasts, her young men. She called them in for iced tea before they left, her voice cracking. She walked into her kitchen and poured herself a quick shot, standing at the kitchen sink, looking out into her empty backyard while the whisky warmed her throat and cleared her mind.

The Allman Joys played their first serious out-of-town gig in Mobile, Alabama, at the Stork Club. They played six nights a week, six sets a night, covering songs from as many varied bands and genres as they heard on WLAC. They mastered Top 40 hits, rhythm and blues, and British rock with equal skill. They could play "You've Lost That Lovin' Feelin'" with full harmonies, and "Walk Away Renée" to melt girls' hearts, then fire off "What'd I Say" and just blow the roof off. They could chase a Beatles tune with a Bobby "Blue" Bland and a James Brown. Working up a set that could last all night took hours of practice. They needed dozens of songs in their pocket to take requests, so they traveled with a portable record player and bought hit singles along the way to update their set.

When they couldn't afford to crash in even the cheapest hotels, they slept on people's floors in a heap under thin blankets and coats. They ate pancakes at midnight and again at noon, and fueled up on Coca-Cola and "blackbirds"—amphetamine pills—just to keep up the pace. They smoked cigarettes until they were hoarse and drank whisky to help them fall asleep. For Duane, it was heaven on earth.

The more Duane played, the greater his need to play became. His life had real purpose and it found its expression in performing. Standing onstage and launching into a song tested him every single time. Once he figured out a riff, he started searching for the next piece of the puzzle, and there were always new passages to learn and new licks to try. The weight of his guitar strap over his shoulder, his instrument's smooth neck gliding under his palm, the thickening of his fingertips and the quickening of his responses, all of it thrilled him. He was doing what he was born to do.

At the outermost limit of their new adventure, they traveled to New York City to play at Trude Heller's, a small club on West Ninth Street. Greenwich Village was a whole new world, teeming with freaks: college girls in miniskirts and black turtleneck sweaters, gay men in dandy suits, and fully tricked-out drag queens leaning in doorways wearing high-heeled shoes and wigs. Duane thought it looked like a damn anthill. Just watching the street hustle was a groove.

They spent their pay on hip bell-bottoms at bohemian boutiques and took their new Beatle boots to the cobbler to have stacked heels added. They stayed at the Albert Hotel on East Tenth Street, a gloomy, Gothic brick structure built by the same architect who designed the Dakota apartments on Central Park West. The Albert had fallen on hard times and become home to poor traveling bands like the Blues Magoos and the Lovin' Spoonful.

The Allman Joys fell into a routine of playing long nights at Trude Heller's, taking home a girl or three, waking up late for a pancake breakfast and an Orange Julius, dropping off their laundry, then heading back to Trude's to practice before dinner, then doing it all over again. To make extra cash, they even took on the role of backup band for a flamboyant gay cabaret singer named Monti Rock III. Monti wore a full face of makeup and loaded himself down with baubles and bangles and worked the crowd at Trude's. Bill Connell, the Allman Joys' drummer, was fresh off the plane from Tuscaloosa, Alabama, and couldn't believe his eyes. Duane, Gregg, and Mike Alexander, their bass player, seemed to take Monti in stride. One look at the expression on Bill's face and Duane gave him the nickname "the Novice."

Duane had already mastered this life. He had taken on all of the responsibilities of a bandleader, from talking to booking agents on pay phones and befriending club owners to planning all travel. He had high standards. He demanded shined shoes and pressed pants, polished instruments and punctuality, updated union cards. Daily practice before gigs was crucial to keep up with the growing demand for new songs. Bill felt it was the influence of Duane's military education showing.

But Duane was also still a kid. The guys made smoke bombs out of toilet paper rolls and firecrackers, using lit cigarettes as fuses. They'd set them in the glass phone booth across the way, then from their hotel room windows watch the smoke pour out, the fire trucks arriving, lights and sirens rolling. They stayed up late after playing, trading stories and worrying about Vietnam and the draft notices that were coming for each of them. Duane sent letters to Jo Jane, full of confidence that they were going to make it; there was no other plan.

Back on the road, they practically wore a groove in the asphalt between New York and Nashville, then St. Louis and Daytona, Mobile and Tuscaloosa, before heading back to New York. All the traveling was wearing Gregg down. He hadn't entirely let go of the idea of going to college, but Duane asked him to give the band one more year and Gregg couldn't refuse him.

Many cover songs the Allman Joys were playing had keyboard parts, and although guitar was his first love, Gregg had been drawn to keyboards for a long time. At Julian's, a restaurant where Jerry now worked as a bookkeeper, a live band played in the bar for the happy-hour crowd. The band's instruments included a Hammond B-3 organ with a Leslie—the special speaker that revolved around inside to create a vibrating sound that Gregg loved. When he was still in elementary school, Gregg had played around on that B-3, waiting for his mom to finish work. When he first sat down, he thought the thing had entirely too many buttons, but he was intrigued with it. Gregg got a Vox organ to help fill out the Allman Joys' sound, and he even found a used Leslie that brought it pretty close to the ideal organ sound he could hear in his head.

Duane knew success was within their reach. He encouraged the parents of the Sandpipers—a singing trio of girls they had backed in a Pensacola, Florida, club—to let their daughters join them in New York. A disc jockey liked the girls' sound and set up an audition for them at Columbia Records with Bob Johnston, a producer who worked with Bob Dylan. The Allman Joys accompanied them, and even if nothing came of it, it was a new connection. John D. Loudermilk, the man who wrote "Tobacco Road" and many other hit songs, saw the Allman Joys play at the Briar Patch in Nashville.

He was impressed by the effect they were having on the crowd and saw their potential. He invited them to hang out at his house in the country and gave them tips on the business and songwriting. He financed their first recording studio experience at Bradley's Barn and introduced them to his influential friends, like Buddy Killen, head of Dial Records, and a fellow songwriter, John Hurley. He even took them out to breakfast with legendary guitarist Chet Atkins, who was so kind and open, the boys were almost able to overcome their nerves enough to talk to him.

With Loudermilk's support, the Allman Joys recorded their first single, a cover of Willie Dixon's "Spoonful"; it was released on Dial Records. Building on the strength of "Spoonful," which was getting decent regional airplay, they filled the Fort Brandon Armory in Tuscaloosa with their biggest crowd yet and earned enough money for Duane and Gregg to buy Triumph motorcycles. The brothers rode out in front of the band's station wagon and trailer, leading the way down the road.

Linda, Berry Oakley's wife, saw the Allman Joys perform when she was seventeen. I had no idea she knew them before Berry became the bass player for the Allman Brothers Band four years later. She told me about the first night she met them, in a club in Jacksonville.

"Me and my girlfriends got to be their squeezes for the weekend. The Allman Joys played at the bottle club, the after-hours club—you bring your own bottle and they sold mixes and sodas, that's when they really cut loose, and played the old blues. The Beachcomber would close at eleven or midnight, and they'd reopen and a whole new crew of clientele would come in. You could buy your mixers and that's when they would really get down to it. They were doing great R-and-B stuff and the best harmonies. They did 'In the Midnight Hour' and 'Reach Out.'

"They came over and sat with us and there were all these waitresses with sailor hip-huggers and lace-up shirts and they were all hot for the band. And here, these little high school girls come in there. It was just a change of pace. I remember Gregg coming up to my friend Marilyn and going, 'Hi, blondie! What's your name?' She just turned into a puddle. They invited us to come see them at their little hotel, the 400 Court Motel on Philips Highway. Here we were, these virginal high school girls . . .

"They took us to Philips Highway Plaza, the mall up there, and they went and bought Geraldine a stereo from Montgomery Ward for Christmas. We went through a package store and they got some Calvert's Extra and some Cokes and we went back to the motel, and they were fixing us drinks. When Duane started to make a move on me, I told him I was dating David Brown. He said, 'Let's reminisce about old Dave.' Your dad was so much fun. They were headed back to Daytona, and me and my friend said, 'Oh, our world will never be the same!' And they said, 'You've gotta come down and see us!'

"They gave us their address in Daytona, and of course we drove down there and it was all these people in and out of the house and their mom was at work, and we sat there and smoked too many cigarettes, and Duane was off with Patti. Nothing could be the same anymore, after you witnessed this. It was something else. There was definitely this magic going on. Things were changing everywhere: Vietnam and the protests and kids getting killed on campus, and peace and love and Jefferson Airplane and Country Joe and the Fish, and it was so intense man, dig it, and 'I Am the Walrus' and Donovan and reefer and laying around on the floor, and let's solve all the world's problems! It was wonderful!"

Soon the turbulent times beyond the music scene touched the brothers directly. Duane's draft notice came. They had to drive home to Daytona to deal with it. They arrived exhausted and loaded down with dirty laundry. They slept all day in their twin beds and happily ate their mama's cooking. She greeted them like conquering heroes and they brought her all of their motel room keys as souvenirs. Jerry draped each plastic key fob through the spaces in a wooden lattice that screened her kitchen from the living room. Soon the whole grid was covered with different-colored, diamond-shaped key chains embossed with room numbers.

As Gregg drove to Jacksonville to the army induction center, Duane shifted uncomfortably in his seat, the pair of lacy under-wear he was wearing digging in under his jeans. It was a cheap trick, but it was worth a try. The brothers sat in their station wagon in silence. Gregg watched Duane hold his head in his hands and was shocked to see a tear drop onto his brother's shoe. He reached for Duane's shoulder and said, "It's going to be all right."

Duane turned his face away and quickly wiped it with his sleeve. When it came time to take the pledge, standing shoulder to shoul-der with a room full of young men with their hands raised, Duane kept his hands in the pockets of his jeans. When he was called out, he simply said, again and again, "I ain't going. I ain't going."

Seated in front of a sergeant who had already dismissed the frilly lingerie with a scoff, Duane gathered his strength and ex-plained that he could not leave his mother and go to war. He knew she would lose her mind if he died in action. She had already lost his father, who had been a dedicated soldier all his life. Duane was allowed to go home that day, but that wasn't the end of it. Jerry and Duane each had to answer questions in front of a panel of of-ficers, and between them they managed to secure his release from his military obligation. They had somehow made the case that he was needed at home.

Almost as soon as he was home, Duane called Bill Cook, the owner of Daytona's hot local club, the Martinique. The Q, as they called it, was a big, dark room with high vaulted ceilings crossed by wooden beams. A girl nicknamed Ringo sat in a curtained-off nook by the entrance and took tickets and stamped hands, perched on a high stool. Bill Cook's office was up a small staircase to a balcony against the club's back wall, next to the long wooden bar lined with stools. Jo Jane and Patti came down to hear them play. A year on the road had made the band so tight it was unbelievable. They were as good as or better than the bands they were covering. They had swagger and style, total command of the stage.

On the way home, Jo Jane sat quietly in the backseat, listening to Patti tell Duane how well he had played. Patti wore a T-shirt she had made herself that read "Allman's Joy." Duane looked at his cousin in the rearview mirror, smirked, and said, "I know your type, Jo Jane. The quiet groupie who stares from the backseat." She narrowed her blue eyes at him and laughed. "You know I love you best," he said with a hug when they got home. The band was going to head right back out on the road in the morning. Duane lingered, saying goodbye to Patti.

Gregg rested a palm on top of Jo Jane's head in the driveway before they left, and said, "As Shakespeare once said: Goodbyes are a bad scene."

Jo Jane was visiting her aunt Jerry again when the boys came home to face Gregg's draft notice a year later. Jerry was nearly hysterical with worry, having no protection to offer Gregory, but the boys had a plan of their own. They had a friend who shot himself in the foot and it worked; he was declared unfit to serve.

They started the day drinking and taking pain pills—Gregg for courage and Duane for fun. Then Duane got on the phone and announced that they were throwing a foot-shootin' party. Vicki came over with a couple other girls, but she left before the deed was done because the thought of Gregg hurting himself made her cry.

Once they were feeling loose, they had to address the fact that they didn't have a gun. They called a neighbor and asked if they could borrow his hunting rifle. He said, "Are you boys out of your minds? Where is your mother?" Jerry knew about the plan, and agreed to act surprised if the police or the hospital called her after it was done. Until then, she would be in her room with the door closed, staying out of it.

Duane drove them to the other side of town to search for a gun. The way Gregg tells it, they asked the first guy they saw hanging out on the street who looked like he was up to no good. "Hey, man, do you know where we could come by a gun?"

"A gun? I might, for a price."

"How much?" Duane asked.

"How much you got?" the man asked with half a smile.

"Thirty-two dollars," Gregg said, pulling the bills from his pocket.

"Well, what do you know? That's just what this gun costs," he said, pulling a small pistol out of his waistband.

Armed with the Saturday night special, two bullets rattling in the chamber, they headed home and straight for the liquor cabinet. Duane filled a box with sawdust and carried it out to the garage. Jo Jane got in the driver's seat of Jerry's white Oldsmobile 98 and backed up the driveway facing toward the street for a quick exit. She opened the passenger door so Gregg could jump right in, and stayed behind the wheel, watching in the rearview mirror.

Duane was hitting that point of drunkenness where he was getting pushy and mean.

He got down on his knees and started drawing a target on his baby brother's moccasin with a Flair pen, laughing in a harsh way. He could tell Gregg was scared out of his mind. His knees were quivering.

"Come on, now! We have all these nice people here to see a foot shootin'! If you can't do it, I will! Now give me that gun and let's go!"

Gregg stomped out to the garage and pointed that gun at the target and pulled the trigger. He fell back into Duane, who was standing behind him, and who yelled, "Bull's-eye! Oh fuck! You did it!"

Duane grabbed a few towels and wrapped up his brother's bleeding foot and half carried him to the car, where Jo Jane was ready to go, then took off with the rest of their friends, fearing the police would come and question them. Jo Jane and Gregg were on their own. Gregg must have been in shock; he didn't scream or cry.

"I guess I proved I'd do anything for the band," Gregg murmured. Then, as they waited at a long red light, he said, "Jo Jane, you are driving like a little old lady. Could you step on it, please?"

"I'm trying to be careful!"

"Yeah, but you don't have to be this careful," Gregg said wryly.

Halifax District Hospital on Sunday night was pretty slow. Jo Jane eased Gregg into a wheelchair and propped up his foot, now bleeding right through the mass of towels.

A doctor motioned them into an exam room.

"What happened here, young man?" the doctor asked.

"I was cleaning my gun, sir."

Gregg came back with his wound dressed in a clean white bandage around his foot. The bullet had passed through without hitting bone, a minor miracle. Although the doctor called Jerry and she corroborated the gun-cleaning story, he wanted to keep Gregg overnight. Gregg was highly intoxicated and they could not be sure that he had not been involved in a crime. A police detective came by the house and interviewed her with Jo Jane by her side. Duane was holed up at a friend's crash pad.

In the morning, Jo Jane and Gregg drove to a funky old house down by the river and gathered up Duane for the long drive to the army induction center in Jacksonville. Gregg had driven for him the year before, and it was just as tense now. There was no telling if Gregg's injury would be enough to get him out of harm's way, and they didn't have another plan. Duane and Jo Jane waited in the car while Gregg told the story of his gun-cleaning accident. Somehow it worked and Gregg was classified 4-F.

The army caught up with the Allman Joys once more when they drafted their drummer, the Novice. Bill Connell was back home in Tuscaloosa to play a gig at the armory when his draft notice came. His father, a major in the U.S. Army Reserve, took Bill down to the recruitment center and swore him in himself. He also pulled some strings with a neighbor who was the commander of the Naval Reserve Center. He helped Bill transfer from the army to the navy, hoping to keep him out of the ground war in Vietnam.

Bill's long hair was unceremoniously shaved on the spot. When he got home from his ordeal, he found Duane and Gregg hanging out with a few members of the Minutes, a local band they had crossed paths with many times in the past year. They played the same circuit of clubs and had similar sets. It seemed that in the brief time Bill was gone it had all been decided. Johnny Sandlin, the Minutes' drummer, would take Bill's place behind the drum kit.

The Allman Joys had lost three bass players in a year and a half: one to marital discord, one to college, and another to Vietnam. The Minutes' lineup had been transient, too, and they were down to three players: Johnny, Paul Hornsby, and Mabron McKinney. They needed a singer and a guitar player, and the timing was perfect to join forces with the Allmans. Duane put his arm around Bill's shoulders and told him it would be all right, but there was nothing anybody could do. He was going to war and the band was moving on without him.

Duane and Gregg spent a couple of weeks crashing at Johnny's parents' house in Decatur, Alabama, rehearsing in their garage. The Minutes had a bluesy set and that suited Gregg's voice. It didn't take long to find songs they all knew and blending the two bands was smooth sailing from the start.

Johnny had dark hair curling over the tops of his ears and a kind face. He was quick to laugh, easygoing, and quiet; Duane and Gregg both took to him right away. Johnny had seen them play for the first time at a little club in Pensacola called the Spanish Village. The Minutes were playing to the kids on the patio behind the club while the Allman Joys played the bar inside to the older set. Johnny noticed that Duane had rigged up an effects pedal and mounted it right on the front of his guitar with a couple of clamps so he could hit it with his hand; it looked so cool. They tore through a slew of British rock songs that Johnny didn't usually care for, but the way they played them, he could feel the excitement of those songs like he was hearing them for the first time. Now Johnny had a chance to play with them, and there was no telling how far they could go together.

In the evenings, as a chill blew off the marsh behind Johnny's house and the pines stood tall and black against the pinkening sky, they rolled up the garage door and played to the empty suburban streets. Soon kids rolled up on their bikes and walked up in pairs, holding hands. Within a few nights, there were a dozen or more people sitting in the paved driveway waiting for them, and Gregg would turn to face them while he sang, smiling.

After practice, Johnny's mom would call them in to dinner and they would sit at her table and toss out new band names.

"What about Allman-ac? Get it?" Duane suggested.

"Or Allman-Act?" Gregg said.

"Gosh, that's terrible!" said Johnny.

"Well, what then? Why can't we keep Allman Joys? We have a following all over," Duane said.

"So do we! We could keep 'the Minutes,'" said Paul. "It doesn't seem right to use the name Allman."

"I never liked the Minutes name anyway. We can change it," Johnny said.

For a while, they used whichever name they thought would bring in the most people. They were the Minutes in Tuscaloosa and Mobile, and the Allman Joys in Nashville and St. Louis. Duane had booked a month of nights at Pepe's A Go-Go in Gaslight Square.

A week or two into their stay in St. Louis, Mabron McKinney, their new bass player, went to the airport to pick up his wife. He ran into a pack of musicians, the Nitty Gritty Dirt Band, who were in town to play Kiel Auditorium. Mabron invited them to come down to Pepe's to see his band, and the Dirt Band's manager, Bill McEuen, actually showed up.

The Allman Joys put on a rocking show. They got so wild at the end of "Tobacco Road," their big closer, that Duane tossed his guitar up in the air over his head and stepped forward, letting it fall flat on its back, then stalked offstage.

Bill McEuen offered to manage them right then and there, saying they were going to be the next Rolling Stones. "What are you all doing playing these little joints? Come to L.A.! You'll be huge there! Go where the people are!"

"The Stones? I don't know about that. More like the Hillbilly Who," Johnny joked.

Duane stretched his arm around Bill and walked him to a table to talk.

"Do you have a tape I can take back to L.A.?" Bill asked.

"Give us a week or two and we'll get you one," Duane said. They would go back to Alabama, cut a demo, pick up the rest of their gear, and head west.

Duane made Los Angeles sound like the Promised Land. The next Rolling Stones? Was he really falling for that line? Gregg was skeptical and Johnny was nervous to go that far west, but Duane was determined. As long as they had people to play for, everything would be great.

The band recorded a few songs at a local studio in Alabama and sent it with a snapshot of them crowded together, leaning on a car. Bill thought that little picture spoke volumes about these guys, no flashy head shots like they practically papered the walls with in L.A., and he kept it.

The drive to Los Angeles was ridiculously long, made longer by the fact that they were too broke to stop and stay anywhere along the way. Duane and Gregg were in the equipment van, and Paul and Mabron rode with Johnny in his car. They fell into goofy moods and passed the time with bad jokes and nicknames. Johnny was "the Duck," for reasons he was too embarrassed to explore. They called Paul "Berry" or "Dingleberry," depending on how mad they wanted to make him. Mabron was "the Wolf," because his beard and hair completely surrounded his face. Duane was "the Dog," because of the way his hair drooped down like hound's ears and for the touch of scoundrel the name implied. Gregg was "the Coyote," wily brother of the Dog.

When they reached Texas, they were greeted at a gas station by a big guy swinging a baseball bat. Their long hair and tight pants were not taken kindly to in those parts. They couldn't get out of

Texas quick enough. Paul, who looked the least freaky, went in to fetch their takeout food and pump gas and did so the rest of the way.

Finally, on the outskirts of Los Angeles, they stopped at a cheap motel to get cleaned up. Gregg traveled with packets of crème rinse to keep his shoulder-length hair shiny. He mixed the thick goo with water in a glass, and then poured the slick mix over his hair in the shower. He left that little slippery glass on the shower floor and Johnny kicked it over, stepped on the glass, and cut his foot, deep and bloody. After he was stitched up, it hurt too much to press his newly patched-up foot against his bass drum pedal, so the Duck had to play with the wrong foot for their first couple of weeks in town. Welcome to California.

A winding road carried them up the hill that ran behind the Hollywood sign, the letters propped up with wooden posts, smaller and
shabbier than it looked from a distance. Miles of houses nested
in thick green trees and tiny cars rolled in the bleach-bright sun
on the highways below. A warm breeze blew the city air out to sea
through a small crop of tall buildings in the hazy distance, peo-
pled by dream weavers and deal makers here to hit it big. Duane
climbed down the steep hill and stood with his arms wide. Johnny
was a little stunned by the scale of it; he knew Paul and Mabron
had never been this far from home, but they were harder to read
and Gregg was so tired he wasn't talking.

The Dirt House was home to the Nitty Gritty Dirt Band, a rambling four-story Victorian in Beachwood Canyon. The guys bunked
there during their first weeks in L.A. They settled into the attic,
where there was plenty of room to set up their gear. They stayed
up late hearing ghost stories about the house and horror stories

about the music industry, and it was hard to say which were more frightening. Duane was lit up from the inside like a kid, all smiles, talking so fast and hugging everyone hello. He looked over John McEuen's banjo with curiosity and asked him to play a little.

They headed out to the Sunset Strip in a big group to check out the nightlife. Young girls in maxi skirts and halter tops stood with their thumbs out, hitchhiking fearlessly. Men with beards and wild eyes paced the sidewalk raving about the war. Guitar cases lay open to gather change in front of passionate folksingers. Everybody had a band—art students with record deals and young runaways at open-mic nights. Club after club was packed into a few short blocks humming with grooves. California's golden sun had kissed the shoulders and noses of the youth in the streets and everyone looked beautiful and turned on, working their wild styles like a gypsy parade, leaning against the walls outside the Sea Witch, the Whisky a Go Go, and Sneaky Pete's. Glancing through the window into Turner's liquor store, you could catch sight of an older gentleman in a suit or a woman with her hair set in stiff sprayed curls and the street life suddenly seemed like a strange mirage beamed from the future. Walking behind Duane, Johnny watched him laugh and rub his palms together. Duane could move at the speed of this new town; he had a chance to be part of something here. He took a passed joint from the Dirt Band's Ralph Barr, the sweet smell wafting out in the open on the street. To Johnny it seemed like a stupid risk to take. You would never do that in Alabama.

Within the month, Liberty Records drafted a contract for them to sign on the strength of Bill McEuen's recommendation. They were christened Hour Glass and slotted into the same arrangement the Dirt Band had: same studio, same producer, same deal.

Once the papers were signed and sealed, they moved to the Mikado, a whitewashed apartment complex on Cahuenga Boulevard up the hill from the Hollywood Bowl. The art deco lobby opened into a courtyard draped with dark pink bougainvillea. Honeysuckle grew wild up the banisters, and there was even a small swimming pool, but the five of them had to crowd into a couple of tiny one-bedroom efficiencies furnished with scratchy couches and twin beds. It felt sort of lonely after the Dirt House scene. Eventually, when the money started coming in, they imagined setting up homes of their own, but that seemed pretty far off. Liberty paid their rent and gave them a little money for food, and their debt to the company began to grow from day one.

Hour Glass played their first show in Los Angeles at the Hullabaloo, a late-night set after the Doors. Movies rolled in a darkened back room and girls danced around a circular stage that spun like a turntable. The Doors' keyboard player, Ray Manzarek, built a long, moody groove, jingling and jangling, old-timey and slow, chased by the piercing whine of a loopy guitar and the swoosh of drums, a dark carnival of sound. The singer was still backstage, leaning against a wall with a girl. If Jim Morrison was choosing his moment, you couldn't tell; he looked like he'd forgotten why he was there. The band was lost in a careening round, playing with their faces bent down out of the lights, waiting for Jim to jump in. He finally strolled into the spotlight and pulled the microphone stand to him, bent his head over it, and breathed a low moaning note that sent a ripple of lust through every girl in the room. It couldn't have been further musically from what Duane was doing, but the Doors' odd power was undeniable. They put on a blurry, sexy, compelling set.

When the Doors came offstage, Gregg walked over to Jim and rested a hand on his shoulder, leaned in, and asked him something. They stepped outside together smiling while Duane watched. Duane kept his eye on Gregg with a sternness that hid his heart. He knew Los Angeles would see the value of his brother shining like a star. Every girl and many guys, too, looked hungrily at his baby brother. Gregg didn't seem to realize his own power yet and Duane worried for the day he would. He'd have to knock him down to keep his feet on the ground. And he'd better get back in there before they had to play.

Paul noticed Gregg's legs shaking when he started singing their first song, but as they rolled through tunes by the Byrds and the

Beatles, he loosened up, and by the time they rolled out "Dimples," a raunchy blues number they had been polishing up, they were smoking. They were tighter and stronger than most bands playing around town and people really dug them, but Duane could see that playing other people's songs in a town where the original artists were potentially playing down the block was a whole different scene.

Working in the studio on their first album was what they all had looked forward to most, but it was an alien experience. Sound Recorders Studios was nice enough, but they were paired with producer Dallas Smith, who had his own ideas about the direction they should take. They were asked to learn songs from a selection of demos they didn't like, so their live set and their album would bear no relation to each other. To Duane's mind, Dallas was a button pusher and a naysayer. The tension building in Duane's jaw was visible when Dallas would interrupt him to make suggestions.

Johnny had worked in studios since he was sixteen years old, playing guitar and drums, but this arrangement felt different. In the studios back home, you jammed until everyone clicked into a groove. The way the room sounded and how comfortable everyone felt was important. But in L.A., it wasn't about working until you knew it was right. Time felt limited and you had to rush through one song to get to the next, with no hanging out or exploring ideas. Dallas was so off base, Johnny started thinking about what it would take to be a good producer, and he knew he could do a better job himself.

It didn't seem to be about their band at all. They had been cast in the role of "Psychedelic Rock Band"—Liberty Records' attempt to jump on the Summer of Love train—and they were expected to play to type. They found the pseudo-experimental tracks embarrassing, but they tried to find the best of the possibilities, songs by Jackson Browne and Curtis Mayfield, and played them with all the strength and energy they could.

Duane's restlessness kicked into a higher gear when he realized he had no control over the songs on their album, or when and where they played live. Duane had worked steadily, traveling to chase opportunities all over the South and up the East Coast for two solid years, and now he was being benched while their label chose only a handful of key gigs, hoping to build a buzz. How was that freedom? How was that anything but jive?

Now that they were managed, Duane lost his sense of control over his own time. They should have been playing every night. Los Angeles was packed with clubs, and great music was happening everywhere. They needed to show everyone who they really were.

He had brought them here and it would be on him if it didn't pan out.

Duane asked the owner of the Troubadour if they could practice there during the day, and that helped him get into a better head. Beyond the well-worn bar, reminiscent of a western saloon, through a door marked with a lit sign that read SHOWROOM, was a cavernous space with wooden walls pieced together like a quilt. The walls radiated a great vibe laid down by hundreds of players who'd passed through. Being together there and running through songs set them back on their path.

In the studio, Duane would rant about Dallas Smith the moment he left the room.

"I am at the top of my game! I deserve a producer at the top of his game and he is not it!" His guitar was being lost in the muddied production under layers of horns, keyboards, and background singers. The rest of the band didn't disagree with him, but it was still shocking to hear him take apart the guy who was in charge. Dallas was in a position to help them; they needed him to change their fortunes.

Duane prided himself on cutting through bullshit with a clear head but this power struggle got under his skin and he started leaning harder on chemical assistance to keep his spirits up. Pills, grass, acid, anything you wanted was easily had and you didn't have to wander into the wrong side of town to get it; you could just nod to the right friend at the bar at night. Pills took hold of Duane, cheap speed from Mexico pressed into powdery white tablets, and blackbirds—glossy capsules that bloomed into a perfect feeling of being in command. Duane preferred the thrill of speed to being lost in a hazy dream. When the jitters kicked in, whisky smoothed them out and brought a taste of distant home to warm him. Duane got tickets for breaking the speed limit and ended up in the drunk tank a time or two. He'd been sleeping late, something he had never done in his whole damn life, and then woke up on his couch with ashtrays on the tables overflowing and empty bottles breaking the afternoon light into green streaks on the floor, his guitar resting on top of him like a lover.

In the incomplete darkness of a city steeped in electric light, Duane climbed down beyond the edge of the road across from their apartment complex to get a clear view of the back of the Hollywood Bowl. On nights with performances, the white shell above the stage launched flurries of notes into the wind, an orchestra of string and brass harmonizing in the breeze, everything happening at once, and he let the music wash over him. The view and the growing orchestral crescendo lured him there, overlooking the canyon and then the city in the distance. He'd smoke a joint and try to will his mind to stay empty. He'd pick up a postcard tomorrow and write to Jo Jane about the music.

In October 1967, the first Hour Glass album came out, and Duane wasn't sure how to feel. He had worked toward this moment, imagining the pride of holding his first record in his hands, but he was only happy with a few songs. The record's release was a nonevent and it didn't change anything. He held the cover: The picture of them dressed up in clashing costumes had been flipped upside down, surrounded by wavy type and swirling colors, some corporate notion of hip creativity. It seemed like a bad metaphor. All the great music being played around town, his band one of the best, and they were being held back. Everything was upside down. They were sitting hungry at the banquet table.

Playing live was the only place he could find optimism anymore. They could set a crowd on fire. Duane would wave up musicians out of the crowd and get them to jam, a rare thing in Los Angeles. One night at the Whisky, Janis Joplin, in blue jeans, with a sweaty forehead and unbuttoned blouse, climbed onstage smoking a hand-rolled cigarette and smiling shyly at a young blond guy down in front. Eric Burdon in a shiny embroidered shirt sang beside her and shifted over to make room for Paul Butterfield, taking up his guitar to tuck into "Stormy Monday." There was a thriving community of players in Hollywood, known and unknown, all passing time together, sharing music.

Although Hour Glass didn't play out as often as they would have liked, they were booked onto some great bills. They played a big pop festival in Sacramento with Jefferson Airplane and opened for Buffalo Springfield and Big Brother and the Holding Company at the Fillmore in San Francisco. Neil Young and Stephen Stills invited Duane to sit in with them after hearing him play. It felt great to see Northern California. The vibe up there was laid-back and the audiences were warm and responsive. It wasn't all about business.

Gregg was beginning to explore songwriting, and hanging out with other musicians, like Stephen Stills and Jackson Browne, who were dedicated writers, was inspiring. Gregg started walking around with a different perspective; he'd hear a turn of phrase or a name that struck him and write it down. He had written a few tunes in his time, but now the desire really grabbed him. He felt like he had opened up a new side of his mind, where moments grew into patterns, and when they finally fell into place, he wrote them down. By the end of the year, he had the beginnings of twenty songs in his notebook, though he wasn't ready to share them.

Sometimes a moment would bring into focus the contrast between where they were coming from and where they had found themselves. While playing a show at Cheetah, a garish dance club on Lick Pier in Venice Beach, they got word that Otis Redding had died in a plane crash. Hour Glass played "I Can't Turn You Loose" in tribute while strobe lights blinded them. They tried to tap into a little of their hero's fire, but home had never felt farther away. After the gig, Duane stood on the pier for a moment and looked out over the dark sea. He remembered seeing Otis as a kid in Nashville, that massive man dancing light and scatting wild with the horns blasting at his back. How could someone so young and strong just disappear like that?

Twiggs Lyndon, a young man who worked for Otis's management company, went with Zelma Redding to Lake Monona in Madison, Wisconsin, to where Otis's plane was lost. He had to be dissuaded from jumping into the icy water himself to search the submerged wreckage. When the authorities recovered Otis the next day, Twiggs accompanied Zelma to identify the body of her beloved and together they brought him home to Macon, Georgia.

Otis Redding's memorial service took place at Macon's City Auditorium. Nearly five thousand mourners gathered in the space built for three thousand. Jerry Wexler of Atlantic Records gave his eulogy. Phil Walden had grown up with Otis and managed his remarkable career; his heart was broken. He told himself he would never take on another artist and give his heart and soul to building a career.

Then he met Duane Allman.

Mabron was getting into strange new interests that were becoming a distraction. He would mention seeing lights in the sky, and sought out lectures by experts on UFOs and alternate realities. He would take time at practice to explain elaborate conspiracy theories and doomsday prophecies in a calm, earnest manner that was worrying. He was less interested in playing bass, so they let him go.

Bob Keller, who had played bass in the Allman Joys, replaced Mabron but not for very long. After a couple of good months, Bob simply didn't show up for a gig. They were pissed off for days, and then they began looking for him. They even searched behind the

Hollywood sign where they hung out, thinking he might have gone up there alone and slipped, or even jumped. He disappeared without a word.

When he finally called Johnny several months later, he acted like nothing had happened, and didn't explain. Between Mabron and Keller, a bad vibe was building around the band.

They had moved to funky apartments on Lash Lane in a bid to keep costs down and it was a definite downgrade. The first day they were there, Gregg passed police in the hallway and looked through an open door in time to see them covering a corpse with a sheet. It really shook him up.

Pete Carr, a friend of Duane and Gregg's from Daytona, happened to be visiting when Keller took off, and he picked up the slack on bass. Pete was only about seventeen and so fresh-faced, they called him the Beaver, but he was a great guitar player. He had never played bass before, but they threw him into the deep end and he swam like a champ. He learned their songs literally overnight and jumped right in to recording their second album.

Duane was so happy to have Pete around. He just had good energy and made Duane laugh. He walked around wide-eyed and amazed by everything he saw. During Pete's first few weeks in L.A., they went to see Taj Mahal. They stood in the crowded club in front of Jesse Ed Davis and watched him play slide. He was a young Native American cat with a constant smile and black hair framing his face in a hip shag. His hands moved with a light, confident ease and he kept his eyes turned down toward his guitar like he was meditating. He pulled startling sounds so coolly out of his Fender with a bottleneck slide on his finger. Duane was mesmerized by it; he had never gotten such a good close look at the technique before.

Taj sat on a stool wearing a wide-brimmed hat that shadowed his face and a red kerchief tied in a knot around his neck. His voice was so rich and warm, a pure blast of home, a shout rooted deep in the ground, real and raw. Taj blew his harp like a train swaying, and not a body in the room stood still. It struck Duane hard like a punch to his chest: This is it. This is the sound of no bullshit, of sweat and fire and home. This was church, a thunderclap, a call to arms.

As soon as he got home, Duane sat down with a water glass and his guitar and tried to find those sounds. Then Gregg gave Duane a bottle of Coricidin cold medicine while Duane was laid up in bed sick as an old dog. Duane dumped out the pills and rested the small, perfectly formed bottle over his ring finger. He soaked the label off the bottle in the bathroom sink, put on Taj Mahal's record, and got to work on "Statesboro Blues," learning Jesse Ed Davis's licks note for note.

The first time I ever called Johnny Sandlin, the sweetness of his southern drawl saying my name brought tears to my eyes. I felt like I was hearing my father's voice sounding out the soft syllables of the name he had given me, for the first time. We felt like family from the first moment. I traveled to Alabama and stayed with Johnny and we spent hours in his studio, talking and listening to music.

Duck Tape Music studio is a cocoon of peacefulness, warm and clean with covered windows and foam tacked on the walls as soundproofing. Incense and candles burn and decades' worth of gear is everywhere. I love the way the place feels suspended in time, a night world where music is king. The main room is dominated by a large mixing board—a panel of dials and faders, inputs, outputs, and wires, and a large leather chair, Johnny's catbird seat. The small kitchen and bathroom look much like they must have in the sixties when Johnny lived here, when it was the in-law apartment to his parents' home.

Johnny plays some tapes I found at Granny's house and listens with his eyes closed, smiling. When Duane really starts to fly, you can see the changes pass across Johnny's face, his hands and feet keeping time unconsciously, a drummer's deep habit.

"It's funny to think about it now, but when your dad was first learning to play slide, it sounded just awful. Paul Hornsby and I used to look at each other with dread. 'Oh no! Here he goes again!' And I'd try to call out another song before he could get going. He had tuning issues. But once he got that straight, he just got so good so fast, it didn't seem possible.

"There was a Murphy bed in here," he says, motioning to a closet door. "And if there wasn't anything going on to hold his attention, Duane would just take a cat nap. We listened to the White Album for the first time in this room. Duane brought it straight over when he got it."

He can see Duane, sitting on the rug with his head tossed back on the edge of the bed, with his eyes closed, engrossed in the eerie new music.

"Duane, are you asleep?" Johnny says.

"I'm just resting my eyes."

I turn my head and try to see him, too, his fingers laced together on his chest, his mouth falling open in a sudden snort that wakes him from a split second of sleep.

"Johnny, did you ever meet Patti, Duane's first wife?" I ask.

"I don't think I ever did."

I know Patti showed up in Los Angeles after hitchhiking all the way across the country with a girlfriend. I had originally thought she and Duane had broken up after she got pregnant, but I learned that they saw each other sporadically for several years more.

"There was a time I knocked on Duane's door to go to the studio," Johnny says, "and he just stood in the doorway and said he had company." Johnny thought that girl might have been Patti. The reunion must not have lasted very long, because no one remembers her being there.

"Duane was private about some things."

Hour Glass started work on their second album shortly after the release of the first. Dallas Smith was producing again, and they were moved to the Liberty Records studio, where they liked the sound even less. They did have the pick of better songs, and Gregg wrote more than half of them, but the experience was even rougher for Duane than the last.

Johnny reluctantly described Duane showing up so high, he couldn't hold his guitar.

He backed up to the wall and slid down into a slump. A few days later, Duane blew up in the studio over some minor frustration and quit the band. He left the studio in the middle of a song. Everyone thought he would check out for a day or two and cool off, but weeks went by and no one heard a thing.

On January 30, 1967, Patti and Duane got married in South Carolina. Their marriage certificate was among piles of contracts and photographs at the Big House on Vineville Avenue in Macon, the museum in what was once our family home. Canceled checks, handbills and receipts, newspaper clippings and old postcards—all manner of documents have found their way back to Macon to become part of the growing Allman Brothers Band Archive. This paper rose up out of the mire of boxes in the attic and spoke to me:

Jasper County, South Carolina, January 30, 1967
To Whom it May Concern, Howard Duane Allman, age 20, Patricia Ann Chandlee, age 19, united in the bonds of matrimony.

Their typed names hover above the printed lines of the form. I don't know how they ended up in South Carolina or why they married there alone, but the date overlaps with the time the band was recording the second Hour Glass album back in Los Angeles.

Patti did not return to L.A. with Duane, and other than that brief time he left the band, I don't know that they ever lived together at all.

The second Hour Glass album, *Power of Love,* came out in March 1968, and the band went out on the road to promote it. They even returned home to Daytona and played the Martinique and the Pier, their teenage haunts. The songs they had worked so hard to craft, Gregg's original songs and the blues songs, didn't quite play in the clubs back home. People wanted the same thing they had always wanted: the hits of the day played for dancing and relaxing. Going from the Fillmore to the Martinique was hard, like stepping back into shoes that no longer fit.

Duane went to shoot a game of pool at Frank's Pool Hall in Daytona wearing a brass bell around his neck on a strip of hide, a trinket he must have picked up in a head shop or a stall filled with junk jewelry in Venice Beach. Walking out on to Main Street, he got heckled by some kid.

"What's that you got on? A necklace? Are you a boy or a girl? I can't tell!"

Duane looked into the kid's eyes with all the dignity and gravity of an elder, slipped the bell over his head and placed it around the kid's neck, patted his shoulder, and walked away. The boy gathered the bell between his fingers and rang it, watching Duane strut up the street, his shoulders squared and proud.

Hour Glass went on to play the Comic Book Club in Jacksonville. That night, Duane and Berry Oakley met for the first time. Berry's beautiful girlfriend, Linda, introduced them. Linda was six feet tall and curvy, with huge blue eyes, and once you saw her, you didn't forget her. Duane remembered her right away. She loved the Allman Joys and had hung out at the Allmans' house a few times. They were really nice guys, and she knew Berry would love their music. Linda dragged him to see them play. He was worn-out from playing with his own band.

Berry was a beautiful, badass bass player from sweet home Chicago, with brown hair flowing down his back, bright blue eyes, and freckles sprinkled across his nose. Berry was steeped in the electric blues. He'd played in bands as a guitarist and a bass player since high school. He had landed in Jacksonville and started another band, the Second Coming. He hoped Duane would come and see them play. He had a hot guitar player named Dickey Betts.

Berry's spacey smile was open and warm, quiet and watchful. He was a fine cat, and spiritual. He talked with total passion about how important it was to spread the love by playing live as much as they possibly could. He wanted to bring like-minded people together and raise them up with music. Duane really dug him, and promised to get in touch soon to jam.

Hour Glass continued on to Montgomery and Tuscaloosa, then took some of the money they were making and headed to FAME Studios in Muscle Shoals. They wanted to record a demo their own way, without compromise, and on their home turf. Coming off the road, they were loose and strong. They played a medley of B. B. King songs and a couple of Gregg's originals. The room sounded perfect, and they were so comfortable, they cut all the tracks in a single night. They were excited by the sound they captured there and couldn't wait to play it for Dallas Smith and the powers that be at Liberty Records. It was a declaration of intent.

Dallas could hardly get off the phone long enough to listen to the music. He wasn't interested in recording a blues band. Maybe it was time for them to part ways, he said. Duane was shaking with anger. It was over.

They didn't have time to dwell on it and get down. They still had some dates to play in Cleveland and St. Louis, where they could hang out for a while and try to think things through.

 10

Donna woke up at the first click, the unmistakable sound of Denny Golden tossing stones against her window. Her sister Joanie sighed in her sleep and turned toward the wall. Denny called out Donna's name in a loud stage whisper that soon became a drunken shout. Ignoring him wasn't going to work. She knew he wanted her to come outside and sit in the backyard in the dark with him. He didn't seem to hear her when she said no. She wasn't sure how she had gotten herself into this situation. They had just met a month or two before, when he asked her out on her first real date.

Denny was a public school boy who came by Incarnate Word Academy, the all-girls Catholic high school outside St. Louis, to meet girls in the afternoon when classes ended. He had a nice enough face, pale and serious, and when he asked her out, Donna was happy. No one had ever asked her out before. As long as they were never alone, her parents didn't mind, which surprised Donna a little. She was sixteen, but they rarely treated her like it. Her father drove them to the Two Plus Two Club to dance with their friends, or to the movies, where they kissed the whole time. Right away, Denny started leaving tightly folded squares of frayed notebook paper in her mailbox, notes so full of yearning she had no idea what to say to him when she saw him after reading them.

"Donna, you are the sweetest and most wonderfulest girl I know," he wrote, as if the word *wonderful* wasn't big enough.

In his school picture, he wore a suit and tie. His dark hair was combed flat and parted on the side, and she thought she could see something like mystery in his eyes, but she wasn't sure. She let him take her to the homecoming dance, but he wrecked it by showing up half drunk. Now he just wanted to apologize over and over again.

Donna had already told Denny she couldn't see him anymore. He was scaring her a little. Maybe scaring wasn't the right word. He was overwhelming her. She couldn't even figure out how she felt about him. Maybe that was just because he drank so much. She didn't like it. She tried to explain that her father had heard Denny ranting in his yard and wasn't happy about it. Denny's next note read, "I am not going to stop until you tell me goodbye, but I hope you don't. I think that [I should] apologize to your dad, and then maybe we could go to a game."

She leaned out the window and whispered, "Denny, go home!"

It went quiet outside, but she stayed by the window, looking at the gray moonlit grass where he had stood until she was sure he was really gone.

After school, the girls in Donna's class changed out of their uniforms and into outfits that followed another sort of dress code: plaid A-line skirts, prim shirts with Peter Pan collars, and cardigans in matching colors. For a really special touch, some girls took their sweaters to a local convent where the nuns carefully embroidered monograms onto them. Hair was worn teased into bubbles and decorated with headbands and bows like Patty Duke's. To maintain the look, you had to sleep in hard plastic curlers and back-comb your hair into a nest in the morning with a rattail comb and blast it with clouds of hairspray. Donna's mother, Tommie Jean, understood better than anyone how important it was to have just the right clothes, but she was working with a very tight budget. Donna would ask for a Villager blouse and her mom would buy a less expensive imitation with an odd ruffled collar instead. She'd ask for a pair of stylish slip-on shoes and her mom would buy gold old-lady sandals that came folded in a pouch like a pair of house slippers. It was humiliating. Donna poked through patterns at the fabric store, looking for pantsuits and A-line dresses to show her mom. Her mom spent hours in the evenings sitting at her sewing machine, its tiny bright light shining on her lovely face. Donna wished she could be as beautiful and glamorous as her mother. Her mom's room was a world unto itself—polished, sweet smelling, and off-limits to her children. When she was very young, Donna would sneak in and sit at her mother's vanity to sniff her waxy red lipsticks and golden perfumes, and look into her tidy drawers of folded stockings and silky things. She would lean into her mother's closet and press her face into the cool rayon dresses and feel a pining pull in her chest like romantic love. Now she stood in her parents' doorway and remembered the feeling sadly, without going inside.

Donna got a summer job at a soda fountain in Clayton to earn shopping money. She made malts and open-faced sandwiches drenched in gravy for $1.07 an hour. She bought herself a shiny green pack of Salems and forced herself to smoke a whole one before her shift. They tasted awful and made her woozy, but she felt graceful and kind of French holding a lit cigarette. No one called her Bean Pole or Bunny Teeth anymore. After years of painful orthodontia, including medieval headgear that forced her teeth into place, Donna was blossoming into a pretty teen.

When her family moved to a new house on Dawn Valley Drive just before the start of Donna's junior year of high school, it was a radical change. She and Joanie were finally allowed to go to a secular school, and the family went to church only on Sunday now, in a modern neighborhood church with none of All Souls' mystery. It was easy to disappear at Parkway High School. Donna wasn't

110

sure how to start up conversations with new girls, and clothing was more important than ever. When she walked down a hallway full of boys, she wondered how she looked or if they were looking at her at all.

She still relied on her friends from Incarnate Word, like Maureen and Mary Jo, who were actually more worldly than most, even though they went to Catholic school. Maureen was a beautiful, rebellious blonde who managed to make her school uniform look ironic and sexy just by standing with her hand on her hip, smiling. She had been suspended from school once for peeking at the nuns while they showered during a school retreat. Donna and Maureen talked on the phone until their ears were hot.

Mary Jo was different—small, dark-haired, and fine-boned. She would bend her head to the side and assess things with serious eyes. Mary Jo knew all kinds of people from hanging out at teen clubs like the Castaway, where she taught Donna how to dance the shing-a-ling, swiveling her hips to the groove. The guys Mary Jo knew made Denny Golden seem like a child. They were mostly local musicians. Mary Jo would light two Salems and hand her one, the smoke ballooning in the colored lights, blue and red. Donna wished they could just stay there, drifting in the streaming songs, dancing together.

Tommie Jean was busy decorating their new house. She picked metallic floral wallpaper for the downstairs bathroom and thick shag carpeting for the den, and reupholstered the sofas in patterned orange velveteen. The house had a modern split-level floor plan; the front door opened onto a wide landing with wrought-iron railings. Swinging saloon doors opened into the kitchen, which had a padded breakfast booth like in a restaurant.

Tommie Jean ruled the Dawn Valley house with vigor and intensity. Nothing could get cleaned well or quickly enough to please her. It was a physical relief when her husband came home at night. She greeted Gil with a long list of grievances. The teenagers were driving her crazy with their smart mouths and loud music. He had to do something. Once the kids were sorted out behind closed doors, she could finally breathe freely and treat Gil like a husband.

Donna did her homework without being asked and kept her grades high. After Catholic school, public high school seemed easy. She took typing and shorthand, which she especially liked for use as a secret code, and home economics, where she learned to sew and bake. Practical subjects were novel and fun compared to her previous school's heavy academics and religious instruction.

Donna was quiet and rarely gave her parents trouble, unless Joanie was driving her crazy, following her around. Donna's worst offense was being moody and withdrawn, occasionally rolling her eyes or being sarcastic. Once she called her brother a fruit and her father slapped her so swiftly she was too shocked to cry. As loose as life seemed now, there were still rules and her mother's yelling and her father's hand enforced them. Donna realized that when either of her parents made quick moves toward her, she couldn't help but flinch, expecting a sudden smack, and that made her very sad. Still, she loved them.

She didn't get to spend much time with her father, so when he offered to teach her how to drive she jumped at the chance. He took her out in his Volkswagen Bug and sat beside her with calm confidence radiating from his eyes. As they rode through their suburban neighborhood on the newly paved roads, Donna found it challenging to maneuver the little bubble of a car; it was hilly and the streets looped around blindly into cul-de-sacs. Her daddy was patient. He didn't yell when she made horrible scraping sounds with the clutch and he didn't let her give up until she could angle the car into a tight parking space and do a three-point turn without stalling. When she pulled back into their driveway, he put his hand on her head and said, "You did good, kid."

By the summer of 1967, Donna could drive herself downtown to Gaslight Square, a long stretch of nightclubs and coffee shops where folk music spilled out onto the street. Boys her age had hair past their collars, long sideburns, mustaches, and trim beards.

Downtown girls wore their hair long and silky with their skirts well above the knee. There was energy all around her.

Mary Jo invited Donna to go to a love-in. Donna wasn't sure what it was, but she wanted to check it out. Young people sat cross-legged in circles in Forest Park, singing songs, hugging and kissing, painting hearts on their cheeks and laughing. Girls danced bare-foot in the grass in colorful patterned dresses, their faces bright with sweet, simple joy. A boy with long blond hair gave Donna a droopy little daisy with a silent smile. It was such a lovely gesture. Her mother was standing in the front yard when she got home. She showed her the flower and Tommie Jean smiled. Donna was kind of surprised, for some reason. Then she asked Donna if she knew the boy.

"No, mom. He was a hippie. You know, a flower child."

Her mother looked at her like she was speaking a foreign lan-guage. Her parents were so straight. They didn't drink or smoke or swear and they could never imagine the way the world was chang-ing, right now. Soon they complained that Donna's bleach-blond bangs were hanging in her eyes and her black mascara was too thick. Tommie Jean would catch her on the way out the door and try to wipe off her eye makeup and tug down the hem of her skirt, until Donna wriggled free and ran to her car.

Life was basically uneventful. School and home, dinner in the kitchen with her siblings, homework and sleep. Maybe one good phone call. She could feel herself outgrowing her family in a way she couldn't explain. She wanted to retreat to her room and lis-ten to the Beatles and Buffalo Springfield. Love songs helped her imagine what love could be and she could feel it, just by closing her eyes.

Daydreaming in class one afternoon, Donna was jarred awake when her teacher asked her to step into the hall. She couldn't imagine what she had done wrong. Her stomach went sour when she saw her father standing tall beside a row of lockers in the hall-way, looking serious around the mouth. He said he needed to take her home. She couldn't remember later exactly how her daddy told her; she could only remember his hand on her back while they walked out to his car, and how afraid she felt not knowing what was going on.

Her father took her out of school to tell her that Denny Golden, the first boy who had ever liked her, had fallen into a diabetic coma and died suddenly after his high school graduation party. Her parents were afraid she would find out at school and decided it was best that they tell her at home. Alone in her room, she took out Denny's love notes and arranged them in front of her on her bed, a half-moon of folded squares. She couldn't bring herself to read them, but she didn't want to put them away, either. She thought of Denny's mother, and how kind she had always been to her. Donna gathered his letters into her cupped palms, a pile as light as the bones of a bird. Poor Denny.

She was almost eighteen when Donna met another boy she liked, a painter named Dennis Gregorian. He wasn't exactly a flower child; he was darker and more mysterious than that, like Bob Dylan, with long brown hair and a full mouth. She thought his face was beautiful. He lived in a rented room in a run-down boardinghouse in Gaslight Square. He and his brother John were runaways, cruising around town in their big all-American heap of a car. Dennis told her they were broke. They siphoned gas from strangers' cars at night to keep their own car running. When Dennis and John picked Donna up after school, girls would stare and wrap their arms more tightly around their books. Sometimes Donna went back to his room and they kissed a little, but usually they took drives in Forest Park and sat in the sun, talking about art and music. Being with Dennis was easy and sweet, with just a faint feeling of something more serious beginning to happen underneath.

On April 4, 1968, a few minutes after six o'clock in the evening, Martin Luther King, Jr., was shot and killed in Memphis, Tennessee. As the news of his murder spread, people began taking to the streets all over the country in outrage and sorrow. The Roosmann house was quiet; no one was talking about what had happened.

Donna had snuck out of the house to go dancing at the Starlight Ballroom with Mary Jo, unaware of the assassination in Tennessee. As people gathered, word of King's death shocked the teen club into silence. No one there was sure how to mark the horrible moment, except to spend it quietly together.

Riots were erupting all over the country. Chicago and Washington, D.C., were burning. Louisville, Baltimore, Kansas City, and a hundred other American cities were overcome by riots that led to occupations by the National Guard, called in to restore order. Thousands of people were injured and arrested, buildings were destroyed, power was knocked out, curfews were imposed, and even as the revolts went on for days, it still felt to many like no response could ever be great enough to express the damage done to the world. King's death was an immeasurable loss.

Donna was only dimly aware of the scale of the trauma that was tearing the country apart, but in a way, it effected a rupture in her life as well. She leaned into her parents' bedroom door late that night, and whispered that she was home. From their bed, her parents could smell the pungent reek of cigarette smoke on their daughter's clothes. Her mother started to shout.

"Donna, where have you been? Have you been smoking? There is a curfew! You should have called! Do you have any idea what you have put us through?"

Her father boomed louder, "While you live in my house, you will live by my rules!"

"Then maybe I shouldn't live here!" she answered, so quickly and firmly she surprised herself.

Just like that, Donna turned on her heel and left the dark house with nothing but a little purse over her shoulder. She walked down the hill past all the silent, shadowed houses, their lawns damp from sprinklers. She was so angry, she felt like screaming. As she turned back to look toward home, her mother's car rolled slowly toward her, Tommie Jean's face peering through the windshield. Donna stepped quickly behind a neighbor's thick hedge and crouched down until the car rounded the corner.

She ran in her high-heeled sandals straight down to the gas station at the foot of the hill, swearing she would never go back again. She called Dennis from a pay phone but he didn't answer. She knew she had to stay off the street because of the curfew, so she hid in the Shell station ladies' restroom. She leaned against the wall by the towel dispenser, then sat balanced on the dirty ledge next to the sink with her legs crossed and waited, looking slowly at each item in her purse, counting out meager change in her palm. She thought of Martin Luther King, Jr., and tried to remember something he had said, some part of a speech she had heard on the radio, but nothing would come. It seemed even more outrageous that her parents were being so unfeeling, on this night of all nights.

A couple of hours later, Dennis finally picked up the phone in the boardinghouse hallway, sounding dreamy and odd, and agreed to pick her up. He swung his big car around the gas pumps and stopped right in front of the restroom door, and Donna jumped in and slid close to him on the bench seat. They drove back to Gaslight Square slowly and carefully with headlights off, rolling through the locked-down city like a shadow.

Donna stayed with Dennis for almost a month. Dennis took her to school in the mornings, and after classes, she took a bus to her job as a cashier and stock girl at Pier 1 Imports. Her mother visited her at work a couple of times and tried to convince her to come home, but she wouldn't. When Donna went home to pick up some of her things, she didn't say a word to anyone. She felt like a thief in her own closet.

Dennis's room had a high ceiling and scant furniture, just a narrow bed, dusty dresser, and wooden chair that looked decades old. He owned nothing but a couple of shirts and some jeans, art supplies he kept in a dented toolbox, and a few canvases leaning against the wall. The room's air was stale. One weak bulb lit the room. The single window looked out over a row of the old gas streetlights the neighborhood was named for, shining on the sidewalks where hip kids walked back and forth all night long. Donna felt time slow down and open up, unfurling empty hours belonging only to them. She wanted to walk outside into the tumult of the street and stay there until the morning, just to feel the truth that no one was watching or waiting for her.

Donna and Dennis slept side by side in the little bed, which she had never done with a boy before. Lying there in their cotton underwear, kissing slowly, she somehow felt he was out of reach. This was the problem with Dennis: Donna couldn't get close to him. She couldn't catch and keep his eye. Sex wasn't even a thought between them; she wasn't ready and he wasn't asking. He had other interests. Dennis was a drug addict.

He and his friends shot paregoric, a tincture of opium. You could get it at drugstores, although they limited the number of bottles you could buy at one time. You were supposed to sip it in small doses for upset stomachs. Donna sat with Dennis in a stranger's dim kitchen and watched him cook down dark liquid in a little saucepan to concentrate the opium and burn off the camphor. Then he wrapped a rubber tube around his arm and slid a needle smoothly into his vein. She watched his expression slip down, then his body follow in a slump. He was more gone than he'd be if he walked out the door; his eyes were unseeing, his back bent low. Donna was alone and could only look at him and wonder what he felt like inside.

When Tommie Jean leaned over the counter at Pier 1 and told Donna she had to be careful, Donna worried for a minute that she had intuited something about the drugs. Then Donna realized with horror that her mom thought she was having sex. She had never talked to her mother about such intimate things, and under the fluorescent store lights with a counter between them, she was mortified by her mother's intensity. It was awful to imagine what her father must think, and in a strange way, her desire to stay with Dennis ended right then. The fragile shell around her new life broke and the fear she pushed away flooded in. This wasn't the life she wanted. She wanted music and dancing and the sun on her face—she wanted her freedom—but she wasn't going to lose herself to get it. So, she went home. If Dennis noticed and minded, she couldn't tell. He just let her go without a word.

Months later, on the day Donna graduated from high school, Dennis finally called her. She was out with her friends and missed the call. She guessed it was sort of a big deal that he called, but she felt different now. She was really over him. She did keep one of his paintings hanging in her room, a portrait of a man in a red velvet cloak, the shadows of the soft folds of fabric rendered in the most amazing way.

In the summer of 1968, Donna's father gave her his VW Beetle. She really got her look together. She bought a pair of knee-high boots and a peach satin minidress and round wire-rimmed sunglasses.

And then she met Duane.

 **11**

Donna went to see the Jefferson Airplane at Kiel Auditorium on July 23, 1968, with her friend Joey Marshall, a musician who played guitar in a band called the Truth. She was hoping it was a date, but it was hard to tell; he was so friendly to everyone. The show was fun, all trippy lights and swaying dancers in the crowd, and it was cool to see Grace Slick, a girl singer for a change, and hear her bold voice thundering out of that tiny body.

As they stepped through the crowd outside, a guy with long red hair leaned out of a car window and called out, "Joey!" He was riding shotgun through the parking lot with Jack Davis, a disc jockey from KSHE. Donna stood back and watched Joey walk up to the car. Joey was so damn cute with bright blue eyes and big white teeth. He came back to her just beaming, saying Duane had invited them to a gathering at Jack's house. A gathering: It sounded very sophisticated.

"Who is Duane?" Donna asked.

"He's a great guy, and a great guitar player. You'll love him," Joey said.

Jack served them cold champagne as they sat around his living room and talked.

She could see the effect Duane had on the men in the room. He had a passionate way of expressing himself, but he was very calm, too, and they listened to him and responded with smiles and silent nods. Duane told road tales about his band in his warm southern accent. He was lively and funny, chain-smoking, relaxing with his arm across the back of the sofa, and then he'd talk solemnly about the commitment musicians make to one another. Donna had never seen anyone captivate a room the way Duane did.

She went to use the bathroom toward the end of the night, when the champagne had run dry. She wiped away the dark shadows of mascara under her eyes and ran a comb through her hair. When she opened the door, Duane was standing right there. They were toe to toe and eye to eye. Had he been waiting for her?

"Hey," he said, and smiled. She smiled back but she couldn't find her voice.

"We're going to Forest Park. Can you come?" His eyes were so keen, she felt like he was touching her. She nodded. "Okay," she said.

"Well, okay!" he said.

They all walked together, Jack and a girl in a little sack dress, Duane and Joey talking with their heads down, Donna close behind in her high-heeled sandals. As soon as they hit the grass, Duane ran over to a giant red oak tree with a few low branches and climbed into its arms like a monkey, the heels of his boots just visible beneath a curtain of leaves. Donna sat on the damp grass and watched his feet swinging there, smoke from his cigarette floating out between his boots, and she thought she heard him whistle a little. She smiled to herself and watched the sky pinkening up with the coming sun.

When she ran into him in Gaslight Square a few days later, he smiled so big it made her blush. They had an easy companionability right away. He pointed out the clubs where he had played and said he'd take her to hear some live music soon, if she'd like. She told him she would love that and smiled. He took her hand. His warm palm was hard with calluses.

"Do you know the song 'Classical Gas'? The other day I watched my little sister Laura riding a horse at the stable, and that song came on the radio. She had sun in her hair and the horse was stepping so beautifully, it was just beautiful . . . ," Donna said.

"Sorry, ma'am. No requests," he joked.

Joey came bounding across the street toward them and Donna dropped Duane's hand when she saw him, then felt bad for doing it. She gave Duane a ride back to the apartment downtown where he was staying with his band. He invited her in, but she said, "Next time."

Next time, they lay on a bed and kissed in an apartment where Duane was staying with his cousin Jo Jane. He told her she would meet his brother soon, and she might decide she liked him better because he was a real looker. She couldn't tell if he was kidding. When she did meet Gregg, there was no question in her mind that Duane was the one for her, and it touched her that he had worried.

Hour Glass played at Kiel Auditorium, opening for Iron Butterfly and Janis Joplin. The gig ran long and the promoter ended the show before Janis's set was over, so she announced that they would play for free in Forest Park the next day. Duane called Donna and invited her. Janis's band, Big Brother and the Holding Company, set up their gear under the archways of the World's Fair Pavilion and a small crowd began to gather. It felt like a secret show for those in the know, and Donna was impressed that Duane knew the band and was greeted so warmly.

The members of Hour Glass started calling her "the girl." They couldn't remember her name, but soon she was always by Duane's side. Duane asked Jo Jane what she thought of Donna. "She seems different," she said, and he replied, "She is."

Jo Jane was renting an apartment in St. Louis because she had fallen in love with a man who was working in town. She planned to be there for the next few months, so her cousins and their friends made themselves comfortable. Jo Jane's roommate wasn't crazy about all the guys crashing with them, but Jo Jane simply proclaimed, "Love me, love my band!" Waking up to find the boys sprawled out everywhere felt like home. She made them hot dogs and Kool-Aid for lunch and it was like being a kid again.

Gregg had brought his girlfriend Stacey with him from Los Angeles, and they fought all the time. Jo Jane and Duane sat on a vinyl couch under the window and heard grumbling and whining through the closed bedroom door. Then Stacey would march out the front door, clomp down the stairs, and head out into the street. Gregg would trail behind, slipping a leg into his blue jeans with a big sigh, careful not to meet his brother's eye. Duane and Jo Jane flipped around to lean on the windowsill, trying to see the couple below them on the sidewalk through the branches of the trees. Soon they'd hear Stacey's little heels on the stairs, marching back up. She'd push open the door with her hip, her arms busily entangled with Gregg's, and they'd head unsteadily back into the bedroom, where Gregg would kick the door shut with a bare foot.

Duane smirked at Jo Jane and she rolled her eyes at him. "Poor Greggie," she sighed.

"It's his own damn fault," Duane answered.

After Hour Glass played that night at Pepe's, Stacey made soulful eyes at Gregg and said, "When Gregg is singing onstage, I know he is singing just for me."

Duane fixed her with a piercing look and growled, "He sings for himself."

Duane took Donna to East St. Louis to see Albert King play in a club that seemed to have once been an old movie theater. He wanted her to hear King play "The Sky Is Crying." She had never been to this rough part of the city before, but Duane navigated the terrain like it was his own neighborhood. She watched Duane's face as he watched King play. His huge dark hands tenderly fluttered over the neck of his V-shaped guitar, sweat beading on his forehead as he followed each phrase he sang with a keening run that seemed to second his emotions. Duane's face was wide-open and winsome. He looked like he was falling in love with every note.

Duane took her to Pepe's during the day when it was empty and the owner nodded to him when they walked in. Duane took his guitar case up on the stage and sat on a stool. He played her Tim Buckley's beautiful song "Once I Was," raising his eyes to her as he sang out into the open room.

Once I was a lover
And I searched behind your eyes for you
Soon there'll be another
To tell you I was just a lie

And sometimes I wonder
Just for a while
Will you remember me?

His voice was strong and full of feeling, drifting in and out of key in moments, earnest and pure. He was blowing her mind.

Standing beside her Volkswagen Bug, he said, "You're a good sidekick." He kissed her forehead and gave her a harmonica in a little box marked "Key of G." Then he was gone, on to another town and another gig. Letters began to arrive, marking the months they were apart. In neat, even handwriting on motel stationery, Duane joked that he should marry the heir to the Holiday Inn chain to secure his band a permanent discount. He told Donna of his travels and said he really missed her, and she began to open her heart.

Duane had asked her to come see his band play in Nashville. Donna had a job proofreading checks at a printing plant. When she told her boss she needed time off, he made an off-color joke about coming back to work pregnant. It made her mad, but she knew she would share Duane's bed for the first time, and she did want to be careful. She made an appointment to see her family doctor, a pediatrician she had seen all her life. When she told him she needed birth control pills, he asked, "Are you getting married, Donna?"

"No, sir."

"Have you discussed this with your parents?"

"No," she answered, more quietly.

With two questions, he denied her birth control pills and ended the discussion. She left his office with hot cheeks. Sitting in her parked car, she cried in frustration.

Duane sent her a ticket for the first plane trip she had ever taken. Her life was expanding around her, opening up like the red rose on the front of the greeting card he had sent her on Valentine's Day. He picked her up in the band's van at the airport and took her back to a friend's cabin where the band was staying. As soon as they were with everyone, his attention was drawn away from her. She sat quietly and watched him laughing and playing his acoustic guitar. Donna felt herself an observer fading into the background.

Everyone rode to their gig in the van, focused on the show ahead. At the Briar Patch, she sat alone by the stage and waited for the music to start. They played so late, she could barely keep her eyes open. She rested her head on her folded arms on the little cocktail table beside the stage and the club's owner himself tapped her gently on the shoulder. "Miss, you need to sit up, please. There is no sleeping in the club."

They made love for the first time that night, awkwardly fumbling while the guys in the band slept in the next room. She wasn't exactly disappointed, just confused. She wanted it to happen. She wanted to feel close to him and she did, but she wasn't sure what would happen between them now. She wondered if he had realized it was her first time. She only bled a little.

She went back to St. Louis feeling uneasy and Duane continued down the road traveling and playing music.

. . .

My mother gives me little moments in soft focus and I can't get them any clearer in my mind. I want to know what they talked about. I want to watch her dark eyes change when she sees him coming toward her with his swaggering gait. I want to see him sitting at the little booth in my grandmother's kitchen and hear him call Tommie "ma'am" and make her smile. I want to hear his laugh and see her blushing, but I know Donna wants to keep something for herself. She closes the subject coyly, saying she will tell me anything, I just have to ask. There are no words to ask her for what I want. I simply want more.

I never realized how quickly it all happened. My parents met and changed the paths of their lives in a matter of months. I thought there must be many stories about their time together before I was conceived, but I had heard them all. It occurred to me with a shock: They were really strangers. When I suggest this to my mother, she bristles and says, "Why does everyone always want to count the days we spent together? Haven't you been in love? Don't you know how important every moment is? How infinite that time feels?"

Duane and Gregg went back to Florida to regroup and figure out their next move. Paul and Johnny returned to their homes in Alabama, ready to settle into the comfort of steady studio work and family life. All the songs they played together, all the exciting possibilities the last two years had brought had come to nothing. It was a very low moment, captured vividly in a letter Jerry wrote to Jo Jane.

....

Daytona Beach, Fla.
Sept. 25, 1968

Dear Jo Jane,
Thank you for your letters. I always appreciate them. I have tried to find the time, energy and solitude to write, and now I have the time and solitude, but out of energy.

125

I will fill you in briefly on what's happening and I do apologize if I repeat what has already been said.

Your mother's vacation here ended on a Sat. and Erskine and family arrived to help escort her to the airport. Erskine and family left about 9 or 10PM Sunday nite and Duane, Gregg, Bob and Pete arrived 3AM Monday.

They were really down. Had just completed worst gigs ever and were on the outs with Paul. So the first few days Paul was let out, Johnny was asked to stay, but declined and in less than a week Mr. and Mrs. Carr had Pete re-enrolled in school—Daytona Adult Classes. The only true thing that came out of that shuffle is that Pete is tired of playing bass. Pete's a good guitar lead and has one ambition, to play better than Duane and maybe he will; but Duane has been a very good teacher to him with no regrets—Johnny and Paul were no surprise—Pete was—to them and me. Of course I got it first from the old lady in an off hand way. I figure Pete will go to school until he finds a good tight group to split with doing lead.

So here we sit, Duane, Gregg, Bob and me and I am yelling "get rid of Bob!" and they say all right. It took about two weeks. Of course all of us were down. I told them I was already so down they would have to keep digging to get to me—of course the disbanding put me further down; but more hopeful. Success comes only with change.

I guess we had maybe 2 days when there were only 4 of us, until Gregg went to Jacksonville and brought back 2 girls and one boy to wait several days until the other members of their band came back from a break. Well it is hard to explain. There are 3 band members and the bad thing is that to band with Gregg and Duane, Roger's "Pete" had to be let out of their band and that was a bad day for all, but he is trying to re-enroll in college so maybe it wasn't too bad a day. The three band members are David and girlfriend Jenny, Butch and Linda (wife), Scott (single). Scott has a friend who lives

126

in Jax and is just back from Vietnam and guess whose floor Barry sleeps on? There are two girls, friends of Linda and Jenny's who come from Jax every weekend, Cathy and Dotty and they sent me flowers this week thanking me for my hospitality, which was sleeping on my floor.

The band is practicing and these boys are seasoned musicians. Scott sings and writes, David helps Duane with the mc shit and Butch is a terrific drummer. They are really a great bunch of young people and you would love them and they would you. You would also love Jenny and Linda and as you know I am not girl crazy.

And as usual Ringo has not quite moved in to sleep and eat, but almost. We have *10* for dinner every nite.

I still go to therapy (for my back) 3 days a week and feel like hell. I stayed up 3 hours Sat. They left to gig in Ft. Pierce and then shut the front door and I went to bed and stayed in bed almost all weekend.

Two nights ago, Monday, I cooked a 12 lb. turkey—roasted nice and brown, slow and tender to have turkey and all the trimmings Tuesday nite. Tues when I came from work, there was another 12 lb. turkey raw. Said they ate the other last night. With 3 or 4 hours to cook a turkey, they ate at 10PM. Band was practicing anyway so it didn't matter. Jenny left today to visit home (NY) and Linda is leaving tomorrow for home (Wachula, Fla, not far) and the band is gigging tonite at the Scene and will gig at either ft. Pierce or Miami over the weekend. As soon as they have enough cash they will be going back to the West Coast. Probably in 2 or 3 weeks.

To say the least, there is no time to be sick or to get well. I am glad to have Duane and Gregg home, but what a price to pay. They are just fine and wonderful, but too many for this house.

Marilyn and Mr. Webster have moved and rented Francis house next door to Max—Duane dated Linda instead of

Penny this time—Dated Penny once I think. I saw her at the Martinique last Friday nite and she is still real sweet to me. Boys packed the old "Q" and Bill screwed them as usual so that's it and I'm glad. That bastard deserves any and all misery he ever gets.

I am sure there is more and I will think of it when I seal this letter but I am so tired it will have to wait.

Love, Aunt Jerry

PS–Would you believe I read the Hobbit book in all these goings on?

After kicking around Florida together for a month or two, Gregg admitted that he was planning to head back to Los Angeles as soon as he could get the money together for a ticket.

Duane accused him of wanting to hang out with rock stars and shack up with Stacey. He said Gregg was thinking only of himself, imagining life as a solo artist. Duane felt completely betrayed. He was relentless, cutting Gregg down like it was his job, saying "Hey, fuck you, man. Get lost, you fucking traitor. Go make your money, baby."

Gregg tried to explain he was doing it for the good of the band. He was working off the Hour Glass debt to Liberty Records by recording for them as a solo artist and he hated having to do it. In fact, he was taking a bullet for Duane, because he knew Duane would never go back there, and someone had to or they would be sued for breaking their contract. But it was suddenly clear to Duane that the label had never valued the rest of them at all. They didn't care about his guitar playing; they wanted to make Gregg a pop star. The band they had built together was dismissed, but their name was printed on the singles Gregg recorded with studio musicians, "Gregg Allman and the Hour Glass." That was just an insult.

Once Gregg was gone, Duane wanted to get out of Daytona,

fast. He headed to Jacksonville to see Berry Oakley, the bass player he had met on the last pass Hour Glass made through town. He was not going to sit around feeling bad. He had to get around people and start thinking about his next band. He'd been thinking about Berry Oakley ever since they met and wanted to get to know him.

The night they met at the Comic Book Club, Berry told Duane about the scene in Jacksonville and his band, the Second Coming. "Man, you have got to come to the park and see my band play. You will not believe the crowds. All those kids were just hungry for some decent music, and we are giving it to them. They show up by the hundreds and we just play whatever we feel," Berry said.

"Music can change the world. It is changing this town, I'm telling you, and playing for free is the way. Just giving away all that good energy, it's different than a paying gig. It's a pure experience."

Duane felt an immediate affinity with him, and his vision of what music was really about. Duane was going to head up to Jacksonville and call him, first thing.

One night Duane brought his axe and stayed. He and Berry sat and talked and smoked, playing all night in the dining room under the dusty crystal chandelier, furnished with a collection of guitars, amps, and cases.

Linda had gone up to bed after a while, she was very pregnant and very tired, but she couldn't sleep. She could not stop listening to the mellow blues wafting up to her bed, directly above them.

"Melodies Berry had created were intertwined with the beautiful voice of Duane's strings. I was witnessing magic, like the blossoming of a love affair. I might have had a tiny twinge of jealousy, though I was thrilled for Berry. He'd been touched by that magic," Linda told me years later in her lovely way.

Duane sent letters to Donna, sharing the changes he was going through. He wrote to her about the Hour Glass breakup and his trip to Jacksonville. He told her he was running out of money and had made a decision to return to FAME Studios in Muscle Shoals. He was determined to convince the owner, Rick Hall, to hire him as a session player. Duane knew he needed to get his head together. He needed to cut out the speed, let go of the bullshit big-city scene, play some real music, and make a regular paycheck.

He wrote to Donna steadily through the fall, into the gray winter.

....

September 4, 1968
Daytona Beach, Florida

Skinny Girl,
I miss you. The band broke up, that is we got rid of Paul and the Duck. We tried to get the Duck to stay, but he wouldn't have it without Paul. Paul's in Tuscaloosa, gigging; the Duck's in Miami in a studio. Gregg, Pete and I are still together. We hope to get this really cooking spade drummer and start over again. It'll take a while but it'll work better than the old group, I think. We've all been writing the new material, and some of it is really good. My writing is pretty stoned today. I really miss my tree a lot. I wish I was in it right now. On the way home the damn bus broke down; it hung us up in Birmingham for two days. Interesting, huh?

Nothing at all is happening here. We're all wanting to get back to St. Louis. Sorry I haven't written before now, but I've been on a gigantic bummer and couldn't write.

Tell Jan, Joe, Bill, Eddie, & drummer hello and tell them about the group. It's hard for me to put thought on paper, and I haven't had the $ to call or I would, but I love you and I think of you often. Behave, and I'll see you when I get there; soon, I hope.

—D.

November 10, 1968
Florence, Alabama

Dear Skinny,
I love you.

This has been a rather slow week here. There were only two sessions, but I'm doing another Sunday. We start on Arthur Conley's new record Monday. I sure wish you were here. As soon as my money starts arriving from New York, I'll send you some to come here on. There's nothing in this place or anyplace I need more than you.

Tell Doris I love her. Tell Joey and Jan to just go for themselves and eliminate Bill. One person doesn't make or break a band. He just gets fired! Fuck him.

There's not much new here, so I guess I'll close for now. I've been smoking the Outrageous Killer Weed today, and I'm really sleepy. Take care of yourself and think of me a little, because I'm thinking of you. Goodnight—

Love, Duane

Last Wednesday
This Year

Dear Donna,
I heard you called my house to talk to me but I wasn't home, so I figured I'd write you back instead of calling. We're pretty short of bread nowadays.

I wish I'd been home because I've wanted to talk to you a lot of times but somehow I never did get to call. I've missed you, and sometimes I've felt that you were thinking about me too, but I don't guess you can be sure about a feeling that you have, ever.

I've been pretty busy lately; I cut Wilson Pickett's forthcoming Album two weeks ago, and it went really well. Since then I've been doing regular session work (playing guitar on other people's records when they don't play or can't play well enough) at the recording studio in Muscle Shoals, Alabama, and it looks like I'm going to have to move up there soon. If I do, there's a good chance I'll be able to cut an album of my own soon.

Gregg is going back to California in two weeks to fulfill his obligation to Liberty Records, too. Did the Truth ever get their album out? If so, I'd sure like to have one. See if Joey will send one to me. Also if you see him or Jan, tell them I'll being doing Mike Bloomfield's new album with him and also that I was on Super Session Vol. II album with Hendrix, Bloomfield, Harvey Brooks, and Barry Goldberg. They'll probably dig that. I did some bottleneck things over some of Bloomfield's things that were pretty nice if I do say so.

They've been having these huge gatherings of freaks in Jacksonville, Florida every Sunday for the past few weeks. Millions of bands play and it's really fun; I wish you could be here to see it, it's a miracle. The cops that go to them really dig it, so it's great all round. I've been living there for quite a while with friends, and I'll probably stay until I move to Muscle Shoals.

Didn't I tell you that Jeff Beck would be a monster? He's so fine, I'm glad he's really making it. I hope you get the chance to see him in St. Louis if you haven't already. I really miss being in St. Louis, I love it there. I miss the boats, the tree, and the bears more than anything.

What's this crap about me getting killed by a train or something? Hearing things like that is really weird.

I know that it is probably hard for you to write letters, because it is for me, too, but I want you to try because I need to hear from you soon. Take care of yourself and those around you, and think of me once in a while because in my heart I love you very much and I think of you often. I'll write more later.—D.

Their correspondence was their courtship. Opening the glass lid of her keepsake box is like opening a time capsule. Each letter has the softened hand of a loved thing, paper folded and refolded so many times they have gone limp. My father's handwriting is neat and even, and his voice startles me, how clearly it reveals him. I don't know if my mother would have been able to hang on to the love my father felt for her without them.

12

On my trip to Alabama, Johnny Sandlin drove me to Muscle Shoals to visit FAME (Florence Alabama Music Enterprises), the legendary recording studios where my father's life really started to change. We passed through the marshy flatland that mirrored the vast sky above. Fenced cotton fields and neatly groomed farmland, brick churches every other mile, and a smattering of small houses rested quietly beside our two-lane road. Picturing Duane in this rural, peaceful place after the constant action of Los Angeles wasn't easy. I figured you had better know how to make your own fun if you move to Muscle Shoals.

FAME Studios is located in the same building it was in in 1968. Walking inside, you hear the voices of Etta James or Clarence Carter singing through the little speakers above the door as a stream of hits plays all day. FAME has two studios, A and B, each room partially paneled in wood, with high, angled ceilings, acoustic tiles, and curtains to buffer sound. Control rooms are visible through large panes of glass. Rick Hall's office is upstairs.

"When I was much younger, much younger," Hall tells me when we meet, "I was hot as a pistol. I had no time for Duane. I had no time for anybody. I was *that guy* in Muscle Shoals, Alabama.

"I cut the first hit record here. It was all black music. It was Arthur Alexander, that was the first one. Then Jimmy Hughes's 'Steal Away,' Joe Tex, Joe Simon, Aretha Franklin, Etta James, Wilson Pickett, Clarence Carter, and Otis Redding. Anybody who was anybody—they were here.

"Duane had separated from his brother. He considered his brother to be very talented, but somebody you couldn't deal with. He was tough and he didn't understand business. He was a kid. Duane from the first was my guy and I was his guy. We loved each other. We cared about each other. He came here and said, 'I want to become a studio guitar player.' My ankles bled most of the time, because he was nipping at them. I'd think, 'Come on! Back off! Don't breathe on me!' And then he'd hug my neck and I'd hug his. I cared for him."

Rick settled back behind his wide desk and jumped right in at the beginning.

"'Duane, I have six guitar players. The last thing I need is a guitar player. I've got guitar players running out my ears. I don't have a place for you.'

"'Would you mind if I just stayed around and kind of worked my way in somewhere? I will set up a pup tent in the parking lot. I want you to use me on something.'

"'Make yourself at home,' I said.

"'I'm gonna burn some ass, you will see!' Duane shook my hand and winked at me."

Duane loved Clarence Carter and when he heard he was coming in, he turned up the heat and Rick told him he could play on the session. They cut a real blues thing called "Road of Love," and Duane's playing really shined. Rick was very impressed. In the

135

middle of the song, Carter even sang out, "I like what I'm listening to right now," after Duane's slide solo, a blast of passion in the middle of a simple, funky groove. Duane brought that track to life.

Duane said, "The blues are coming back, Rick. It's gonna be big and you can be big with it."

"I'm tired of that shit," Rick said.

Rick was a rhythm-and-blues innovator: horns, funky piano, and an all-important singer out front, bursting with personality to really put a song across. Duane was from another planet, walking in with tight striped pants and bowling shoes, his hair down to his shoulders, looking like it had never met a brush. He played so loud the shingles on the building rattled. Rick would say, "You're killing me! I'm gonna go deaf!" And Duane would say, "But that's it, Rick! The strings sound wider when you play loud. It overdrives the speakers in the amplifier and gives you that growl!"

Duane's talent was undeniable, and the artists who came through and the guys in the rhythm section respected his ability and enthusiasm right away. Rick signed Duane to a contract, but to Rick's mind, Duane's solo project was a mess.

Duane wanted to sing, play guitar, and do everything on his own, but he didn't seem to be getting anything accomplished. He bedded down in Studio B and he'd sleep half the day away and smoke pot in the alley for the other half. They were in a dry county, for God's sake, even alcohol was forbidden, and he's lighting up without a care in the world.

Duane convinced Rick to do seven or eight sides of him singing. Some weren't quite finished when Rick's close friend Phil Walden came by to check him out. Phil had been Otis Redding's manager from the beginning of his career, when Otis was playing at school dances in their shared hometown of Macon, Georgia. Phil was a self-made industry man, a kingpin in Macon who signed promising black artists and worked hard to help them cross the color divide. Phil managed musicians and brought them to Rick to record. He and Rick shared a sense of themselves as Modern Southern Aristocrats and they had found incredible success. Phil saw Duane's value right away, a white kid who could bring southern music into the rock scene; he was a dream come true.

"Rick, you're going to be rich!" Phil told him. "You've just got to hang in there. Just go in the studio, light up a cigarette, get you a Coca-Cola, turn the machine on and sit back, and when he gets ready to do something, let him do it, and don't worry about it."

Rick was not built that way. He lived an orderly life and ran an orderly studio. His sessions ran like a well-oiled machine. The rhythm section came in day after day and worked regular hours. They knew those rooms intimately and how to get the best sounds out of them, and they wasted no time fussing with any of it. Then here was this skinny dude, curled up on the floor taking a nap in the afternoon. Rick would wake Duane up and Duane would say, "The stars aren't lining up."

Twiggs Lyndon was one of the first people Phil Walden introduced to Duane. The buzz about the white guitar player who could really play the blues had reached Twiggs in Macon, and he traveled to FAME to check it out. Twiggs was a musical purist, raised on the real shit; he had no interest in rock and roll, and he truly believed black musicians were tapped into a source white players would never find. Twiggs was a tenacious and brilliant guy who worked as a road manager for several of Walden's artists. He was born and raised in Macon, although he was cut from a different cloth from most of Macon's upright citizens. He walked with the swagger of a cowboy and dressed the part, too. Twiggs wore a cowboy hat and a long ponytail, a holstered pistol on his belt. He tucked his blue jeans into knee-high boots. To top it off, he raced through town in a beautiful 1929 Ford Opera Coupe, which he treasured. He had bright blue eyes and great white teeth that flashed in a winning smile. He could talk his way into and out of almost any situation.

Little Richard gave him his first job in the music business when he was not long out of high school and had gone AWOL from the navy. Twiggs met the legendary R&B powerhouse at a club in California and told him they were from the same hometown. Twiggs offered his services doing whatever Little Richard needed doing.

The story goes that Little Richard gave Twiggs a suitcase full of money and told him to bring it back the next night, and when he did, without a single bill touched, he was hired on the spot.

Duane flat out blew Twiggs's mind. He almost didn't have words for the way Duane's playing made him feel. In his experience, no white musician he had ever heard was able to play with the soulful feeling that Duane conjured. He said that the first ten minutes he spent in Studio B hearing Duane jam made all the bullshit he had been through in the music business thus far well worth it. He made up his mind right then and there that Duane was his way forward. Just hearing him play would be payment enough for whatever Duane's band would need.

Rick let Duane play with Wilson Pickett. Rick and Pickett had listened to a bunch of songs, demos from sixteen writers out of Memphis and more in Alabama, but they still didn't have that one song that felt like a hit.

"Pickett was brutal with songs," Rick explained. "He'd reject them and was apt to throw the guy who wrote it out and whip his ass. That's why we called him the Wicked Pickett. But he loved me, and he liked Duane."

It was Duane's idea that Pickett record "Hey Jude."

"Would you stop that? That's the craziest thing I ever heard in my life! That record is number five this week with a bullet and will be number one in the next two weeks and will be there for eight weeks. And we're going to cover the Beatles with Wilson Pickett in Muscle Shoals, Alabama?" Rick fairly shouted.

"That's exactly why we need to do it!" Duane said. "We are going to let the world know we're not afraid to produce anything on anybody. We'll cover it and it's going be a big hit!"

Pickett and Rick laughed and told him he was crazy, but then he started to play the riff, and it seemed like a different groove. Pickett warmed up to it and Rick motioned for him to sing along. He sang, "Hey Jew," and Rick said, "It's Jude! It's a name!"

On "Hey Jude," Duane sounds like he's being released, clearly excited by the energy radiating from Wilson Pickett. Duane sat on a small amp facing him and they locked in, matching each other's intensity and driving each other to a fever pitch.

That feeling, of expanding the possibility of a song with his playing, pointed the way forward for Duane. His fierce solo on the end of the cut was the true beginning of his career; everyone who heard it wanted to know who he was. It opened doors for him.

The sessions came one after another after that: Arthur Conley, King Curtis, Soul Survivors, Otis Rush, on and on. And that was just the first month.

FAME Studios ran like a top, clean and even, tight and satisfying. The session players worked regular hours, arriving in the mornings ready to work, and leaving in the evenings, going home to their families. Then Duane blazes through the place, restless and road-worn. Working a routine schedule wasn't in his nature or his experience. He wanted to jump into sessions, add his own touch, and leave.

Rick wasn't going to wait around for Duane to find his identity as a solo act. Phil asked Rick what he was going to do with Duane and if he would sell him Duane's contract.

Jerry Wexler of Atlantic Records stayed dialed in to the music that was being made in the South via Phil Walden. Shortly after the song was cut, in the last days of October 1968, Phil played "Hey Jude" for Wexler, who couldn't believe what he was hearing. Atlantic offered Rick ten thousand dollars for Duane. Rick said, "Write me a check."

Duane played his final session at FAME in February 1969, and Rick never saw him again. Duane's continued session work happened in New York or Miami in Atlantic's studios, or at the studio on Jackson Highway in Sheffield, Alabama, where the Muscle Shoals Rhythm Section, also called the Swampers, set up their own shop.

Rick ended his story with a sigh. "Duane was always very up.

He was not a downer. He was pleasant, soft, and tender. With me being the reverse of all that, we related well. I had had so many conflicts with tough people, but Duane wanted everybody to be in harmony."

We walked back downstairs to FAME's lobby; Johnny was waiting patiently for me. I was wrung out like a rag. Rick had told me the whole story almost without taking a breath.

....

December 6, 1968
Muscle Shoals, Alabama

Dear Donna,

What do you mean, I might not have been good? If I don't get no sled, fuck Santa Claus!

I'm sorry I didn't get to talk to you when you called. I called back but you were gone, so I'll call you again later.

Things here are going very well. In about a month I'm going to start getting my gigging band together. I can hardly wait. I love working in the studio, and it is very valuable experience, but I know I was born to play for a crowd, and I'm really itching to get started. I'm pretty sure the Duck will be with me, and maybe Paul. I hope to get a couple of black cats, too. They're definitely good to have.

I received some letter from this band that I was living with for a while, and they want me to produce a record for them. I really want to do it, because it'll give me a chance to help them out, and myself, too. Man, I'm gonna be some kind of busy.

I should be back from New York by the fifteenth, so shortly after that I want you to come down. I can't set any exact date because I don't know what might transpire between now and then, but as soon as it's possible, I want you to be here with me. Find out how long you'll be able to stay when you come and tell me. I hope a long time.

I'll close for now. I love and miss you Skinny, and think of you often—

Love, D

P.S. Last Day of Scorpio (ooooo!)

....

[mailed December 12, 1968]
Sheffield, Alabama

Last Wednesday
This Year

Dear Skinny,

Thank you for your little letter, I didn't think it was ugly at all; I loved it.

It's getting real cold here now. We're supposed to have snow pretty soon. I can't wait. I'm gonna get a sled for Christmas; Santa already told me.

I just signed a personal management contract with Phil Walden. He used to manage Otis Redding, and he still manages Arthur Conley, Clarence Carter, Aretha Franklin, and a bunch of other people. I'm going to New York in January to cut Aretha Franklin's new album. I don't remember if I told you that or not, but I'm so excited about it, I'll tell you again. I want you to come up as soon as you can after that, because I'll have plenty of bread and we'll be able to do whatever we want.

It looks like I'm going to get some time off for Christmas, but I'll probably go home to see my mom. I still want you to go with me to Miami to the Pop Festival. I'll make the necessary arrangements.

I'll write more later. Remember that I love and miss you and want to see you very much. D

· · ·

Duane began 1969 by writing in the new appointment calendar Rick gave him for Christmas, his name embossed on the cover. He wrote:

This year I will be more thoughtful of my fellow man, exert more effort in each of my endeavors professionally as well as personally, take love wherever I find it, and offer it to everyone who will take it. In this coming year I will seek knowledge from those wiser than me and try to teach those who wish to learn from me. I love being alive and I will be the best man I possibly can—

Duane used his appointment calendar for most of January, and then his notes dwindle down to nothing. The empty pages that follow the last entry speak to how busy his life became. You can already see his frustration with the limits of session work in his entry on January 5, when Rick wouldn't let Duane change his guitar part. It does contain a few entries that recorded significant moments, like his sessions with Aretha Franklin, and his first meeting with both Jerry Wexler and Tom Dowd, the Atlantic president and the legendary producer, respectively, who would become two of the most influential men in his life.

JAN. 2: I spent today driving back from Daytona with Mike and Vance. A nice day.
JAN. 3: Clarence Carter Session. Clarence cancelled today. Moved into my lake crib and it's a gas. Spent the day fixing it a little.
JAN. 4: Clarence Carter Session
JAN. 5: Clarence Carter Session—Leave for New York for Aretha Franklin session
First part of session terrible. Couldn't get Rick to accept new idea for guitar parts. The other cats said I was learning fast when this happened. What a drag.
(make a car payment)

JAN. 6: Begin Aretha Franklin Session—In New York. Aretha wasn't available to record today, so we cut this girl Donna Weiss from Memphis. She was a really nice chick, but I'm afraid not much of an artist. I met Jerry Wexler. What a good cat. Saw Tom Dowd and met Arif Mardin and all the Atlantic folks. A damn good organization.

JAN. 7: Aretha showed today. We cut some things. Nice session.

JAN. 8–9: etc etc

JAN. 13: Wait for Sally's call at Fame

JAN. 17: Been busy and haven't been keeping this book up. Need to get some bread from sessions soon. Session tomorrow. Received 18 sessions in New York.

Duane was flown to New York City to play with Aretha Franklin at Atlantic Studios.

She didn't make it into the studio the first day, which was a real disappointment, but when she got there the following day, everything pulled together quickly. She was a country girl in many ways, comfortable in her own skin and easy to be with, but she didn't waste time. She hit her stride, singing and playing piano. Duane and Jerry Jemmott, the bass player who was already legendary for his powerful, fluid, and funky session playing, were set up in front of Aretha's piano, facing away from her behind baffles to keep their sounds clean.

The songs they were working up were closer to pure blues than any other work Duane had done for Atlantic. He pulled back and let a single note ache, resting on his warm tone and touch. The sound of his slide was well suited to her tone; their interplay was a conversation. Duane was confident enough to echo the feeling and richness of her voice. When he was done with his part of their session, he went out and bought a bottle of wine, returned to the control room, and listened to Aretha sing out for the rest of the night. It was an incredible experience for him.

143

While he was in New York, he went with Jimmy Johnson, a fellow studio guitarist at FAME, to see Johnny Winter play at the Fillmore East. Johnny was playing great, and Jimmy loved it, but Duane seemed restless and distracted. He leaned in to Jimmy and said, "Just you watch, this time next year it's going to be me and my band up there on that stage."

Jackie Avery was a singer and songwriter working at Redwall, a recording studio Phil Walden had built and dedicated to the memory of Otis Redding in Macon, Georgia. Some of his songs made their way to Muscle Shoals. He was hoping a song of his would end up on Duane's solo album. When Duane heard the demos, there was only one element that stood out—the rhythm of the drummer. Whoever he was, he had a whole other sense of timing. He was moving everything forward without force, but in a kind of shifting changing progression that was both reliable and surprising. Duane couldn't tell if this cat knew what he was doing and was amazing, or if he was getting into that sweet current accidentally. Either way, that drummer had potential. His name was Jai Johanny Johanson, also known as Jaimoe.

Jai Johanny was from Gulfport, Mississippi, by way of the moon. When he was in high school, he found a buried treasure in the school library and came to believe it was sent there by God just for him, via the U.S. Postal Service: *Down Beat* magazine. The magazine revealed the wider world: Chicago, New York, Philadelphia, and more. It was filled with sharp-dressed black musicians with goatees and little glasses, berets and Mohawk haircuts, pressed suits and smiles. Jai found himself a pair of clear glasses without prescription lenses and wore them as a talisman, a taste of cool to call his own. He even shaved the sides of his head into a Mohawk.

Jai Johanny played a drum in the marching band. He practiced next to the football field and watched the team run in swerving patterns, tackling each other and sweating, and it felt like he was missing out. He looked down at the still, pocked white circle of his drumhead, and the bandleader, Mr. Willie Sydney Farmer, saw him.

"Go play football if that's what you feel like doing," Farmer said.

Jai Johanny lasted three days at football practice and then returned to the band room ready to learn. Football was something he could figure out how to play, but drumming felt like a riddle that kept shifting. Farmer played Charlie Parker albums for Jai Johanny, engaging his ear on a deep level.

A few years later, when Jai Johanny was playing in a nine-piece band fronted by Otis Redding, Otis told him he needed to learn about time. He was rushing the beat, he said. Jai Johanny couldn't feel it happening. His next gig was playing with Joe Tex, who fired Jai Johanny three times. After the third time, Jai went home and turned the washhouse behind his grandmother's house into a studio. He set up his kit and a record player and listened to John Coltrane. He played along with the music, five, six, seven hours a day. One afternoon, he was playing and hit the zone. He can't say what was different or why it happened that day, but he hit a point beyond which everything became clear. He could not make a mistake if he tried, and time as he once chased it disappeared. He was the time. It was in him.

Charles "Honeyboy" Otis played drums with everyone—Lightnin' Hopkins, John Lee Hooker, so many players a list would be too long—and he took Jai Johanny under his wing. Jai could rely on him and look up to him. He listened carefully to the things Honeyboy told him. When Jackie Avery told Jai that he needed to go hear a white guitar player who was working at FAME Studios, Jai remembered something Honeyboy once said to him. He said if Jai Johanny wanted to make good money, he needed to find some white guys to play with. Instead of heading to New York to play jazz, which was his dream, he decided to head to the Shoals and meet Duane Allman. He could go to New York a little later.

When Jai Johanny Johanson walked into FAME and introduced himself to Duane, it changed both of their lives. Jai was every inch the rebel Duane was, and they recognized each other as kindred spirits before they played a note together. Jai had the physique of a bodybuilder from working out with railroad ties when he couldn't afford weights. He wore round sunglasses, a string of beads around his neck, and a close-cropped natural haircut. He was a bohemian, tuned in to improvisational jazz, and had spent years holding it down behind some of the best R&B acts in the world.

He and Duane jammed together in Studio B, and Jai Johanny moved into Duane's cabin by the lake right away. He brought albums by John Coltrane and Miles Davis, and together he and Duane began to explore the universe. Neither of them had ever played the way they were playing together. Each one led, then followed, the music expanding around them like an endless field of play. It was a joyful, powerful experience to play with another man who didn't impose limits on himself. They improvised, feeding off each other's energy. From the first time they played together, they were close as brothers.

Duane wanted to get Jaimoe and Berry Oakley together as soon as possible.

He was feeling confined by the daily routines of session work, even though he was playing with some of the most talented musicians in the world. David Hood on bass, Jimmy Johnson on guitar, Roger Hawkins on drums, Barry Beckett and Spooner Oldham on keys: Those session cats were undeniable, and they made the best-sounding records anyone could ever want to hear. The experience of playing beside them had shown Duane what he could handle. He had learned how to get the sound he wanted out of his guitar. His tone was leaps and bounds closer to the sound in his mind. But all those guys were too comfortable. They were living like all the other working stiffs, day in and day out. Duane needed an audience. He needed to move people. He needed to move, period.

The Muscle Shoals Rhythm Section had shown him that he played best when he played with the best. He wanted to keep that feeling of being driven to the edge of his gifts by the players around him, and the cats in Jacksonville had that ability. When Berry came to jam, their vibe flowed right away, with wild, powerful riffing that scared the other studio players in the building. No one else would pick up their instruments and sit in with them; they were grooving on a whole other level. They followed each other into new musical territory none of them had been able to reach alone.

In January 1969, Donna flew to Alabama to visit Duane. It had been months since they had been together in Nashville and she was nervous. Duane picked her up in the Dogsled, a white two-door Ford with a black hardtop that used to belong to Rick. He traded for it by playing guitar. Duane could talk anyone into anything.

He had to go back to the studio, so Donna waited for Duane in the diner of a motel near FAME Studios, where he was in a session. She sat alone and ordered a cup of tea, feeling like a real lady. When it came, she poured in the milk and squeezed a slice of lemon into her cup and was disgusted to find something was wrong with it. She sent it back and asked for another cup. She did this twice more before the waitress explained that she should choose one, milk or lemon, since both together would curdle.

On the way home, they heard the high moan of a freight train rolling across the narrow road. Duane, Donna, and Jai Johanny were sitting shoulder to shoulder on the bench seat of the car. The train's whistle rose round and clear in the air as if blown through a horn's brass body. My father asked Jai what key it might be in, that perfect note? He guessed G sharp and the train passed on into the Alabama night. My mother was eighteen years old that winter. This moment stayed with her, proof of Duane's musician's ear. He heard the world blowing cool licks all around him. He saved them up and gave them back, streaming freely out of his guitar. She watched it happening, his inspiration forming, and his strength gathering.

Duane's cabin by the Tennessee River was small and very homey. He had painted a winding vine of colorful flowers on the paned windows of the French doors between his bedroom and the living room and hung an Indian tapestry on the wall. Donna leaned against a post of Duane's four-poster bed and described a passage she had read from Kahlil Gibran's *The Prophet*.

> *Give your hearts, but not into each other's keeping.*
> *For only the hand of Life can contain your hearts.*
> *And stand together yet not too near together:*
> *For pillars of the temple stand apart,*
> *And the oak tree and the cypress grow not in each other's*
>   *shadow.*

She described how love could be between them, how they could stand beside each other like two pillars, not leaning or overpowering, but together. She could see by the look in his eyes how impressed Duane was by this idea, and she panicked for a moment. She did not completely understand the words she had just said.

Donna was still and quiet; a world of words could be imagined in her silence. Her eyes were guarded, as difficult to read as the flat glass eyes of a doll, but her lips were by turns nervy and tight, occasionally venturing between her teeth, where one cheek would pinch back into a half smile of distress. She wasn't going to give in to Duane right away; he could tell. She ran the back of her hand against his cheek, like a gorilla preening her mate. He reached toward her and stroked the back of his hand against her cheek, his Gorilla Girl.

So many things went unsaid between them, and it was better that way. He seemed to know her thoughts. They lay quietly, curled around each other, and talked about what they would be like as parents if they had a child someday. Duane joked that he would be so hip, he'd give his daughter's boyfriend a key to the house. Donna squeezed his cheeks together and said, "Say funny bunny." Through his squished lips he said "Fuck you," laughing, and they rolled together on the bed. Their thin bodies wound around each other in light sleep, folded thigh to thigh. His fingers moved even while he slept, pushing the patterns of invisible chords against Donna's skin as he dreamed, his body spooned around hers.

The next morning, he jumped out of bed and began to write "Happily Married Man," a mean little early rock-and-roll riff with tough and funny lyrics: "My new old lady is out of sight, loving me every day and night. Oh, I haven't seen my wife for two or three years, I'm a happily married man. . . ."

Donna smiled, slipping his blue jeans on. They fit her perfectly.

Berry was traveling back and forth between Muscle Shoals and Jacksonville, returning with stories and tunes they'd been working on for Duane's solo album. He was especially excited about the jams he and Duane had with Jaimoe. He told Linda about this tall pretty blond girl Duane had there with him and how he really seemed to be into her. He knew she and Linda would love each other.

When Donna got home to St. Louis two weeks later, everything felt empty and small. Then a letter came and she held it against her, ran to her room, and closed the door. A delicious ache suffused her chest and raced in tingling streaks through her arms and legs, as if every place he had ever touched her were suddenly alive in the sight of his words. If she had ever doubted what this was, she was sorry, because of course this was love. Lying on her bed, she read:

February 4, 1969
Muscle Shoals, Alabama

Skinny Gorilla Girl That I Love,
You've been gone three hours now, and I'm nice and drunk trying not to remember that you're gone. I thought about cutting my house in half and sending half to you so at least we'd be under the same roof, but my heart's aching so bad I don't think I could pull a saw to do it. Jai Johanny took two of those blackbirds and he's really flying and doesn't know it; what a groove. He's sure a fine friend. I sure do love you and miss you and I just wish that this pen would say what I want to say. Oh mama, I need you so bad this minute I could bust. Don't ever make me watch you leave me again. I don't

think I could handle it at all. I'd better quit this before I get in my car and come after you.

> I'll Love You Till
> There's No Till,
> Duane

Duane sat on the bank of the Tennessee River, high and feeling so at ease. The sun weakened into pale syrup by the water's reflection, the trees murmured and shimmied, everything was encouraging a sense of completeness. The little bottle on his finger was cool and thick. There was a world of sounds between the known chords, whole realms beyond the clean and distinct notes found by pressing and strumming alone. These fluid cries felt so true and sad and human to him: odd notes, long notes, voices pulled out of his hand's movements. The river smiled up at him and the trees applauded Duane sliding home.

He grinned and ran his calloused fingers over his mustache and rough cheeks. He needed a shave. He looked over his shoulder to Jai Johanny, who was growing thick roots into the ground around the bend. His small leather hat was over his eyes and the corners of his mouth formed a sleeping frown. Jai Johanny's fingers were interlaced over his chest and spots of sun flickered over him like blown bubbles on the breeze.

Duane played the opening riff of "Statesboro Blues" as Jesse Ed Davis played it, over and over with the stamina of an athlete and the monomania of an addict, the siren call, then the quick run of notes flowing; every change, at first as jagged as rock, was soon worn smooth by his fingers.

Songs are maps, and once you have traveled the route they describe, you can find your way in daylight or darkness alone, no longer thinking as you point yourself toward home.

Duane found his sound at the water's edge. It was resting in his hands.

13

Jo Jane sent Duane a Yeats poem that reminded her of him:

THE SONG OF WANDERING AENGUS

I went out to the hazel wood,
Because a fire was in my head,
And cut and peeled a hazel wand,
And hooked a berry to a thread;

And when white moths were on the wing,
And moth-like stars were flickering out,
I dropped the berry in a stream
And caught a little silver trout.

When I had laid it on the floor
I went to blow the fire a-flame,

But something rustled on the floor,
And some one called me by my name:
It had become a glimmering girl
With apple blossom in her hair
Who called me by my name and ran
And faded through the brightening air.

Though I am old with wandering
Through hollow lands and hilly lands,
I will find out where she has gone,
And kiss her lips and take her hands;
And walk among long dappled grass,
And pluck till time and times are done
The silver apples of the moon,
The golden apples of the sun.

He replied from Jacksonville on March 20, 1969:

Dear Jo Jane,

I got your letter a little late because I'm down in Jacksonville and I had to get all my mail shipped here and that's always a drag because my replies are always late.

That poem was sure nice; I get high every time I read it. Old Aengus must've been a guitar picker for sure. I wish I shared his optimism.

I'm down here getting a new band together, as usual. This one is stronger than anything I've had so far, and I've got some high hopes for it. I have two lead guitarists (me and another guy), two drummers (one is black, he worked with Otis Redding right up till when he got killed), bass, and Gregg playing organ and singing. Sounds good, huh?

I quit my staff position in Muscle Shoals because all these people up there kept telling me how rich I was gonna be in a few years from just kissing the boss's ass and playing EXACTLY WHAT THE BOSS WANTS. I told the motherfuckers that I was the boss in that department and would they excuse me but I heard the highway calling me. Probably a stupid move. PROBABLY A STUPID THING TO WRITE

Poem: I love and miss you everyday more than I could ever say

Hotcha, D

I'll write more later.

Freed up from the confines of FAME, Duane began focusing on building his gigging band. He didn't entirely close the door to session work, but he was through living in Alabama now that he had Phil Walden behind him.

He considered almost every talented musician he came across as a potential bandmate. Listening to demos, or seeing a gigging band live, he would say to Jaimoe, "What about that guy?" and Jaimoe would answer, "Duane, that guy isn't fit to carry your case."

Duane would be surprised. Jaimoe saw that Duane didn't entirely realize how remarkable he was. Berry's talent was equally undeniable; his approach was both powerful and melodic, and emotionally expressive, qualities rare to find in a single bass guitar player. He, Duane, and Jaimoe quickly recognized that they had chemistry, and Berry's interest was more than piqued.

Playing with Jaimoe and Berry in a power trio modeled after Cream and the Jimi Hendrix Experience seemed like the way to go, although Duane was not sold on being the front man. He knew he had passion and guts as a singer, but he didn't possess the stability or control he needed vocally. Phil Walden tried to put Duane at ease, pointing out that singing wasn't the focus of either popular trio he was inspired by; it was more important to showcase his guitar playing and build a vibe.

As far as Duane was concerned, he had found his new band. Jaimoe and Berry were the ones, and he was ready to move forward.

But Berry had already met his match in Jacksonville—a guitar player named Dickey Betts.

Dickey had crossed paths with Duane and Gregg many times in the clubs Duane referred to as "the Garbage Circuit of the South." Dickey was quiet, well spoken, and totally passionate and knowledgeable about music. He loved everything from Django Reinhardt's wild and free gypsy jazz to the Grateful Dead's psychedelic, folksy sound. He was versed in bluegrass and country swing as well as the blues. He had an incredible ear and his touch could go from a gentle melody to pure aggressive fire in an instant. Dickey was raised in central Florida and started playing music as a kid with his family in a road show called the World of Wonder. His father played mandolin. As a teenager, he developed a real wild streak, and got into riding motorcycles wearing a vest with "Eat Shit" emblazoned on the back. His first band, with his childhood friend Joe Dan Petty, was called the Jokers and they worked the clubs. He and Berry met and started jamming, and formed a band of their own called the Blue Messengers. The owner of a Jacksonville nightclub called the Scene took a shine to them and hired them to be his house band. He had poured money into the place, installing an elaborate dance floor and swirling lights, and he wanted them to be his house band, with one change: He thought Berry looked like Jesus Christ, and wanted them to rename the band the Second Coming, which they did.

At first, their gigs at the Scene were sparsely attended. Jacksonville seemed an unlikely home for a long-haired psychedelic rock band. They nicknamed their town Jackass Flats for a reason, for the conservative guys working the naval base and the shipyard and the rednecks living in the backwoods. Berry was confident that there were young people like them hiding out; they just didn't have a meeting place. He suggested that they play Willowbranch Park for free, saying all the freaks would come out of the woodwork, and sure enough they did. They began to play shows each weekend, and within a couple of months, thousands of kids came to sprawl out on blankets and dance in circles, passing joints openly in the park, and the Scene was packed all week, too.

Jaimoe and Duane traveled back to Jacksonville for longer stretches of time between Duane's remaining sessions at FAME, and Berry welcomed them into his home and to jam. Jamming with the Second Coming was a gas, turning on all the local kids, riffing on songs like "Hey Joe" and "Hoochie Coochie Man."

Dickey was a mysterious dude, open and charming at times, then deep within himself and impossible to read at others. He wasn't as forthcoming as Berry, and it was clear it would take time for Duane to get to know him. Dickey could not help but be a little wary of Duane, this strutting, arrogant guitarist who had appeared in town out of nowhere, clearly hoping to poach his bass player. Dickey could see right away that the band was dialed in. He was trying to be patient, feeling out the situation.

For all the caution, their playing took off from the start. They had chemistry. Dickey's strengths and style were different than Duane's. Dickey had a kind of fight in him that set off Duane's fluidity in a remarkable way. Dickey's tone and attack drew from a country root, while Duane was digging deeply into the blues. The conversation between their sounds was dynamic and fascinating and the music that unfolded during their Jacksonville jams began to shift the direction Duane thought his band would take.

Duane realized he had been preparing for this band forever. He had gathered ideas about what he wanted it to feel and sound like all along the road. Carlos Santana was coming closest to what Duane could envision. The band could expand into extended, exploratory jams onstage, and tap into different influences. He started to imagine a band that could really open up a song and strive together like the jazz cats did. Jaimoe played John Coltrane and Miles Davis records at their crib all the time, and anything less than that level of ambition and innovation started to seem like a waste of time. Duane also wanted two drummers. If James Brown could do it, so could he. Instead of switching between them like Brown did, Duane could almost hear the interplay in his head, if the drummers riffed with each other the way the guitars did.

His band would be together, man. Duane took Donna to see

Procol Harum. When Gary Brooker, the piano player, bent his head over the keys, and the band started in a perfect synchronized moment, Duane leaned in and said with excitement, "That's just how my band will be—that tight!"

Duane and Gregg met a great drummer named Butch Trucks in 1965 when his folk trio, the Bitter Ind, came to Daytona Beach looking for a gig at the club where the Allman Joys were booked. Duane made a few calls for them and turned them on to a club owner in Jacksonville who Duane knew would love what the Bitter Ind were doing. The Bitter Ind got the gig. By 1968, Butch had moved on to a Byrds-inspired band called the 31st of February, and Duane and Gregg were briefly tempted to join them when Hour Glass ended. They even cut a few songs together. The brothers joined Butch in a studio down in Hialeah, Florida, and recorded "Melissa," a pretty song Duane particularly liked that Gregg had written just after high school. Butch thought it was sounding great, but soon after, Gregg slipped away, back to L.A. when it was just coming together. Gregg sold the publishing rights to two of his songs, "God Rest His Soul," about the death of Martin Luther King, Jr., and "Melissa," to pay for his plane ticket.

Butch had trained as a percussionist at Florida State University. He played drums with amazing power and his timing was perfection. Jaimoe had an uncanny intuitive flow like no one Duane had ever heard. He was truly a jazz drummer at heart, with a unique approach. What common ground could Jaimoe and Butch possibly have? They were from different worlds, literally and musically. But Duane had a strong sense that they would complement each other.

Now that they were all in Jacksonville, Duane headed to Butch Trucks's house with Jaimoe by his side. Butch opened the door to Duane standing on his porch with a muscle-bound black man wearing a necklace made out of bear claws and a dark pair of shades, as intimidating a person as Butch had ever seen. Butch was raised in a conservative, Southern Baptist family and carried all the racist fears that came with this upbringing.

"Hey, Butch, this is my new drummer, Jai Johanny," Duane

said. "Jai, this is my old drummer, Butch Trucks." Duane walked through the front door.

Duane liked testing people, liked to watch them cope with being thrown into deep water. Jaimoe was completely silent and sat on the sofa without a word. It was a long afternoon. They could find very little to talk about, but when they finally sat down to play, that didn't matter at all.

All of the inspiration Duane had carried for years came to fruition in Butch and Linda Trucks's living room in Jacksonville, Florida, on March 23, 1969. Duane returned with Dickey and Berry, along with the Second Coming's keyboard player, Reese Wynans. Once they set up and began playing, everything quickly began to gel.

This is the moment everything that followed flowed from: an afternoon in a living room, furniture pushed to the walls. They tuned their guitars, chords snaking around their boots on the floor, and sipped from cans of beer. They began to jam on a simple twelve-bar blues shuffle. Within the first few turns, it was clear they were communicating. Their eyes locked and they smiled and nodded. They were together in a new sonic space, and it was sprawling. It was as if they had wandered into a field of tall grass together and were lost in dense waves of green until Duane and Dickey together cut it down, revealing a clear view of blue sky for miles ahead. Berry stepped confidently into the breach, fearless and funky, with the power of the drummers at their backs like a gathering wind, and suddenly everything was possible. Even if they wound up in a tight spot, a moment hot with tension, they could turn a tight corner together and the song would open up again. Melodies would build and grow, then pass away. It was a journey.

The minute sensitivity of every note danced across their faces. Dickey's blackbird-wing hair swung over his face, his eyebrows arched over his closed eyes. With his shoulders grooving, hips shaking, Duane's mouth formed a silent O, his head shaking no, and then yes. Duane would wander off course and hit a note that at first sounded out of place, then bend it, pull it, and stretch it until he could use the tension in it and suddenly somehow it was right, more right than perfect would have been, because you could feel the wheels shaking beneath him, the danger and fragility, and it was exciting to know he was taking you out on a limb with him. Duane's tone was incredible, round and warm, full and rich. He turned up his amp until it was fairly straining, a careening brightness he could tease and ride hard.

They didn't have to talk about it. They played a reeling, endless jam that touched on the lives they had all lived separately and it took off like a rocket. Together they had all of the ingredients needed for greatness, and they were hungry for it. Their experiences were pressed into the service of their songs, every hard time useful now as grist for the mill and transformed into something beautiful, full of pride and longing.

The men played without speaking or wondering how they had gotten to this new place. Nothing had ever felt like this before. Not to any of them. Duane told them that if they wanted out of this band, they would have to fight their way through him to get out the door.

"This is *it*, man!" Duane was over the moon. He had found what he was looking for. They all felt it.

Lying in bed, Donna knew something felt off. Her body was heavy and her mind kept drifting, settling on Duane, then flying off into vague worry. As she wondered what it was, she rested her hand on her flat belly. She decided she needed to take a pregnancy test.

Her sister Joanie came with her to the doctor's office. Donna panicked and tore up her first form when she realized she had filled in her true name and address. Joanie stuffed the pieces in her purse. She knew her sister was pregnant; she could just tell. The air around Donna seemed still and charged, and her face looked serious and beautiful. She was different somehow.

Joanie was right. At eighteen years old, Donna was pregnant.

Donna lay in a warm bath and looked down at her long legs. She covered her breasts with her palms. Somehow she wasn't afraid.

Her body finally felt like it really belonged to her, and it magically knew how to make a baby. Her life was opening up before her and although she couldn't see what it was becoming, she could feel it expanding. She would finally have space to maneuver and to grow. Telling Duane was the only worry. She had no idea how he would react.

Her most recent letter from him was postmarked Miami, Florida, so sitting in her friend Maureen's living room, she dialed the operator and asked for help calling recording studios in Miami. The operator placed four or five calls and Donna left messages for Duane at each studio, and it worked. By the end of the day, Duane called her back.

"Come to Macon as soon as you can," he said. "Everything is going to be all right. I love you."

He sounded really happy; he made it feel easy. She was so grateful.

With her mother's help, Donna packed the suitcases she had been given as a graduation present. They folded her nightgowns and underthings, her new navy blue crepe dress, and a hot-pink mini with fancy white stitching all over it. The dresses would in no way adapt to her growing belly, and Donna assumed they were her mother's way of saying she wanted Donna to keep dressing like a proper young lady.

Donna fit in a neat stack of parenting books, including Dr. Spock's *Baby and Child Care* and A. S. Neill's *Summerhill*. She took little else. Tommie was surprisingly accepting and promised she would come to Georgia when the baby was born. Her father, on the other hand, stopped speaking to Donna for several weeks when she told him she was pregnant and going to live with Duane. As she was leaving for the last time, they met at the front door. He was moved to tears.

He quietly said, "Goodbye, Buttons!" He had never called her Buttons before, and there were tears in his eyes. Donna had seen her daddy cry only once before, when his father died.

. . .

Donna walked down a flight of rolling stairs onto the tarmac at the tiny airport in Macon, balancing her little cosmetics case against her hip. She wore her new prim minidress and her blond hair brushed silky straight. Duane was there to meet her.

As she walked shyly beside him through the parking lot to his car, the weak latch on her case sprang open and her books tumbled out at their feet. A smiling pink-skinned infant on one cover, a doctor in a white coat and a woman with a huge belly on the others, scattered facedown and pages flapping. It was mortifying to her. They hadn't even had the chance to ease into the idea, and there it was.

Duane took her to a small apartment on College Street that Phil Walden had rented for the band, a real hippie crash pad in the same building where Twiggs had an apartment.

The only furniture was mattresses on the floors and a Coke machine filled with bottles of beer. Duane offered Donna no comfort on her first night there. A kind word and his arms around her would have gone so far, just to curl up together and dream of their future, but he stayed up late, talking to Twiggs and Jaimoe in the main room of the apartment, and left her alone in the one bedroom. As she unpacked her nightgown, she could hear Twiggs and Duane talking through the door. She heard a rumbled, garbled question from Twiggs, and then Duane's answer:

"How do you ever know if they're the one?"

He made her wait most of the night before he climbed into bed smelling of beer and pulled her body into his. The way he felt against her almost made her forget what she had heard him say.

Their first weeks together were spent in constant motion. Just a few days after her arrival, Duane told her he had to go to Jacksonville to take care of some business. Duane and Donna drove the Dogsled down to Jacksonville to Berry and Linda's house. On the drive, Duane told her the Oakleys were expecting a baby of their own, any day. It was comforting to know Linda was already a couple of steps ahead of her on the path. Duane and Berry thought it was so cool they were going to be fathers together. Everything they were going through felt connected, new, and hopeful: the band, the families, the budding spring.

Donna looked at Duane's profile in the dark car as he leaned forward to light two cigarettes at once on the glowing coil of the lighter. He handed one of them to Donna with a wink. Sly and the Family Stone came on the radio and he sang along in a sweet and funny falsetto, "I . . . I . . . I am everyday people. . . ." Donna didn't know if she had ever felt freer.

They pulled up in front of a gray house where the Oakleys and Dickey Betts lived. It was late, but all the windows were blazing with light and you could hear music and voices from the street.

"Are you ready to meet everybody?" Duane asked. Donna nodded and ran her fingers through her hair.

Berry's sister, Candace Oakley, opened the door. She was one of the most beautiful and hip girls Donna had ever seen. Candy was not much more than five feet tall, with bronzed skin, bright blond hair down to her waist, and smart blue eyes that flashed over you so quick, you couldn't even imagine what she was thinking. Berry's wife, Linda, walked up behind her, almost six feet tall with long, wavy light brown hair, dreamy blue eyes, and full lips curved into an easy smile. Her hands perched proudly on her big round belly. They both had a refined hippie girl style that Donna couldn't imagine pulling off: They wore strings of colorful beads around their necks, open silk blouses, tight cutoff jeans aged to pale perfection, and handmade sandals. The little blue crepe shift dress Donna's mother bought her suddenly felt like a costume straight out of a Gidget movie. She felt like a square. They led the way into a small living room with people sitting on every available surface: draped together in armchairs, cross-legged on the floor, separating stems and seeds out of a pile of marijuana on an open record album cover. The room was smoky and smelled like spices.

Linda thought Donna looked like a fashion model, standing just behind Duane with her chin resting on his shoulder, looking around with dark, calm eyes. She was so thin and tall, ladylike, looking just like Joni Mitchell on the cover of her first album, with

161

long blond bangs and delicate wrists. Donna noticed another very pretty girl with dark brown hair down her back and an incredible tan. She stood up as soon as she saw Duane. When Donna asked who she was, Linda smirked and said, "Oh, you mean the Polynesian Princess?"

Donna watched Duane walk after the dark-haired beauty, down a dark hallway and into a bedroom, and a chill ran through her. When he pulled the door closed behind them, Donna's first instinct was to bolt. She wanted to run as fast as she could under the rustling palm trees, out into the night. Looking at the closed door that separated her from Duane, she suddenly knew her new life could disappear before it had even started. Duane could easily follow any girl through any door at any time and never come back. It would be that simple. She wanted to be alone, so she could shake the sinking feeling in her belly, but there was nowhere to run to. When he opened the door and returned to her side, she couldn't bring herself to look him in the eye. If she was going to be part of this world of his, she was going to have to be cool.

She was shocked out of her reverie by a deafening crack that could only be a gun. Berry loped into the room laughing. "Damn! Dickey just shot his gun off the porch!"

The police were at the door within minutes, just long enough for someone to toss the baggie of pot out the back window into the bushes while everybody tried to fan the smoke out the back door. Donna was terrified. Two uniformed officers passed through the house quickly, asked a bunch of questions, and left without hassling anyone too badly. Dickey was polite and calm with them, and then lit a joint the moment the door closed behind them.

Berry, Duane, and Dickey took turns singing, but they clearly needed a stronger vocalist. Duane knew what he needed to do. He had been telling Jaimoe about his brother's voice for months; it would fit perfectly on top of the music they were playing.

Gregg's time in Los Angeles had been hard on him. Liberty was no more tuned in to his real potential than they had been with Hour Glass. They made a few mediocre singles and nothing much came of them. He was humiliated by the choices the label made for him, like the Tammy Wynette song "D-I-V-O-R-C-E." He was feeling pretty low. He was so depressed he even contemplated putting a gun to his head.

He had made a number of friends and solid connections with other musicians, including the guys in a band called Poco, and he was considering joining their band when Duane called. It was the first time they had spoken in eight months, and it was all business. "Baybro, I'm putting a band together with two drummers, two guitarists, and a bass player, and I need you to get your ass down here, round it up, and send it somewhere." Gregg thought it sounded like a train wreck, but it was the highest compliment to hear Duane say he needed him to be his singer. Gregg left for the airport that night.

When Gregg arrived at the gray house, it was packed with people he either didn't know or knew only dimly. He followed the sound of his brother's voice out onto a screened porch. He set eyes on a little beauty who took his breath away. Good God! Hair past her waist as blond as sunshine and a tight little body! She laid a smile on him that made his knees go weak. Duane stepped between Gregg and the girl and gave him a big squeeze. "Baybro, that is Berry's baby sister Candy. You best behave!"

Back at Butch's house, Gregg sat and watched his brother tear into "Statesboro Blues," the same tune he had started with back in Los Angeles. During their time apart, Duane's slide playing had taken an astounding leap forward. If Gregg hadn't heard it for himself, he wouldn't have believed it was possible. When the band all kicked in, the playing was so powerful, Gregg felt the hair on his arms stand up. Then he started to feel like the odd man out.

In anticipation of Gregg's arrival, they dusted off an old country blues tune that Muddy Waters had electrified first, common ground for them to stand on together, a song called "Trouble No More." Duane handed Gregg the lyrics he had written out by hand.

163

"Bro, I don't know. I need some time to get comfortable here, you know? You guys already have it together and all."

"Oh no you don't, man. You are *not* going to embarrass me in front of these people. I have been telling them for days how you are the only one who can sing for us. Now get your shit together and sing." Duane's eyes burned through him. There was no way out, so Gregg sang. He poured his anger and stress into the song, and it fueled him. He dug into the deepest, most guttural and bluesy side of his voice and unleashed everything he had. The smile that spread across Duane's face flashed all the way across the room. Duane was so thrilled when he was done; he grabbed Gregg's face in both hands and kissed him on the lips.

Gregg's power and soulfulness were beyond anyone's expectations. He sounded amazing. All fear was gone. All that was left to do was pull together six or seven songs and get in front of a crowd. Gregg told them he'd been writing steadily in L.A. He had twenty-nine songs in his notebook, and a few might be just right.

They also had to decide what to call themselves. The first band name they lit on was Beelzebub, but the potential for calling down bad juju was discussed and the name was scrapped. The Allman Brothers Band seemed like a natural choice to everyone, except for the brothers themselves. Duane and Gregg didn't want the band to feel like they were not six equal partners, but everyone else thought it was a great name, and it meant something: All men are brothers, and that was what they were all about, spreading the brotherhood.

Duane explained to Donna that she would stay upstairs from Linda and Berry, with his friend Ellen Hopkins, whom everybody called Hop, for a few days while the guys practiced and traveled to a few gigs around Florida. Ellen was a young graphic artist who worked at a local television station, another one who seemed to have a proprietary eye on Duane. Ellen watched him walk through her house with something like hunger. Donna could feel that she was not entirely welcome. She didn't know what the story was there, but she could feel something.

When the band returned to Jacksonville after a week away,

Duane and Dickey took Donna to Sarasota for a quick visit. Dickey's wife, Dale, had family there. Duane told Donna, "You are really going to like Dale. I like Dale. She's a solid chick."

Donna didn't care for the word *chick,* but she wanted to be solid, too. That sounded just right.

Florida was a world away from Missouri, the air and light gentle and lulling. She and Dale spent most of their time in the swimming pool talking and soaking up the sunshine. Time with Duane was very scarce. After a few days, he said it was time to continue on to Daytona to see his mother. Donna's head was spinning; in less than a month they had visited four new towns and met most of the people who would fill her new life.

They stayed with Jerry for several days, and Gregg came and joined them. Jerry was clearly thrilled to be with her sons, but Duane seemed nervous. He had planned to tell his mother about the baby coming, but he couldn't bring himself to do it. He pulled Gregg aside and asked him to tell her, but he didn't do it.

Jerry was very welcoming to Donna, talking over her shoulder at the stove, asking Donna if she liked to cook, too. She even insisted that Donna sleep beside her in her queen-sized bed, saying it would be more comfortable than the living room. Jerry got a little tipsy at dinner and while they were falling asleep told Donna she loved her. It was incredibly sweet.

Out in the garage the next morning, Duane got down on one knee and slipped a beaded Indian ring out of his pocket.

"Donna, will you marry me?" She smiled and said, "Well, I don't know. . . . How do you feel about babies?"

"I feel good about 'em," he answered, kissing her belly. He slipped the toy ring on her hand. He stood up and wrapped his arm around her, whispering, "I love you," into her hair. She was so relieved she thought she might cry. They didn't say a word to Jerry about the engagement or the pregnancy.

14

Macon is beautiful in the spring, white magnolia blossoms hanging heavily in the trees, fallen pink cherry petals swirling on the cobblestone streets, and new grass growing in so green it hurts to look right at it. The Ocmulgee River and the train tracks run side by side, the twin means for carrying King Cotton to market back in the day. Together they mark the far edge of Rose Hill Cemetery, a magnificent rambling city of the dead where marble stones rest in the shade of grand old trees.

Duane and Dickey walked to Rose Hill together with their acoustic guitars and sat in the shade of a tall elm within sight of the river. They smoked a joint and started to play, rambling country blues that wandered between them like a trail. Once their high and their song had faded a little, they lit cigarettes and started to talk. Duane knew that he and Dickey had to support each other, actively. They would have to protect each other. He'd say, "When I listen to you play, I have to try hard to keep the jealousy thing at bay and not try to outdo you when I play my solo. But I still want to play my best!"

"That's a thin line," Dickey said in agreement.

They were equals, both powerful lead guitar players in their own right, and the music would come off only if they both blazed as brightly as they could. Competition was inevitable and it wasn't a bad thing, it would help them both get stronger, but resentments could never grow. Duane loved the way Dickey got sounds out of his guitar that Duane could never replicate, and he told him so. Dickey said he felt the same way about Duane's playing. They raised the bar for each other. They vowed to keep talking as things arose, if either of them felt the need to.

Duane was bound to get the lion's share of the press attention. His session work was being steadily released and would continue. Some songs were even charting. He was becoming known, and while he was at ease representing the band in interviews if need be, he would not allow them to be divided. If the focus stayed on making one another better and pushing forward as one, they could really grow.

When Duane came back home from Rose Hill, he told Donna that they all had to protect one another, no backbiting or gossip. They were a family and that was a serious and profound responsibility. No one could be left out or left behind. If she saw anyone struggling, she was to help them out. He was such a beautiful man, she thought. She promised she would be the best friend she could be to everyone.

The Allman Brothers! Appearing at the College Discotheque, featuring Duane Allman on guitar! Nicknamed Skyman by Wilson Pickett after his fantastic guitar work on Hey Jude! It's an experimental blues-rock music feast that your mind won't believe. Skyman will be playing slide guitar using the neck from a wine bottle! That's tonight at the College Disco- theque on Mulberry Street above Guy White TV and Radio. 8pm until midnight. Don't miss it! Heads welcome.

The promo was rolling out on the radio for the Allman Brothers Band's first advertised show on May 4, 1969, while they were busy recording their first demo at Capricorn Studios. (Phil Walden had renamed Redwall Studios after his and Jerry Wexler's shared astrological sign, Capricorn. With Jerry's support, the studio had undergone a major renovation at Atlantic's expense.) They cut four songs: "Don't Want You No More," "It's Not My Cross to Bear," "Trouble No More," and "Dreams." The demos are tight and clean, composed and fluid. It astounds me how complete they sound, and how quickly the band found its voice.

A rough tape of the show at the Central City Park in Macon, recorded just a few days later, blazes with life. The funky swagger of the demos is amped up to a nearly frightening pitch. It is instantly clear that playing live was the thing that would set them apart.

In the roughly six weeks since their first jam session in Jacksonville, the Allman Brothers created the body of work that appeared on their first album as well as other songs that wouldn't emerge until later, like "Mountain Jam" and "Melissa." The speed at which they worked and the quality of the music they made seem almost impossible.

The challenge would be to re-create the fire they found onstage in a soundproof room with a tape rolling when they set out to record their first album at the end of the summer at Atlantic Studios in New York City.

Duane's joy was evident; he had finally found four men to join him and Gregg in their lifelong musical conversation. Each player was so seasoned, they could read one another and follow one another anywhere. Duane could ride the groove he built. He could rest his weight on a melody drawn out and explored, and picking up speed, he cruised toward the horizon line with the pedal pressing ever downward. Dickey would fall in beside him and Berry would ground them with a counter-melody, heavy and hard driving. They would move together at the same clip, running hot and swerving wildly into one another's lanes, passing leads hand to hand while switching positions in the pack. The drummers rumbled fiercely behind them with all the building propulsion of a charging train—get on or get out of the way. Gregg's voice would break through in a ragged cry, while he played an eerie humming organ that wound its way through the fray. The band tapped into a higher mind, their songs sensate and immersive.

Now that the band was in place, the wider circle around them started to form: a road crew, a management team, the powerful businessmen at Atlantic Records, and a legendary recording engineer. The power of the music inspired all of them, and Duane's profound belief in his band made them confident that they would all succeed together.

Twiggs Lyndon made good on his promise to stay close to the brilliant guitar player he had met at FAME and became the band's first road manager. He arranged everything the band needed to tour. He wrangled everyone; collected the money, booked hotel rooms, arranged meals, and rented gear. Every logistical consideration fell on him. It was an immense job.

Duane met Joseph "Red Dog" Campbell at a be-in in Jacksonville behind the Forest Inn. It was such a life-changing moment for Red Dog that he even remembered every detail of what he wore, from the strand of wooden beads a girl had made for him, down to the brown moccasins on his feet. His dense orange curls wandered down his neck, escaping the black hat he wore low over his intense eyes. He sidled up to Jaimoe after the band played and introduced himself. He told him he wanted to meet Duane, and Jaimoe said, "Just go talk to him." In his gruff drawl, Red Dog told Duane he recognized the sound of his slide playing from a favorite Aretha Franklin song, "Is that you on 'The Weight'?"

"Yeah, man! That's me all right! I loved doing that cut, and I'm so glad you like it. Hey, you know where I could get a joint?" Duane asked.

Red Dog turned a sly eye on Duane. "You have come to the right place!"

He strutted off to the side of the crowd with a huge smile.

Red Dog was enrolled in Florida Junior College, hoping that after a couple of years he could transfer to law school. He was doing pretty well, but he was getting deep into codeine cough syrup and smoking dope. He was a true hustler, selling dime bags on the side from a newsstand where he worked when he wasn't in class. The newsstand was next to a go-go bar, and he also had a financial arrangement with some of those sweet girls who wanted a little work on the side. He'd arrange a date or two for them to make ends meet, but that's a whole other story. He was recently back from his second tour of Vietnam, by way of the Panama Canal. He told Duane that if he had never smoked Panama Red, well then, he ain't never smoked. He also tried to explain how it felt to hear him play. The sound of Duane's guitar really spoke to him. He felt it coursing through him like an electrical charge. He had never experienced anything like it before. He didn't even pay that much attention to music most of the time. Duane turned a real smile on him and thanked him for the kind words. They went down to the basement of the inn. They found a couple of crates to perch on and shared two joints.

"They call you Red Dog? They call me Skydog!"

"No shit?"

"I did this session with Wilson Pickett and he started calling me Sky Man, and they called me the Dog before that, so it came together."

"What, cuz you was so high?"

"Nah, man. Cuz I played so high and pretty with my gi-tar!"

They laughed until their eyes started to water, passing the joint between them.

Red Dog and Duane got deep real quick. Red Dog wiped his eyes and started to tell Duane he was overcoming some serious shit, walking around with dark memories. He didn't usually tell anybody about the war, but this guy was the real deal. "You run, you die. I don't care if you are my brother. You put a hole in my line, and I'm puttin' a hole in your ass. There is a code."

Duane understood. Red Dog was all about loyalty and he had seen real shit.

"Hey, are you looking for work?" Duane asked. Duane told him his deal was with Phil Walden, the same dude who managed Otis Redding, who owned a recording studio in Macon, Georgia. He was financing Duane's new band, and they were going to hit the road hard and soon. He was going to need a road crew. If Red Dog was interested in a gig, he could set up the drums and generally do what needed doing. He could also drive and help haul the gear around.

Red Dog never really went home again. He could feel the beginnings of a brotherhood forming with a pure mission. Together, they would take the music to the people.

It took a year and a half before Jaimoe would let Red Dog do more than take his drums out of their cases and set them carefully on the ground, but Red Dog made himself indispensable to everyone with his personality alone. He had the biggest heart, a miraculous gift of gab, and amazing dope.

Donna heard a knock on the door at College Street and opened it on a handsome man with the pale blue eyes of a husky and the wild curls of a cherub. He was completely covered in dust and had dark circles under his eyes, but his smile was very sweet.

"Hey, I'm Kim. Is Gregg here?"

Kim Payne and Gregg had hit it off right away when they met in Los Angeles at the end of 1968. They were introduced by the singer of the band Kim roadied for, the Rockin' Gibraltars. Kim was from Montgomery, Alabama, and had the loose-limbed gait of a man used to straddling a motorcycle. His voice was the sound of home to Gregg, that soothing southern sound girls out west couldn't resist. They became running mates immediately, and they were never alone for long. Gregg knew lots of girls, and some of them were willing to put up Kim and his friends for weeks at a time. But Kim said, "You can only puke on someone's rug so many times before you're not welcome."

Like soaring birds suddenly slicked up with grease from a polluted sea, it wasn't easy to stay free in that dirty town. In a blink you'd go from riding high to having nothing. They'd run out of money, and Gregg would sell a song for a couple hundred bucks, and they'd keep partying for a month or more, drinking Red Mountain Wine, which had no mention of grapes on its label and cost $1.49 for a gallon. That and a handful of the 'nal sisters—Tuinal and Seconal—and they'd have a nice buzz. Mornings were rough, especially when you weren't sure where you'd sleep that night.

They were both getting burned-out and down to no money when Duane called.

Kim asked Gregg with a little smile, "You ain't gonna give all this up, are you?" Gregg said he wasn't sure he was ready to go back to being in a band with his bro, but in the end he couldn't resist.

Kim drove Gregg to the airport in a borrowed car dragging its front bumper, and when they said goodbye, Gregg told him that he would send for him as soon as his band was up and running. Kim was sure he'd never see Gregg again, but a couple of weeks later, Gregg called him and told him to head to Macon, Georgia, if he wanted a gig as a roadie. Kim told him he'd need gas money, and Gregg wired him fifty dollars.

"Well, that was more money than I'd seen, almost ever," Kim said later, "so I went out and busted up my head and my bike. I had to replace my clutch lever and my brake pedal. I had thirty-seven dollars and eighty cents to make it three thousand miles."

Just outside the city, Kim got pulled over by a California Highway Patrol officer for riding someone's bumper. Kim had paid a visit to a gal he knew to get some provisions for the road. She was a nurse and had given him some "diet pills." He was in a hurry. The cop asked him where he was headed so fast, and Kim told him he was southbound. The cop let him go once Kim promised him he had no plans to return to California.

172

The first day, the ride went from eighty degrees and sunshine in Los Angeles to snow in the San Bernardino Mountains. Kim was wearing all the clothes he owned. "I had on three pairs of blue jeans with so many holes I could scratch my ass without touching thread. The warmest thing I had was a denim jacket and that was full of holes, too." By the time he made it to Odessa, Texas, snow had eased into hours of icy rain. He had been driving for more than fifteen hours and couldn't feel his hands. He was soaked to the bone. The only place in Odessa that wasn't closed down was a filling station and a twelve-room motel that backed out into the silent, dark desert. He decided he didn't care what it cost; he needed to get dry and sleep.

He told the Mexican man running the place that he wanted to roll his bike into his room for the night, but the man wouldn't let him. He offered Kim a spot inside the work bay of the gas station, and Kim warily accepted. He took his bedroll, a wool army blanket wrapped around all of his worldly possessions, and headed to his room. He stripped off all his clothes, wet, stiff layers of denim caked with drying splatters of mud, and hung them on the gas wall heater to dry, then hit the bed.

Kim was asleep in an instant, but it didn't last more than a couple of hours. He was shocked awake by the blast of his door being kicked in by a huge silhouette of a dude in a cowboy hat. He cocked a shotgun with an evil crack, a sound you don't want to hear in the dark when you're naked and alone. His son was behind him, a gangly teen ready to kick some ass. Then, at the same instant, the man and his boy both turned tail and ran. They had seen that there was just Kim in the bed. They had the wrong room. Kim decided to get back on the road, and would skip motel rooms for the rest of the trip. He was grateful to see his bike still parked where he had left it.

The drive took him four and a half days. By the time he hit Alabama, he had a quarter in his pocket and his bike was held together by baling wire (he'd crashed four or five times). He was also half crazy with the stress of trying to decide which was worse: blowing money on gas by driving without stopping and saving money on food, or blowing money on food and wasting time. He had stopped talking entirely, refusing to answer the same damn questions he was asked at gas stations every seventy-five miles when his tank needed filling.

"Where you coming from?" He'd point behind him.

"Where you headed?" He'd point ahead of him.

When Kim finally made it to Montgomery, he collapsed on his mother's front lawn. His brother took one look at him and said, "Get a haircut and a job, and you'll be all right."

Kim borrowed five dollars from his mama and headed on to Macon.

The first person he saw when he pulled up to 309 College Street was Michael Callahan. Mike walked around Kim's trashed bike a couple of times and said, "You must be Payne. Come on in. . . . Pretty hammered."

Kim never knew whether Mike meant him or his bike.

He slept on one of the many mattresses for two days straight, and met Dickey, Duane, and Jaimoe, in dreamlike intervals broken by deep sleep. Mike had heard about Kim from Gregg, who had been talking him up like he could move mountains with his bare hands. For some reason, there was a lot of lobbying going on for spots on the Allman Brothers crew. Every band member had a friend or a family member they liked for the gig.

"Why everyone was clamoring for a job that paid nothing and kept you living on peanut butter and hot dogs for a year and a half, I'll never know . . . but it was magical. As Linda says, we didn't have nowhere to go but up," Kim said.

Michael Callahan was the guy Berry wanted to bring on board. He had worked in the road crew for Tommy Roe and the Roemans, the band Berry played bass with out of high school. Callahan grew up in Tarpon Springs, a small Florida fishing town. He was a biker with a huge smile and a quick mind for solving technical problems. He was also a bit of a wild card, with the playful spirit of a kid.

Callahan became the Brothers' front-of-house man, running the soundboard.

Together with Kim, Red Dog, and Twiggs, Callahan completed the original group of crew members who became legends in their own right, known as much for their loyalty and their work ethic as for their unchallenged ability to party harder than anyone else on the scene. They were not hippies. They were veterans and bikers, pure badass survivors looking for a new band of brothers. The crew weathered all the same severe conditions as the band without the glorious payoff of playing, and was satisfied with having a remarkable vantage point from which to watch the show.

In this lean early time, the crew was crucial to the band's survival. While Phil Walden had invested a considerable amount of money into new equipment and vehicles for the band, he wasn't giving them money to live on in Macon and they hadn't started to earn by gigging. When they were on the road, everyone got a dollar a day, and you had to choose whether you wanted to eat or smoke. Phil was used to working with black artists who had small bands and operated on a shoestring budget. He hadn't adapted his thinking to supporting ten men and their wives and kids. Everyone felt there was a real disconnect between them and Phil when money was the subject. Red Dog kicked in his disability check from the marines, Twiggs shared his modest salary from Walden, and that's how everyone ate and stayed high.

Duane earned the lifelong loyalty of the crew in the earliest days by taking everyone to a business meeting called by Phil Walden. When Phil said he only needed to speak to Duane, Duane made it clear that these ten men were the band, and if Phil needed to talk band business, they would all be present. Duane knew that standing up to Phil and taking an active role right out of the box was crucial. And when money started coming in, Duane made sure that the crew was always paid first, even before the band. He respected how hard they worked and knew how much they'd sacrificed.

. . .

Macon was a quiet college town, mostly filled with clean-cut kids and working families, both black and white, and the eccentric personal styles the band and their friends were rocking caused quite a stir. Their hair was long and their facial hair elaborate. Their tight blue jeans were perfectly faded, thanks to an arrangement Twiggs made with the ladies who ran the laundry downtown. He asked them to throw their denims in with every load they did all day long, and he'd be back around in a couple of weeks to get them. Cowboy hats and big brass belt buckles, windbreakers covered with motorcycle patches, suede fringe jackets, and tough motorcycle boots. Walking shoulder to shoulder, they were a gang. Their *old ladies,* a term Donna didn't like at all, were just as eye catching in their tiny miniskirts and long flowing hair. Pulling up to the Piggly Wiggly grocery store with Twiggs in his curvy Depression-era coupe and stepping out into the parking lot in their low-cut blouses and cut-off jeans just blew people's minds. At one point, there was a petition to have them all removed from the College Street apartment. The Manson Family killings hit the national news in March 1969, and "hippies" suddenly seemed dangerous.

They didn't pay much mind to the hostility around town, and it didn't last forever. Once the band started to get a little recognition, things eased up. They also began to draw more of their friends to Macon, including three members of Hour Glass—Johnny Sandlin, Paul Hornsby, and Pete Carr, who were offered jobs as the rhythm section at Phil Walden's studio at Duane's suggestion. Johnny told Phil he wanted to start producing, and Phil agreed to give him a shot. Duane was so happy to have them close by.

Joe Dan Petty, a lifelong friend and former bandmate of Dickey's, moved to Macon and came on as part of the road crew as soon as there was money to pay him. Ellen Hopkins, their friend from Jacksonville, moved to Macon, and the feeling of family deepened for everyone. They formed the boundary of one another's world, and soon needed almost nothing from beyond that perimeter other than a crowd ready to receive the music with open ears and open hearts. As Jaimoe said, "There was no outside world."

The Brothers were taking a lot of people on their journey: Women and children, friends and fellow musicians all had a stake in what they were doing, and that pressure rested squarely on Duane's shoulders. He was their driving wheel, and their connection to Phil Walden. Duane wanted to push through every impediment, and if you didn't have something positive to add, if you couldn't see the big picture and get on board, he wanted nothing to do with you.

Sometimes, they found support in unexpected places, like at Twiggs's favorite restaurant in Macon. The H&H was housed in a former filling station, just a few tables and a window you could walk up to from the street side, named for the proprietors, Mama Louise Hudson and Mama Inez Hill. Mama Louise passed them plates heaping with fried chicken, collards and rice with gravy, corn bread, biscuits, and black-eyed peas. One plate could hold two grown men all day. As money dwindled, the Brothers tested that theory, bringing everyone in the band to gather around the two or three plates they could afford, and when it tightened further and they stopped coming, Mama Louise noticed those skinny little white boys had gone missing and told them never to stay away for lack of money. They were so polite and warm, she had taken a real interest in their welfare. She kept a running tab for them, and they made good on it eventually.

Gregg was more productive as a songwriter than ever before. Words and melodies came to him, easy and often, as if the seeds of songs were carried on the Georgia breeze. He'd bring his lyrics to rehearsal, and throw down the tune, and soon it rose from the glowing glass tubes in their amplifiers to fill the room. First one player then all would find their way in and meet you there in the flow. Something was tried—Duane breaking off in a spree of joy, a melody that loops around Gregg's like an embrace, followed by a countering wave from Dickey, another voice weaving in, yes, you all could see at the same time where he was going, and you go in together, six abreast, shoulders squared, strutting fine. Gregg had a different sensibility than the rest of them, preferring the tight arrangements of traditional songs to the free-form jams that the guitar players were driving, and it wasn't always easy for him to accept the changes they wanted to make to his tunes. Songs he imagined as ballads became driving rock epics and three-verse blues became twenty-minute-long journeys. It wasn't comfortable for Gregg to push back too hard, and Duane was more than confident in the direction the songs were taking.

In the middle of a jam, Duane heard Butch holding back. When things became unfocused and started to bog down, he looked over and saw Butch hesitating and saw his brow knitting and Duane glared at him, a look as strong as a slap upside his head. Butch was indignant and kept on. Duane tore into a little lead, an aggressive pitch to the center of Butchie's chest, and then he did it again, until Butch could feel the heat rising through him; he was getting pissed-off. Duane was trying to call him out in front of everyone. What an asshole, he thought, and Butch started hitting like he was hitting Duane back. And in the instant that he was really giving it to him, Duane's face bloomed into a huge smile. He nodded and pointed at Butch, and cried out, "There you go!"

With Jaimoe, it was about totally valuing and trusting whatever he was doing. Dickey needed respect and praise sometimes, but Duane could get after him a little, too. He was about the only one who could. Dickey was changeable, with weather of all kinds, and when he was winding down Duane could say, "Hey, Hoss Fly. Something eating you?"

Berry was usually in a deep groove of his own and he played happy, all the time, a wiggle in his hips, one toe patting, a wild knee rising and a smile as big as the world. Sometimes Gregg just needed to be chewed out like a kid, and Duane didn't hold back. But Duane also listened to Gregg seriously and believed in him completely; he just wanted him to stay focused and give everything. Everyone wanted to keep pace with Duane. They were doing the best work they had ever done, and in some way, it was for him.

Duane believed as he always had that if they pleased them-selves, they were on the right track. If they played as if every show could be their last, nothing and no one could stop them. He could articulate his confidence, not just in words but also in the ferocity of his playing, and when he played strong, no one could deny him, and all of their excitement built.

In addition to the songs Gregg was bringing in, they were riffing on several old blues tunes. In the blues, the strongest man would lay himself bare; the kind of man who would never let you see him hurting was welcoming you in. Duane wanted to be that naked and honest. He sought his tone in jazz horns and in the rawest blues singers who would tear themselves up for you, unafraid to look ugly or sound desperate. He wanted it: the heart torn out and still beating in his hand to offer up.

The hard heel of Duane's boot knocked out rhythms on the floorboard, calling on the many players before him, thumping and strumming, moaning out their words in an endless incantation of longing and betrayal. The Brothers knew the debt of inspiration they owed the bluesmen of the Mississippi Delta and Chicago, black players whose influence could easily be erased by white mu-sicians covering their songs. When it came time to play songs like "Stormy Monday" or "You Don't Love Me," Duane would announce the artists' names out loud into his microphone before they played their songs at every show: Elmore James, T-Bone Walker, Bobby "Blue" Bland, Blind Willie McTell, Muddy Waters. It was the very least he could do, giving credit where it was due. As Gregory said to me, "Music is all fathers and sons," songs passed hand to hand, bridging divides in time, place, and race.

Duane's slide playing was a kind of haunting ventriloquism; he made his guitars speak in a human voice. When he moved glass against steel strings, it felt like conjuring, like a magic trick. Jo Jane said the first time she saw Duane make that ghostly sound, he was pressing a water glass against the neck of the guitar in a hotel room while they sat and talked. She thought he had invented this brilliant technique, and he didn't disabuse her of that notion.

179

Duane played to pull people in close, and he had hooked her with those moaning melodies unlike any she had ever heard.

The earliest slide players wanted to do something their fingers wouldn't do, so they found an ingenious way to use a tool to carry them over the frets of their guitars.

Craftiness was born of their need to express pain, and it made use of objects that could have been weapons in a bar fight—a knife, a broken bottle, a bone.

Duane was a curious and hungry young man who tapped into an aspect of the culture in which he was raised. White culture seemed to offer only escapism and denial in the form of pop music. Duane's quest led him to the other side of town, to black culture, where a deeper communication was happening. White artists like Duane have been relying on black artists to lead the way forward, always. Creativity isn't born out of comfort and ease; at its best and most moving, music is a means of survival. Blues artists understand that best. Duane needed to play. He played to live, and you can hear him living in every note he ever played.

On breaks from long hours of practice at their warehouse space, the guys drank wine and took mushrooms, listened to records while mesmerized by the flashing trip light in the College Street apartment. They were living in each other's pockets, sleeping on mattresses on the floor, riding motorcycles down country roads, swimming at the quarry. They were never apart, and they easily built a shared vocabulary they could rely on, while they told tall tales and made each other fall down laughing.

They invented a game of cork ball. It started as a game they played in the crash pad when they were too high to venture out, and eventually they moved to the patch of grass in front of the yellow house on Orange Terrace where the Oakleys and the Truckses lived. They would take a cork from the hardware store and rest a penny on its narrow end. You had to keep the coin still while you bound it down with tape, making a small tight ball that felt solid and unbalanced in your hand. Then you'd get yourself a pool cue, cut it down to the length of a bat, and hit that ball with the business end. Gregg described the game in great detail, miming the shape of the cork and turning it invisibly in his fingers before pitching it away. "It was a precision game, a musicians' game . . . you know, with no running! No way! We stuck wire signs in the ground and they were set spaced at a good distance, labeled one, two, three, and 'H' for home run, and you scored by distance hit. Duane was a great hitter, and I must say, I had a great pitch."

While Linda was still in Jacksonville recovering from the birth of her daughter, Brittany Anne Oakley, and getting ready to move, Berry rehearsed in Macon and he wasn't always alone. A young Mercer College student knocked on the apartment door at College Street, and stood shyly in the hall in front of Donna.

"Is Berry here?" she asked. Donna let her in and watched Berry's face light up. Duane coaxed Donna back into the bedroom, saying, "Let's give them some space."

Just as he was closing the bedroom door, Donna saw Berry kissing the girl. She was so shocked, her face flushed hot and her eyes welled up.

"Duane, how can he do that? He has a new baby! Linda is so beautiful!"

"Well, he's a man, honey. He's up here alone now and he's lonely. A man needs company sometimes. Let's mind our own business." Donna made up her mind to tell Linda as soon as they were together again. She had a right to know.

Phil Walden soon rented a furnished apartment on Bond Street for Duane and Donna so they could have a little privacy, and so could everybody else.

Duane wrote a letter at this time to Holly Barr, who was married to Ralph Barr of the Nitty Gritty Dirt Band. For some reason Duane nicknamed her Polly. The letter is a perfect snapshot of this time in Macon.

181

May 16, 1969

Dearest Polly,

I hugged your letter for about ten minutes when I got it. I was just laying on my old bed and somebody came into my crib and says "Mail call Mail call" and I got it!

I LOVE YOU

I'm really happy here in old Macon, Georgia. The country is beautiful and the air is clean and the old magnolias are a-bloomin' and I got a Les Paul of my very own and my old lady whom I love more than anybody is gonna have a baby this coming November and Gregg's here gigging with me and I got about the greatest band I ever did hear together and a Marshall amp and two drummers and I quit taking speed and I been going swimming nekkid in the creek.

I quit my session job to get into this group thing again and we'll probably be moseying on out to California in a month or so. I even bought a car and a box guitar a Gibson Heritage and it sounds real pretty but I can't do the things ya'll do with it. The name of the band is the Allman Bros. and we mostly play music to fuck by and it's too loud but it's sure fun. My old eyeballs are drooping down so I'm gonna go to bed, but write to me real soon and God bless you and yours. My address is

309B College St.

Macon, GA

Oh yeah! I got to take Zelma Redding (Otis's widow) motor-cycle riding last weekend. She's really great.

Love Always,

Duane

I had a picture of me I was going to send you but I can't find it. I'll send it next time. My best to lucky old Ralph Barr.

Duane didn't have all that much time for cork ball and fishing. He was still taking on session work and the offers kept coming. On May 5, just after the Allman Brothers' College Discotheque gig, he returned to Muscle Shoals to record with Boz Scaggs, a member of the Steve Miller Band who was coming from San Francisco.

Jann Wenner, the founder of *Rolling Stone* magazine, was producing Boz's first U.S. solo album, and he took him to Jerry Wexler at Atlantic Records, who suggested recording in the South. They had a choice of studios: Stax in Memphis, Phil Walden's studio in Macon, or Muscle Shoals Sound, a new studio founded by the rhythm section from FAME Studios. Boz and Jann listened to everything that was coming out of those studios and they soon knew they wanted the Muscle Shoals Rhythm Section, and they wanted Duane.

His playing really stood out to Boz.

Boz visited Memphis and Muscle Shoals without declaring

who he was. He soon found out that Duane had left Alabama for Macon, so Jann called Phil to see if Duane could take a break from Allman Brothers rehearsals to make this record. They were depending on Duane to make the record what they wanted it to be.

The core men of the rhythm section at FAME had struck out on their own and opened a new recording studio at 3614 Jackson Highway, in the neighboring town of Sheffield. Boz's album would be the second project recorded there; Cher's album *3614 Jackson Highway* was the first.

Boz didn't know a lot about Duane's background, but he got a good sense of his stature by spending that week with him at Muscle Shoals Sound. Duane's work with Wilson Pickett and Aretha Franklin had preceded him, but Boz was most struck by who Duane was to the players at the studio. They lit up when Duane walked in the room; their respect for him was clear.

Talking to Boz, I was struck by the lasting impression my father had made on him. It was still fresh and detailed.

"Duane had a profound effect on that album. One of the real revelations to me was Duane's character, seeing him in the South hanging out with those guys. In his appearance, he looked like he was from New York or L.A., with long hair. It was a brave statement in itself in redneck America. You could get in trouble just driving around in his car. It was an occasion, and a homecoming. They held him in very high esteem. He was the dude. He was the natural leader, and he made everyone laugh. It was a side I didn't see in Macon, where he was much more serious and focused."

Boz described the week for me.

At ten o'clock in the morning, they started rolling in: David Hood, Roger Hawkins, Jimmy Johnson, and Barry Beckett, and they went straight to work.

"You'd go through a song, no rush but no wasted time. Beckett was the leader. They had their unspoken communication. It ran like a top. Very focused and light but serious, pitching in and making suggestions, songs they would like to try. It was a camaraderie, very comfortable," Boz said.

They had a control room and one main recording room, and an additional sitting room with a Coke machine and a small bathroom; they used every bit of space. It wasn't built to be a studio, and from the outside, you couldn't tell what was going on inside. They all understood the acoustics and the eccentricities of the rooms. They'd modify the sound by moving the baffles, or they'd pad a corner and experiment with mics, and once they got each instrument sounding the way they knew it could, they could get to work.

"Then you can arrive like it's your office," Boz said. By midweek, they were ready for overdubs, and horn players and background singers arrived as the rest of the players were going home for the night like a second shift.

Boz was open to including additional songs, and Jimmy Johnson suggested a song by Jimmie Rodgers, "Waiting for a Train." Johnson called in a fiddle player from the local barbershop, and he was great. It seemed the quiet Alabama town was full of world-class musicians.

Boz took great care to describe the recording of the crown jewel of his album, the song "Loan Me a Dime." They knew they wanted to break into a jam at the end of the song. The idea was just to let it slowly fade out, but once Duane started to solo, it began to build with an internal groove that no one had anticipated, and as Barry Beckett started soloing with him, everyone followed them in and it just kept growing.

Boz said, "Rarely do they come back in to listen to the playbacks. I mean those guys have been in the studio for years and they don't have to go back into the room to listen; they know what they've played. But they all came in to hear what they'd played, and while they were listening to it they were looking at each other and going, 'God, man,' and grinning at each other.

"The first time we did it, it lasted twenty-five minutes and everyone thought it was such a gas, they trouped back in and did it again and we ended up with about forty minutes of 'Loan Me a Dime' and we wanted to use at least twenty minutes of it, but we had to use the shorter version, but that music is in the can somewhere in Muscle Shoals, and Duane was really rockin' out."

I was there in my mind, down in the bathroom with my father, his preferred spot so he could really crank up his amp without bleeding into the other mics in the room. He was in his zone, the sound of him ringing off the walls of the tiny room, his mouth moving with his hands, his foot tapping.

"Loan Me a Dime" is one of the truly astounding performances of his life, and I can only imagine how Boz must have felt, hearing that song played back for the first time. Duane elevated the whole process, the vibe and the music. He and Boz had formed a fast friendship.

Kim was enlisted to drive Duane down to Muscle Shoals in the Dogsled for the session, because Duane didn't have a valid license just then, for reasons that Kim wasn't privy to but might have had something to do with speeding. Kim spent much of the sessions in the room with the players, sitting on the floor listening, which was unusual. You usually had to stay in the control room, but it was too full, so he had an incredible vantage point. When the horn players really hit their stride, it blew his hair back.

After a few days, when they were ready to head home to Macon, Kim got back behind the wheel. A couple of hours down the road, Duane got a thirst, and although Kim did his best to dissuade him, he finally put his foot down and made Kim pull into a market for a six-pack of tallboys. By the time Duane had polished off a couple, he had another great idea.

"Lemme drive."

"Duane, you don't need to be doing that," Kim said.

"Pull over and let me drive. It's my car, now pull it over!"

There was no point in trying to argue. It wasn't but a mile farther down the road when they got pulled over and busted. Duane was arrested and put in jail, and the police said Kim could leave only if he left something of value behind as collateral. So Kim took Duane's Fender Twin amp out of the Dogsled and left it with the cops. He headed back to Macon to let everybody know they had to bail out Duane. When he told Callahan what was up, Michael said, "Man, Duane can stay down there, but we sure as shit need the Twin back!"

Boz didn't want to let go of the good feeling he had found in Muscle Shoals.

He went to visit Duane in Macon, and was drawn by the laid-back beauty of the place, and the sense that music was flowing free and easy and friends were there for the asking. Boz and his wife, Carmella, rented a house there for a time, bringing their worldly California style and gypsy ease with them.

Mom swears one day they had a bare apartment, and the next it was painted six different colors and decorated like a magazine. Carmella had a magical touch, and she was such an exotic beauty, with dark hair and eyes, people would stop in the street to watch her as she walked by. When strangers asked her where she was from, she would make up crazy answers like Istanbul or Cairo and they would just stare. She wanted to see everything Donna and Linda could show her, especially the antiques stores and tiny boutiques they'd discovered.

Carmella and Boz were part of the Allman Brothers Band extended family for a time, soaking up the gentle vibes of the Deep South. The concentration of musical energy and experience in Macon, the legend of the local R&B greats, added to the mystique. Boz went fishing and played poker with the guys late into the nights, drinking beer and telling stories. He said, "It was a remarkable slice of life."

Boz watched the Brothers rehearse; the investment Phil was making was apparent.

"I have a sense that between Phil and Duane, the scope of the project was developed. The model for the band was Duane's vision, not to be popular but to give him artistic room to grow. I think it was a really important vision because a lot of musicians at that time, of our generation, West Coast guys, all over, were not as experienced as Duane. He'd been at the heart of the contemporary recording scene with Atlantic. He'd had more going for him. He'd been to California and knew the scene. Most of them were still learning their instruments. Duane and the rest had already been through all that. They knew they had to make a statement, and make a career. . . . Duane was intelligent, and had a focus that most people didn't have."

Boz had just bought a car with his first check from Atlantic Records for the album they had recorded together in Muscle Shoals. Duane asked Boz to take him up to Nashville, probably still wary of his brief trip to jail. He wanted to meet a guitar dealer named George Gruhn, who specialized in vintage acoustic guitars. Duane wanted a Dobro, an acoustic guitar with a metal resonator they called a spider bridge in the center of its hollow body. Nothing sounded like a Dobro; it was like a time machine, right back to the Delta, that warm rattle vibrating under your fingertips. Duane was so excited.

It was a three-hour drive and they left in the early morning, down the two-lane country roads and onto the highway to Nashville. On the drive, Duane talked about what his new band could be. He said that besides the process itself, which was powerful, everyone had a real strong and obvious sense that this was an important new venture.

He was inspired by what Santana had done; it was the best guitar-based band around.

Carlos Santana left room for songs to grow and change in the moment, and extend into musical explorations anchored by his guitar. He was also using percussion in innovative ways that rock acts weren't doing. Duane wanted the Brothers to have room to stretch out like that.

Donna rode quietly in the backseat. She was so quiet, Boz doesn't remember her being there, but she was. The road trip made a big impression on her. They stayed at Tracy Nelson's farm on the outskirts of town, and slept in a beautiful brass bed piled with quilts. Tracy was a singer and guitar player in her own right, and a close friend of Boz, but she was out on the road.

They spent a few hours in George Gruhn's darkened apartment and he was really a character. Duane seemed to know George, at least by reputation, and this guy was an expert. Duane was something of an expert, too, and he played almost every guitar that seemed to have potential, his head bent and patient. Every single guitar came out of the case to be looked at, tuned, and played for a while, so it was hours and hours. There were hundreds of guitars stacked, case upon case and bag after bag of guitars, every surface of the room piled high. Duane had only enough money to buy one, and he was being meticulous, going through all of them until it came down to a choice of several.

It was a very careful process, and he finally did arrive at the one. Boz played a couple himself, but mostly he watched attentively while Duane played. As their eyes began to adjust to the dim room, it seemed there were slow-moving forms around the perimeter. It took a while to make them out. George collected more than guitars; he was also a serious collector of snakes. Glass tanks were stacked among the cases and Boz recalled several giant pythons curling slowly and gently around Duane's boots while he played, a very vivid scene.

The first thing Gruhn disputed to me was that his snakes were crawling free that day.

"Do you have any idea how many places a snake can hide or be trapped in an apartment? They were all kept in tanks. I was known to carry a guitar case full of vipers to guitar shows. I didn't have a car alarm or anything like that, but there is no deterrent quite as effective as a case full of poisonous snakes."

Gruhn is still selling fine guitars in Nashville, and he is a highly educated and published herpetologist. He has even written a book about guitars that borrowed from the taxonomy he was familiar with from studying snakes and reptiles.

I called him one afternoon on a whim and we had a great talk.

I asked him if he remembered what my father was looking for in a Dobro.

"Not specifically, but he knew what he wanted. He played until he heard it. A good player can play any guitar and make it sound good, and your father was certainly that, but a *really* good guitar makes suggestions."

I loved the idea that fine guitars have ideas of their own, things they want to try and to which they can lead a player who is tuned in to them.

Maybe there were melodies and feelings held in the hollow body of the Dobro my father finally chose that manifested as songs. Coiled songs were waiting for him in the body of that old instrument, nestled in a roomful of snakes.

I asked Boz about the naked picture of my father that was included as a poster with Boz's eponymous album. The photo was originally taken during a shoot for Allman Brothers publicity, and when Boz needed a shot of Duane for his album, he couldn't resist using the naked image as a kind of centerfold. When I was a kid, I was welcomed by the picture of my grinning father, holding a strategically placed leaf, the image framed or pressed under thumbtacks in friends' bathrooms and hallways, and it would embarrass the hell out of me, and fascinate me, too. Boz wasn't there when the picture was taken, but he knew the story.

The Brothers went out to Otis Redding's farm with Stephen Paley, a young photographer who shot for Atlantic Records. Boz said, "They got naked and it was a riot to hear about it. We were looking for pictures of each person on the album, since there were no shots taken during recording. It was part of the spirit of the package. Duane was a unique individual in the scheme of things, and the picture reflected that. He was funny and could be really clever with the jokes. It was a sunshine feeling in that studio. It was a frivolous side you didn't always see. He was respectable, gentle, highly focused, and completely without pretention. I can't think of higher things to say about anyone. He was a serious man. He was brave enough to pull it off."

The Brothers gathered bare-assed and smiling, no head trips or hesitation.

I have seen photocopies of the outtakes from that afternoon, and they are even more remarkable than the iconic color image that became a promotional postcard and ad for their first album. The band stands together, relaxed on the stream bank with nothing to hide. The moment looks like a scene from some sun-kissed utopia where there is trust and ease among the strongest men. It brings home in a single image how close they were, and how much they shared.

My young, pregnant, and midwestern mother was shocked when Duane came home and described the day.

"Du-*ane,* what will I tell our child?"

"Tell 'em 'Your daddy got nekkid in a crick!'"

When he brought home a demo of the Boz album, Donna put it on their turntable before she started making supper. Duane always listened to himself play with a critical ear. He rarely said much about the tapes and test pressings he brought home. But when "Loan Me a Dime" came on, his face changed. A little smile perked up his left cheek and took over into a full-blown toothy grin. He was happy with it and he couldn't hide it.

He put his arms around Donna from behind as she stood at the stove, resting his chin on her shoulder, and said, "I have to admit, that sounds pretty good."

. . .

Duane and Donna's new home on Bond Street was only a couple of blocks from 309 College Street, but it was a different world. Their place was one of two in a Victorian house that had been divided into apartments. Their door on the second floor was up a wide wooden staircase that turned sharply at a landing, beneath a many-paned, multicolored grid of stained glass that cast psyche-delic shadows on the floor when the sun angled in. The ceilings were tall and fireplaces with brick chimneys stood in every room. The glass windowpanes rippled with age like water, and blurred the street views of the other grand homes around them.

When a session check came in, Donna decorated around the furniture that was already there: brown vinyl couches, a bare mat-tress, and a couple of shabby tables. She and Duane shopped for tapestries, astrological posters, and paper lanterns to cover the bare lightbulbs.

It was a more intimate life for Donna and Duane, and it brought them closer.

They would stay up late in bed reading novels to each other aloud. Donna noticed he always flipped to the ending of a book and read the last few pages before they started.

"What are doing? You'll spoil the story for yourself if you start at the end."

"I've always read the end before I start. I want know what hap-pens and I don't want to wait," he said.

They took long hot showers together and Donna shared her special hair conditioning technique with Duane. It was an elabo-rate process involving heating a glass bottle of amber-colored oil in a pot of water on the stove, then massaging it into his scalp and hair while he sat on the floor between her knees. She wrapped his oiled-up head in a towel like a turban and he had to keep it that way for half an hour. He was a good sport about it, and was so happy with how silky his hair felt afterward.

At night, Macon was so very quiet, only the singing insects in the trees and an occasional low growl from a passing car would accompany Duane's acoustic guitar. Donna sat beside him while he played and he looked up at her and asked if she'd like to learn a song.

She went to their room and returned with a Joan Baez songbook and turned to the song "Wildwood Flower."

"Oh, that's an old Carter Family tune! I love that song!" Duane said, and started to play it without looking at the lines on the page. She set the book aside and he passed her the guitar, angling his body around her back and resting his left hand around hers. He carefully placed her fingers in a neat pattern, then suddenly grabbed her wrist and shook her hand until her fingers were flapping like a wing. "Relax! That's the first thing," he said.

Donna laughed. "Okay! I'll try. Show me again."

He was so patient with her, sitting like that, leaning in to smell her hair, and praising her when she strummed the strings just right. When he left for practice the next day, he called out, "I'm leaving my acoustic behind for you! Practice your song!"

Phil Walden had a dock on a lake, a quiet place to wet a line, and Duane loved to go there with his fishing pole and a few free hours at dawn, or in the evening when the air started to cool and insects would settle onto the water's tense surface and skim, luring the fish out of the depths. He and Butch would go together, and talk would turn to books, their favorite shared pastime. They passed each other well-worn copies of J. R. R. Tolkien's Lord of the Rings trilogy, and volumes of philosophy by Thoreau and Rousseau, drawing out themes of free will and brotherhood from each of them, and always coming back to music. Butch quoted Nietzsche saying, "Without music, life would be a mistake."

They felt the true revolutionary potential inside the music they were creating with the Brothers. Music was the only communication pure and strong enough to really be regarded as universal, and so it had a special power to bring people together. It actually articulated a higher state of being everyone struggles to attain.

Sometimes Duane brought Donna to the lake, and their talk

193

tapered down to a sweet murmur while they watched the sun brighten the tops of the trees. Donna knew how to put a worm on a hook from fishing trips she had taken in high school. She never asked Duane questions about the past, or wondered aloud what the coming weeks or months would bring; it was one of his favorite things about her. She stayed in the moment, watching the long muscle in Duane's arm wave the pole behind him, then cast the line smoothly out over the water, the hook barely disturbing the surface as it dropped in. He was so beautiful to her, his frizzy red hair catching rays like a crown.

He held the slick speckled bodies of the fish they caught firmly in his hands and freed the tiny silver hook from their flexing mouths with expert ease, telling her he'd been doing this all his life. When they got home he showed her how to clean a fish. He dragged the back of his knife against the scales, quickly stripping them all away, then flipped the blade between flesh and bone, peeling them apart into even fillets with a wink. Donna's try was less fluid and fast, but she figured it out.

They dredged the fish in flour and set the fillets into bubbling butter in a frying pan. Donna made grits and biscuits from a simple mix and Duane danced a little jig around the table saying, "A breakfast fit for a king!"

Some mornings, Gregg would come over and sit with them at the kitchen table in the sweetness of the morning light. Gregg's mail was delivered at Bond Street and he would go through his letters with great ceremony and share them with Duane. There were notes from friends in Los Angeles and the occasional card from their mama, telling them about high school friends of theirs she had seen on the beach and asking them to come home for a visit as soon as they could manage it. Once a letter from Stacey came, and Gregg groaned loudly as he opened the envelope. Things had not ended well with her. He'd gotten some great song lyrics out of their breakup, though. Gregg read the first line out loud: "'You can tear this up if you want to.'" And he tore it up right then and tossed it over his shoulder. The three of them laughed so hard at that one, they shook the table.

They had serious talks, too. Not long after Brian Jones of the Rolling Stones died, Gregg, Duane, and Donna sat around the coffee table on the floor and talked about death.

"You better not die before I do, that's all I can say. I couldn't stand it," Donna said. "Well, you can't leave me here, either," Duane answered.

"I guess we all have to jump off a cliff together," Gregg said.

They lingered on the subject for a while longer. Duane said, "Just throw me in a pine box," but then he hesitated and said he could not stand the idea of being buried deep in the ground. He made Donna promise she would find another way, and she asked them if they could please talk about something else.

Kim's first duty as a roadie was to pick up their new white Econoline van and bring it over to Twiggs's folks' house to park it—easy enough, and everything was fine, until he was standing inside with Twiggs, giving him the keys, and noticed movement in the steep driveway. He said, "Hey, somebody's van is . . . oh shit!" Kim had forgotten to engage the parking brake, and the van rolled down the hilly drive and smacked into a tree.

Kim was not looking forward to telling Duane about his first day on the job, and he could already tell Duane was the one to impress. He was more than a little surprised when Duane stretched an arm around Kim's shoulders and said, "That's okay. You're my hoss even if you don't ever win no race."

That white van would become their home for the better part of the next year. It was a bare metal shell with no insulation at all inside. Two mattresses filled the back, curving halfway up the walls to hold six grown men lying head to toe. Red Dog usually drove, and Twiggs took turns riding shotgun with Jaimoe. Kim and Callahan would take turns driving the reclaimed U-Haul truck with all the equipment, riding caravan-style. They had painted it black and named her the Black Hearted Woman after their song. If there was any harder or cheaper way to travel, they didn't know of it.

In late May 1969, Duane went on ahead of everyone to New York City and played three sessions in three days with two legends: Aretha Franklin and Percy Sledge. Then he met the band in Boston to play their first major gigs outside of the South, at the Boston Tea Party, May 30–31. Boston proved to be a real trial, but it also gave the first indication that the right people were getting behind them.

After driving all day piled in the van like a cord of wood, then humping Gregg's four-hundred-pound Hammond B-3 organ up two impossible curving staircases, the Allman Brothers opened for the experimental New York band the Velvet Underground at the Boston Tea Party. The pairing was completely misguided; there have never been two bands with less in common. The Brothers knew the crowd wasn't with them, and the music never quite got off the ground.

Phil had arranged for an industry-heavy crowd, including Frank Barsalona, the head of Premier Talent, and Jon Landau, an influential rock journalist. Bunky Odom, who helped Phil, said Barsalona was used to working with famous European artists and that he was less than impressed by the Tea Party shows. He thought the Brothers were too bluesy and advised them to dress better and jump around onstage a little, put on a show. Bunky says Duane, in colorful language, told Frank that wasn't going to happen.

Instead of writing them off, Don Law, the owner of the club, agreed to book them in an opening slot for Dr. John, a like-minded musician. But it meant hanging around Boston for a couple of weeks.

They were too broke to stay in a hotel for that length of time, so Twiggs did a little investigating. He found out the J. Geils Band was staying in an old abandoned apartment building. It was pretty rough, with filthy spaces and not a stick of furniture. They'd be sleeping on the floors, without power or water, but it was free.

Otherwise they'd have to spend the gas money to drive to Macon and back again, and that didn't seem wise. They took a vote, and everyone was game to squat at the building. They explored the empty flats and found dead rats big enough to saddle up and ride, but not much else.

Twiggs had a suitcase filled with a collection of 45-rpm records, organized with labeled cardboard dividers, and he had real treasures. Red Dog went begging electricity for their record player from a girl next door. She agreed to thread their extension cord through the window, but her old man wasn't happy about it. Maybe Red Dog offered his thanks in a way he couldn't abide, and the guy threw a cherry bomb in behind the cord, the acrid smoke driving everybody out yelling on the sidewalk. It was a rough couple of weeks. The next time they passed through Boston, Don Law let them crash at his apartment. They slept on every available surface, although mostly they didn't sleep at all. They stayed up listening to Law's records and talking. It was a great time, and a big improvement in circumstances.

Berry sent letters home to Linda from that trip in the sweet and silly language they shared. She read them out loud to Donna and Candy. Phone calls were a luxury none of them could afford, and letters were treasures beyond compare.

....

June 12, 1969

Beeg Leenda,
What you doin? Nuthin probably, you so lazee. How is the little Peeglet doin? Is she bein good? I sure do miss her. You take good care of her but don't spoil her too bad so she be a brat like you. OH B.O., what you say? You steenk.

As you might be able to tell B.O. ees flipping out up here. We are ending up paying more dues than we figured on before getting off the ground and we still don't have a definite date set for the album. We were supposed to have a job in New York this weekend & next week but that fell through and the thought of just hanging till next week's gig is a drag but there doesn't seem to be anything I can do about it or anything else and that is fucking my mind up too. Fuck!

I am writing by candlelight so I can't see very good but I'm trying. You know what a fine writer I am. Boston is really a cookoo place, it's different, really different, everybody here is a freak and nobody gives a shit, it's nuts. And boy do they talk funny. Kind of like New Yawkas. It is also very funky, at least most of the places we've been. The place we've been staying in for the last week is as hammered as the Pick Wick without furniture. Yeach.

We've been practicing every day but not getting much done. The lethargy rate is too high.

Tomorrow Johnny Winter is playing here for the whole weekend. I guess we'll be around the club getting drunk watching him. The guy that owns the club has about four cases of beer and some wine in the big old band room each night when there's a gig so we go there and drink it all up ha ha. There was a neat band there last weekend. Delaney & Bonnie & Friends and the Serfs. So we sat around and got drunk with them and rapped.

Tell everybody I said Hi. Sure wish we could play down there. I miss it.

I thought of a new lick today for a song so I'm going to go get the guitar and see if I can remember it.

Be good and take care of the little one.

Love

B.O.

Duane took one look at the tiny blonde sitting on the couch backstage and said, "Hey, I know you!" Bonnie answered, "Is that my

Geraldine "Jerry" Robbins,
1945.

Willis "Bill" Allman, in his official
army portrait, 1945.

Duane Allman
with his parents,
Bill and Jerry,
Nashville, 1947.

Duane, Gregg, and cousin
Jo Jane Pitt, Fort Story,
Virginia, 1950.

Gregg, Jerry, and
Duane Allman,
Nashville, 1954.

Duane Allman,
Castle Heights Military
Academy, Lebanon,
Tennessee, 1963.

Donna Roosmann,
Parkway Central High
School, 1967.

Gregg and Duane at the
Martinique, Daytona Beach,
Florida, 1966.

Aretha Franklin and Duane, Atlantic Studios, New York City, 1969.

Duane and King Curtis, Atlantic Studios, New York City, 1969.

Duane playing cork ball on Orange Terrace, Macon, Georgia, 1969.

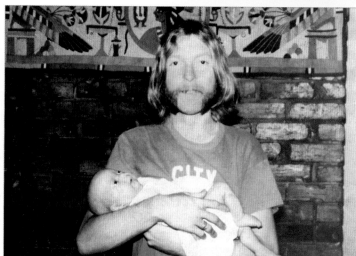

Duane and Galadrielle, Macon, Georgia, 1969.

Donna and Duane, impromptu baby shower, 1969.

Jerry and Jo Jane, Daytona Beach, 1970.

Duane and Gregg with "Mama A," 1970.

Duane and
his Dobro,
1971.

Donna wearing Duane's pants in their bedroom at the Big House, 1970.

Linda, Brittany,
and Berry Oakley
in the yard at the
Big House, 1970.

Twiggs Lyndon
and Candy
Oakley, 1970.

The Winnie: Jaimoe,
Dickey, Gregg, gas station
attendant, Joseph "Red
Dog" Campbell, Butch
Trucks, and Duane, 1970.

Jaimoe in the Winnebago, 1970.

The whole crew. Back row (left to right): Michael Callahan,
Kim Payne, Berry, and Duane; front row (left to right): Butch,
Dickey, Red Dog, and Gregg; Jaimoe is down in front.
Los Angeles, 1969.

Duane and the goldtop Les Paul, 1970.

Bonnie Bramlett, Delaney Bramlett, and Duane at WPLJ radio station, New York City, 1971.

John Paul Hammond and Duane, California, 1971.

Duane trading the cherry-burst Les Paul for the tobacco burst, June 1971.

New York City, 1970. Back step (left to right): Dickey, Gregg, Butch, and Jaimoe; front step (left to right): Duane and Thom "Ace" Doucette.

Goofing with Eric Clapton, Criteria Studios, Miami, 1970.

The Allman Brothers
Band, in an outtake
from the *Fillmore East*
album cover shoot,
Macon, 1971.

The road crew, *At Fillmore East* cover shoot, Macon, 1971. Left to right: Red Dog Campbell,
Kim Payne, Joe Dan Petty, Michael Callahan, Willie Perkins, and photographer Jim Marshall.

Berry (right) and Duane, wearing the shirt Eric Clapton gave him at the *Layla* sessions, 1970.

Jerry and Gregg Allman at the annual Capricorn picnic in Macon, Georgia, 1973.

Donna and Galadrielle, St. Louis, 1971.

Donna and Galadrielle, St. Louis, on the day Duane died.

Twiggs Lyndon, with
tattoo of Duane, at the
Capricorn picnic, 1977.

Gregg, Jo Jane's daughter Eden, and Galadrielle, Greensboro, North Carolina, 1972.

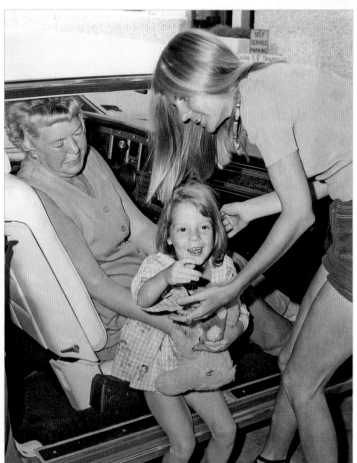

Jerry, Galadrielle, and Donna, Macon, 1974.

Donna Allman and
Linda Oakley on
the ferry to
Gibraltar, 1975.

Brittany Oakley and
Galadrielle Allman,
the Sahara Desert,
1975.

Duane?" He picked her up off the floor with the strength of his hug.

Bonnie Bramlett had been singing behind legends since she was a teenager in East St. Louis. She sang with Albert King when she was only fifteen years old, and that was like a college education in how to handle yourself. You dressed up, even for band practice, as a sign of respect, none of this rock-and-roll blue-jeans stuff. But King also taught her that if she really wanted to belt, she had to let herself look ugly, no worrying about the expressions on your face or whether or not you were sweating. When Bonnie met Duane, he was hanging out in St. Louis with the Allman Joys, doing a week or so of gigs at the Peppermint Twist, and she was singing with the Billy Peek Band across the street at the Living Room. Duane would never forget hearing that great big, bluesy voice rising up out of that tiny little white girl. Duane started running over after the Allman Joys' set with his cord dangling from his guitar to plug in and jam with her group, and she'd come sit in with him.

Bonnie went in for a jam once and said, "Just a blues."

Duane asked, "What key?" and she said, "Huh?"

He said, "This is what you gotta say: twelve-bar blues shuffle in A. That's your key. If you're gonna go up to a band to sit in, ya gotta know what key, or they're gonna think you're a nitwit."

One weekend night, he went to see Albert King and Bonnie was singing backup, and he was blown away. She never mentioned that she had a history with him, and they sounded so great together. Bonnie and Duane were part of the same tribe, following the same path deep into the blues. They talked about it. He asked her if singing came to her as easy and free as it sounded.

"Oh yeah, it's mine," she said.

"Yup, I know what you've got. I've got it, too. It's just in me. I see people struggling to play, and I don't have to. Not anymore. When I want it, it's right there," Duane said.

"Yeah, but you can find a note with your fingers and it's always right there, right where you left it. I don't always know if I can get where I need to go, and I have to know another way in, just in case," Bonnie said.

Bonnie had been through Los Angeles just like Duane had, but they didn't cross paths there. She had heard about a white guitar player who was shaking up the Shoals, and she wondered if it was the same Duane, and now she knew.

She introduced Duane to Delaney, her husband and partner, and they fit like hand in glove. Once Duane heard their band, he made it a priority to keep in touch with them.

During that first spring in Macon, the band impressed the legendary producer Tom Dowd without even knowing it. Tom stopped in his tracks outside their rehearsal room as he walked down the sidewalk leaving Capricorn Studios. The band was playing only for themselves, and Tom loved what he heard. They had all the swing of jazz, the fire of rock, and the grit of the blues; he had never heard the likes of it. Tom turned around and told Phil to send them down to him in Miami, and do it now. He didn't want to lose the immediacy and power of the sound as it was. They were ready. But, a month or so later, when the time came to record their first album, Tom was already booked.

Phil Walden reached out to another producer he felt would work well with the Brothers, and he aimed high. He wrote to Glyn Johns, the British producer who had worked with every serious English band you could name: the Stones, the Beatles, the Who, Led Zeppelin, and Clapton. Johns wrote Phil that he would be free in October 1969, and he even came to see the Brothers play when they crossed paths in California, but Wexler didn't want to pay to send the band to England and shut the idea down. Instead, they worked with another Atlantic producer, Adrian Barber. They recorded and mixed the album during the first week of August with Barber at Atlantic Studios in New York City.

The band arrived on a Saturday morning, after driving in the van from Macon, and by that evening they were running down some tunes. Sunday morning started with "Trouble No More" and "It's Not My Cross to Bear" and finished with "Dreams." They had worked everything out so thoroughly in the demos and in practice, they needed very little guidance once they got going. They just went through the songs a time or two and ran tape. Monday was spent on "Black Hearted Woman," but they struggled with the arrangement and didn't finish it.

Still, they hoped to be done tracking and mixing by Wednesday.

They stayed in a run-down hotel called the Wellington, where Atlantic put up lots of bands, but they had to leave because another group left without paying, and the management had had it with rock bands. They moved on to the Holiday Inn on Fifty-Seventh Street, which was a little less depressing.

Linda got a letter from Berry that read, "Leaving our great little apartment and checking into a funky hotel just spaces me out too bad, you know. It's like being in an old movie."

....

Hey Beeg,

What you doin' huh? How is leetle peeg? I sure do miss you both. By the time I mail this I don't know if it will get to late so I'm sending it to Gregg House. Okay.

We've got the album cover pretty well done and it's going to be nice. Nothing far out or anything, just simple and nice. They're all in color slides and they're all good. Really nice colors. They are going to start work on it right away and we are going to have it mixed before we leave we hope. We are going to cut Outskirts of Town as soon as we go over this afternoon and then we're done. Cutting and start mixing it so it sounds intense when it goes on the record.

Twiggs and Gregg are out talking to some folks about ways for Gregg to get out of the Army and I've just been laying around all day. I can just barely get this letter together. I've got spaced out lethargy so bad. This place has got the best of me today. Oh well. I can't wait to get home.

Twiggs is getting some dates booked for when we get home so we will be playing for everybody and having fun. Yeah. Tell everybody I say hi. Specially Beeba.

Love ya, B.O.

They finished the entire album in roughly five days, and it was as exciting a first album as any band had ever recorded. It was original and powerful and they knew it was only the very beginning. What they could do with those songs in front of a crowd was where it was at, and that's what they hoped the record would win them: more people to play for. All they wanted to do was play.

Around June, the whole band signed a management contract with Phil.

When Duane told Donna about it, he asked her if she thought he could get out of it by changing his name.

"If I recorded under a pseudonym, what do you think they would do? Would that get me out of my contract?"

"Why would you want out of it?"

"I don't like the idea of being tied down," he said.

16

Dear Donna,

I love you and good morning, too! Things are going so good here it's amazing. I'm so proud of the stuff we've done I could bust. All the time and bread we've spent is really sounding like it's worth it.

Yesterday, a few dudes from Three Dog Night came by the session. They really went nuts when they heard the stuff. I can't wait for you to hear it.

Tell the old Duck that I'm bringing a winner for him to dig when I get back.

The food here is so shitty that I can't even hardly eat. The tea tastes like hell, too, but we are getting what we came here to do done. Man, I'm digging it so much it's about all I can think about at once, except that I miss you and home and Rosie. I'll write more when I can. We moved! We're in the Holiday Inn on 440 West 57th Street. Write soon. (I've got a surprise for you when I get home. Tee hee)

All My Love Always,

D.

"Joanie, I think I just started my period!"

"Very funny!" Joanie said. Donna's little sister was visiting Macon during her summer vacation, and they were cleaning the Bond Street apartment because Duane was due home from New York.

While leaning down to scrub the bathtub, Donna's water broke. "Well something is happening. . . ."

Donna called her doctor, who told her it might be her water breaking and she needed to get off her feet. The baby wasn't due for another nine weeks.

When Duane arrived, he found Donna in bed. He pulled rolls of bills out of his pockets and tossed the money in the air, a cascade over her pink satin coverlet. He had gotten paid for several sessions, and it was a huge windfall for them. He climbed into bed beside her and presented her with an elaborate silver bracelet from Mexico. They spent the afternoon making love (not the best idea, she concedes now, considering her fragile condition).

Later that night, Duane decided to go by Phil Walden's and pick up a bottle of wine.

He came home with a police officer.

Duane had come from Phil's full throttle, raced through a stop sign, and got pulled over right away. He told the cop his wife was going into labor at home. The officer threatened to impound the car. Duane told him to come home with him and see for himself, and so the cop followed Duane home and walked right into their bedroom to find my mom resting serenely in a yellow baby-doll negligee, certainly pregnant but barely showing. She was stunned to see a uniformed officer standing by her bed, looking at her body.

The cop impounded their car.

At dawn, the sharp pressure of cramps in her back and sides pulled Donna out of sleep. She woke Duane and asked him to go to Jackie and Ella Avery's house to borrow their telephone. He called her doctor, who said to call an ambulance. Mom was carried down the zigzagging steps from their apartment on a stretcher, with Duane following behind. She grabbed for his hand and asked him to pray for her, and watched with chagrin as he stayed on the sidewalk while she was loaded in. He said he would follow in a taxi, but she didn't see him again until after she had delivered. When they lifted her out of the ambulance, she looked up at the very blue sky and thought, *It's a beautiful day to have a baby*. She was still a child herself.

Dr. Grossman explained that giving birth nine weeks prematurely was dangerous, but since her water had broken the risk of infection was also very high. He said the baby would only have a 50 percent chance of surviving.

After she was given medication to induce labor, Donna was put in a room divided by curtains, where other patients also waited. There was a large clock on the wall, and time seemed to crawl. A woman behind the curtain next to her started chanting, "Oh Mama! Oh Jesus! Oh Mama! Oh Jesus!"

Donna knew she would be in that kind of acute pain soon, but she told herself she wouldn't scream and yell like that.

When Dr. Grossman finally came to check on her, Donna's pain was mounting. She asked him if she could have a cesarean. He laughed and assured her that recovery would be much harder from that procedure. He wouldn't give her anything for pain because he didn't want to slow down the contractions. She asked for Duane but got no answer.

She was left alone for what seemed like hours. Then she was moved to another room, given a drug through an IV, and wheeled into the delivery room, still confused by what was happening. Her last thought was that she had just cut up the waistbands of her good blue jeans and stitched in elastic panels for her growing belly, expecting another two months of pregnancy. The drug in the IV drip knocked her out, but she still heard voices. She was told to push but she wasn't sure how. She felt like she wasn't entirely in her body.

When a nurse set me on my mother's chest, I was covered in afterbirth and I looked so dark, she wondered if I belonged to the black woman who gave birth behind the partition beside her. She was very confused. When she opened her eyes again, she was alone in a small, dim room filled with supplies. She thought they had left her in a storage room by mistake. Another nurse gave her pills to dry up her milk, since she wouldn't be able to take me home and nurse me, but she didn't explain that to my mother. Donna took the pills without question and fell back into a deep sleep. When she woke up, my father came to her side.

"It's beautiful," he said.

"What is?" she asked.

"The baby!"

"I had it already?"

"It's a girl!" he shouted.

"Is that all right?" she asked.

"Yes! I named her Galadrielle."

"You named her what?"

The nurse handed my mother a small piece of paper with the letters of my name carefully spelled out: G-A-L-A-D-R-I-E-L-L-E. Donna couldn't make sense of it.

"Galadrielle," Duane said. "I added the L-E on the end. That's French feminine." He sounded so proud.

"I told him you can't name a baby that!" the nurse said. "How will she ever learn how to spell it . . . or even say it?"

My name was taken from the Lord of the Rings trilogy, my dad's favorite books. Galadriel is the Princess of the Elves.

"Well, I would have named her Les Paul Allman if she was a boy," he said.

It was August 25, 1969, my birthday, ready or not. I weighed three pounds, two ounces, and I didn't look ready for the world. I was kept in an incubator for five and a half weeks, until I weighed five pounds and could be safely taken home. Until then, I stayed in the hospital, too fragile to touch.

When Donna came home from the hospital, Tommie Jean came to look after her. My grandma walked across town every day to visit me in my glass box at Macon General Hospital. It took Duane longer to let Jerry know I had arrived, and she came to visit once I was home. I looked fetal, pale and thin. The smallest available diaper was still much too large. My plastic ID bracelet looked huge on my wrist.

My mom says I made faces and moved my mouth in wild expressions that looked exactly like my father when he played guitar—my eyes closed and my mouth a quivering O, my arms suddenly thrust over my head. Duane looked at my open hands through the glass and said, "Look at those long fingers. She's going to play guitar someday."

Jerry Wexler sent flowers with a card: "Congratulations on the little picker!"

The Brothers were back on the road for a few shows in September, and while passing through Florida, Duane visited Penny, his childhood girlfriend, and together they wrote to Jo Jane. Duane sent Jo Jane a picture of himself smiling with his arms crossed, marked "the proud papa."

....

September, 1969

Dear Jo Jane, my tight partner and incidentally also distant (700 miles) relative,

Me and Penny are sitting here loaded and also have the sillies, so we wanted to tell you how we love you so, and miss

207

you. When can you come? My daughter was born August 25, and she's a beaut. Please have a little silent one for her just for luck.

ALBUM FINISHED,
ATCO 33-308 order number
Very Good

I love you, Duane

At the beginning of October, while I was still in the hospital, Duane went to Miami for a session at Criteria Studios and took Donna with him for a little vacation.

The hospital finally called a week later to say I was ready to go home.

Duane and Dickey walked into the hospital lobby with Donna. She went directly to a phone booth, called Dr. Grossman and asked, "What should I do?"

"Keep her fed, keep her clean, and keep her dry," he said.

The nurse handed me to my father first, and my mother said, "Hey! I've been waiting for her for weeks!" and took me from him. Dickey and Duane went downstairs to take care of the paperwork. They were joined in the hospital elevator by a couple of rednecks who mumbled the word *hippie* a few times, like a dare. Something even worse was said in the office while Duane was handling our bill. Duane never told Donna what it was, but someone must have said something terrible to him; he was very upset.

Later, Duane traded his car to Joe Dan Petty in exchange for Joe Dan taking over the remaining monthly payments of seventy-five dollars for the hospital bill. Duane didn't want the bills to remind him of the way he had been treated.

Dr. Grossman warned Donna not to tax me with too much contact. I needed to rest and get stronger. My worried mother listened, and set me in my little pumpkin seat on tabletops where she could look at me. Duane just scooped me up in his big hands, my dia-

208

pered bottom fitting easily into one palm, and cradled me as he walked through the house, talking in a looping, goofy voice. I love to imagine his smile shining down on me like the sun, my legs stretched to the crook of his arm.

Mom would panic a little. "Du-ane! Where are you taking her? Let her sleep!"

Gregg was afraid to hold me, too, but Duane set me into his hands and said, "Come on, now. You won't break her!" Sometimes Gregory still stretches out his forearm to me and cups his hand and says, with the sweetest smile on his face, "The first time I held you, you fit right here. You were so tiny."

Jaimoe brought a Pharoah Sanders record over to Bond Street for Duane to hear, and held me in his arms by the speaker, whispering into my tiny ear, "What's that? It's music!"

The first time Mom left me alone with my father I had a crying jag. When she returned, I was wailing and Duane was sitting beside me on their bed, playing guitar, trying to soothe me. Mom scooped me up and refused to listen when Duane said he was just comforting me.

"There was an armchair in our apartment on Bond Street and I was sitting holding you," she tells me years later. "I told Duane, 'I could do this forever,' and he said, 'I'm so glad she's a girl, 'cause I've been kissing her so much.'" A mother and a father together, kisses, and the word *forever*. This is every child's first and most perfect wish.

A few years ago, I spent a rainy afternoon in Jacksonville visiting with my aunt Joanie, Linda Oakley, and Linda Trucks, Butch's ex-wife. Big Linda, Little Linda, Joanie's daughter Rachael, and I happily drank wine and listened to their stories. Big Linda even read a few of her letters out loud. The one she wrote to her parents about her surprise birthday party on October 29, 1969, was so vivid, listening felt like time travel.

Dear Family,

I was really surprised this week. We were up all night Tuesday talking, drinking wine and listening to records, then Berry and I were going to bed at around 6 AM and who should wake up early but Beebop. She had her bottle, and I was trying to get back to sleep when BO walked in and handed me a package.

As the sun came up, I opened it to find a beautiful pair of pants. They're like tapestry with pink, blue, black, and ivory woven into the material. I can wear my pink blouse with them, too. Nobody came around during the day except Callahan who brought me a bottle of wine, so I drank most of it and ironed and cleaned the messy apartment alone because Candy stayed gone all day. She finally came home that night after I fixed chicken and dumplings for supper which BO, Rhino and Callahan said were delicious.

So, BO and I went for a walk while Candy watched Brittany. Somehow we ended up at Duane's house. Strange. We went up and knocked on the door and Duane said, "Who is it?" And BO said, "BO and Beeg Leenda." After five fishy minutes the door opened to reveal a room full of streamers, balloons, music and everybody I knew and some I didn't in Macon blowing horns and whistles. Duane grabbed me and ushered me into the dining room and sat me down to a table laden with many gifts and a large glass of Kool Aid and Port punch.

Duane and Donna gave me a small oriental rug, which now hangs above the fireplace in the bedroom. Carmella, the freaky chick, and Boz Scaggs gave me an antique blue dress, like from the 20's with embroidery down the front. Butch and Linda gave me a large English teapot also antique with enamel scrollwork on it. Lisa from Jacksonville gave me a small glass and ivory bottle which now contains straw flowers and an old crocheted French handbag. Candy gave me a tiny teacup and saucer with a pearl enamel finish and Dolores gave me a silver antique salt and pepper shaker. Carmella made three cakes from scratch: tangerine, yellow and fudge and we had tacos and fruit salad to munch on. I sure missed one of granny's good cakes, though. Twiggs gave me a wooden fish. Everybody was so sneaky. While BO was giving me a tour of Macon on foot, Candy had dressed Brittany and the whole crew from the yellow house as well as all the guys from the Boogie Chilin' and assorted freaks rushed over to Duane's. I didn't know everybody cared so much. You and all the rest of the family as well as my Macon buddies really made this a super birthday. Just think! Next year I'll be 21!

They're playing cuts from the Allmans on the radio in Atlanta and Macon now. Pretty soon we'll get some copies of the album to keep for ourselves and also to give away. How's the weather? It's been pretty cold here and sunny, except today is kind of foggy. Very appropriate for Halloween. I hope everyone has a nice Trick or Treat. Brittany is still her jolly, spoiled self. She's been trying to crawl. Eats toast and jelly, grits and scrambled eggs, and other assorted tidbits. Her teeth bother her a lot so she chews on everything, including me. Those teeth really hurt. She sits in her crib and hangs her legs through the slats, and flops her feet. Her favorite thing besides drinking and chewing is squealing shrilly. With the money you sent me, I got Pudge some high meat dinners, junior custard and toddler cookies with vitamins in the icing. Some powder and lotion for her rotund little body and a yellow and blue striped t-shirt for me. It's in the picture I am sending which I would like back. Bo's hammered self, my hammered self with a mouth full of cake and a piece of green yarn which BO tied around my neck, and guess who? It was taken just before the shebang was over. The empty glass in front of me had previously been filled with punch.

The Bugs Bunny cups were for use by the commoners. Ha! I still miss you all and hope to see you by Tuesday but I'll call and let you know. Take care and be good. Say Hi to everybody. I hope Daddy can find work at home.

Love Linda, BO and
Brit.

Linda told us the band had been home for a good long stretch from September through mid-November, but after that, the traveling started in earnest.

"They'd head out on the road for three weeks, then come home exhausted for a few days and head out again." Little Linda said, "That winter, they were gone for months." My father was even busier than the rest of the band; Duane was still playing sessions.

When Duane heard John Paul Hammond was scheduled to record an album at Muscle Shoals Sound in November, he headed down to meet him. Hammond, son of famous record producer John H. Hammond, was a true blues player, and he was also white. He'd come down from New York City to cut a record with Marlin Green, a producer who had worked with Aretha Franklin and Wilson Pickett. He didn't know what to expect walking into the studio, but he felt an immediate chill from the musicians he had come to play with. He had expected the Muscle Shoals Rhythm Section to be black, and they expected the same of him. Duane showed up in the middle of this awkward realization that they were a bunch of white dudes. Eddie Hinton, the guitar player and songwriter, was the one guy who was nice to Hammond and understood what he wanted to do. He wanted to record Howlin' Wolf and Muddy Waters tunes.

"I was getting very frustrated," Hammond recalled. "On the third day, Duane arrived with Berry Oakley. Duane said, 'I want to meet this John Hammond guy! I have one of his records!' Everybody loved him, and when they heard Duane wanted to meet me, they looked at me completely different. The whole mood of the session changed; everything changed. Eddie Hinton turned to me

212

and said, 'This is Duane Allman. He's a phenomenal player, and you're really going to like him.'

"Duane started to play and my mouth dropped open, he was so good. There was a break at the end of the day, and I had an old National steel guitar with me. Duane had never seen one, so I gave it to him to play, and it was in open tuning. He said, 'Gee what is this?' And I told him it was an open tuning, an A. He played slide in a straight tuning.

"'You know that Taj Mahal tune, "Statesboro Blues"?' he asked me.

"'Duane, that's not a Taj Mahal song! That's a Blind Willie McTell song,' I said."

They recorded four tunes the next day, and every one was a winner. In fact, Duane inspired the whole studio band to get it together.

"All of a sudden they understood exactly what I was talking about the day before," Hammond said. "Duane was born with that magnetism." It was the beginning of another important friendship for Duane.

....

Virginia Beach, VA
Holiday Inn

Thanksgiving Day
[November 27, 1969]

Dear Donna,

Well, our tour got off to a really great start, we didn't even play our first date here in Virginia. I am not feeling too good at all about the whole thing tonight. I guess I'm pretty disappointed and more than a little homesick for you and the baby. I guess I'm tired, too.

Did you have turkey? I sure hope so. They had a giant spread here at the Holiday Inn and it was pretty good.

I'm too sad to write, I'll write more later after something good happens.

All My Love Forever,
Duane

The Brothers left home for most of December and January, and even missed Christmas. In letters home, Duane and Berry both hedged, saying maybe something would change and they'd get back to Macon in time for Santa, but seeing as they were booked to play the following day at the Fillmore East, that didn't seem likely.

Donna, Linda, and Candy would all head to their families for the holiday.

This was the first taste of what 1970 would be like: a constant tour with short runs home.

Donna's dad, Gil, drove for eleven hours from St. Louis to Macon to pick Donna and me up and take us home for Christmas. He turned right around after we were loaded into his car and drove all the way back without a rest. Mom sat me in my pumpkin seat between them and enjoyed the funny faces her dad kept making at me, and the high, silly voice he used to talk to me while he drove. By then I weighed twelve pounds and had started to get little chipmunk cheeks that my daddy would squeeze, saying, "Spit out those nuts!" Mom was proud and happy to take me home to her brother and sisters. She felt like a grown woman.

On December 26 the Allman Brothers played the Fillmore East for the first time. Bill Graham's fabled theater on Second Avenue and Sixth Street in Manhattan's East Village was the perfect size, just over two thousand seats, with great acoustics and character. The theater had a high ceiling with a chandelier, a deep balcony, fancy gilded woodwork everywhere, and rows of velvet seats, all a little shabby and comfortable.

Graham was willing to take risks on musicians he believed in, and often paired rock and blues acts together. It could make your career to play well at the Fillmore East. The techs in the theater were mostly New York University students, and word of mouth in the city was a powerful thing; Bill Graham's personal support was even better. He was the most influential and respected venue owner in America.

The Allman Brothers opened for Blood, Sweat & Tears, another band they had little in common with. As with Don Law in Boston, Phil had called in a favor with Graham, and he booked the band without hearing them. The outcome was just as disappointing as the Boston Tea Party shows with the Velvet Underground. The crowd even booed the Brothers, although they were happy with the way they played. Back in the dressing room, Gregg said, "Man, I don't want to play if they don't want to listen," and Duane laid into him.

"What's the matter with you? I don't care if there's a goddamn brick wall out there, you play to that wall just like you'd play to anyone."

After the show, Twiggs went to collect their pay from Kip Cohen, the managing director of the Fillmore East. Kip told Twiggs he thought the band was great and everybody had enjoyed working with them. He recognized that the bill had worked against them. He wanted to have them back as soon as possible. Then he asked Twiggs, "Who do the guys like? Who are they listening to and influenced by? Who would they buy a ticket to go see?"

"Well, I don't know. B. B. King . . . the Grateful Dead . . . Buddy Guy . . . ," Twiggs answered.

Within the month, Phil got a call from Bill Graham offering the band a gig at the Fillmore West with B. B. King and Buddy Guy. When Twiggs went to collect the money in San Francisco after that show, Bill Graham took Twiggs into his office and asked, "How did the band enjoy playing here? I love your band."

"Oh, it was great," Twiggs said. "Being able to work with B. B. King was like heaven. We never thought we'd be on the same bill with him."

"He was your first choice, wasn't he?"

"First choice? What do you mean?" Twiggs asked.

"Well, I asked Kip because I felt so bad that I put you on the bill with Blood, Sweat and Tears. I wanted to make it up to you. I asked

Kip to find out who the Brothers like and he said the first band you said was B. B. King, and the second was the Grateful Dead. Well, you've got two weeks to get back to the Fillmore East. I've got you booked with the Dead."

Twiggs couldn't believe it. He had never known anyone in the music business to be generous. From then on, the Brothers had a strong bond with Graham; he was a champion for them. They called him Uncle Bill.

Driving from Macon to New York City in the dead of winter in that goddamn van was inhumane. Ice formed on the metal walls inside the van, and the windshield would fog and freeze. At one point, Red Dog had to hold his lighter against the glass, trying to melt a hole in the frost big enough to see through while he drove.

At the end of that cycle of shows, Twiggs told Donna and Duane he wanted to take Phil Walden at gunpoint and drive him to New York in the freezing van; that man had no idea what it was really like.

Duane had grown very comfortable in New York over the years of working there, and one of his closest friends there was Thom Doucette, a blues harp player he had met in St. Louis's Gaslight Square. He could blow so fine, he'd kept pace on stage with Buddy Guy and B. B. King, among others. Duane loved playing with Thom, whose nickname was Ace, and he welcomed him onstage with the Brothers whenever their paths crossed. Duane's own sound was influenced by the sound of blues harmonica players like Little Walter and Sonny Boy Williamson, whose improvisations had the same fluid, vocal sound Duane could get from playing slide. Onstage, Ace and Duane had great chemistry, leaning toward each other, bending low and rocking back and forth.

Ace was an interesting guy, with his finger in a lot of pies. He was into real estate, renovating raw lofts in SoHo into artists' spaces. He was also a leather worker and made beautiful sandals. Ace seriously practiced yoga and meditation.

Ace knew everyone: painters, sculptors, writers, musicians. Ace thought Duane had a brilliant mind and a very clear eye; he never missed a thing. Duane loved hanging with him so much, Donna eventually came to see Ace as a rival for Duane's time and attention. As soon as Ace showed up, there went Duane.

Duane asked Ace to travel with the band for a few more gigs and he agreed, but when Duane opened the back of the van, Ace couldn't believe it. Six grown men crowded into that dark little space, sitting on a couple of mattresses, facing east and west. He told Duane he would drive him instead, and Duane reluctantly agreed.

"Ace, I didn't know you had a car," Duane said.

"I have eleven thousand and they're all yellow," he said, putting his hand high in the air, hailing a cab to the airport. You could buy an eighteen-dollar ticket for the flight from New York to Boston right from your seat after getting on the plane in New York.

Duane was a little embarrassed, as if he had not seen the conditions clearly until he saw them through Ace's eyes. As soon as they were back home in Macon, Duane told Phil they needed a better mode of transportation. Blue Walden, Phil's eldest brother, fronted the money for a Winnebago, purchased from Bud K's Kamper Korral. It was a big leap forward. Elbow room and insulation, hallelujah!

And just in time for their commute from New York to California.

Everyone made it back home to Macon for New Year's Eve. They threw a party at Idlewild, a rustic one-room cabin on the edge of a pond, deep in the pines in Forsyth, Georgia, where Dickey lived with his wife, Dale, and daughter, Christie. It was a country getaway for the band, and they gathered there for the peace and quiet, often practicing outdoors.

The women made a huge feast and filled the bathtub with ice and beer. At the turn of the New Year, everyone gathered in a large

217

circle: the band, the crew, the wives, babies, and friends. Everyone held hands and sang "Will the Circle Be Unbroken." It was a perfect way to mark the end of 1969.

On one of their last nights at home together before Duane returned to the road, Donna decided she needed to tell him how hard it was to be separated for such long stretches of time. When he didn't come home with everyone else and jumped into a session or sat in with another band, it was so deeply disappointing. He sat close to her and looked into her eyes.

"Duane, you must go through a hundred changes while you're away, traveling and meeting people and having adventures. I go through maybe one or two changes."

"I guess this is what you'd call getting to know each other," he said quietly.

Still, the tour schedule only got more intense. In the second week of January, the band headed to Philadelphia for a few shows, and then drove straight on to California for their first gigs at the Fillmore West. Playing on the same bill as B. B. King, the first guitar player who had set Duane and Gregg on fire at the first real show they ever saw in Nashville, was a major milestone. He was incredibly gracious, and Duane actually felt a little starstruck. After their set, as he was walking offstage, Bunky Odom told Duane how well he had played, saying, "Man, you were great! You cut B. B. King!"

"No way!" Duane said. "B.B. cut me—he opened his mouth and sang!"

February at the Fillmore East with the Grateful Dead was the trip you would expect and hope for. Their soundman, Owsley Stanley, was also the preeminent LSD chemist who had made it his merry mission to dose everyone he met. He poured liquid acid into the trash can full of ice and beer in the band's dressing room. It was so strong that holding a wet can was a ticket to a crazy trip. Kim didn't notice what had happened until he had to go looking for a cord in Gar, their nickname for Gargantuan, their enormous custom road case, and found it crawling with black snakes. Even

Bill Graham got dosed, and stood behind a stack of Marshall amps playing along with a cowbell during the Dead's set. The two bands were coming from the same place, wanting to lift people up with their music, and they formed an immediate bond. (The next time they played with them, at the Atlanta Sports Arena in May, Duane took me out of my mother's arms and carried me off. "Duane! Where are you taking her?" my mother asked. "I want her to get blessed by Jerry!" He took me into the Dead's dressing room, and Jerry Garcia rested his big palm on my tiny head.)

The band was on the road for the rest of February. They came home for just a few days, but spent most of it recording demos of a new song or two for their second album at Capricorn.

Donna's sister Joanie had decided to move to Macon after her visit when I was born. She graduated from high school a semester early, and in February 1970, just before her seventeenth birthday, she left home. When she arrived in Macon, no one was there to meet her.

"I sat at the little Macon airport all alone, completely freaked-out. Nothing like that had ever happened to me before. I didn't know what to do, so I just waited."

The night before Joanie's arrival, Big Linda, Donna, and Candy got together at the Oakleys' little flat in the yellow house on Orange Terrace. Linda, Donna, and Candy spent a night making elaborate valentines for Berry, Duane, and Gregg. They cut pictures and phrases out of magazines and made collages on poster board, lacquered shiny with layers of glue. Donna pasted down the handbill from the Jefferson Airplane concert where she and Duane had met, a little picture of a VW Bug like hers back home, and pictures of a starry sky. She added a small picture of Duane over the words "For the man with a lot of living to do," and a picture of herself in a leather skirt and big round sunglasses. Cherubs and roses danced at the perimeter of her psychedelic love letter. A Dr. Seuss dog strutted with a guitar above the caption "Dog of

Distinction." Naked ladies lounged on a beach, chubby babies sat in swirls of color, and a picture of a bride stood under the heading "Why I was an unwed wife." (Duane's divorce from Patti had not been finalized yet, but Duane had asked Donna to take his name and always introduced her as his wife.) The valentine told the story of their love.

The girls had taken LSD and the paper images danced and winked under their sticky fingertips. They felt like they were floating above themselves, and when they looked down together from the ceiling at their little bodies working with scissors at the table far below, it made them laugh. They played music and smoked cigarettes and watched the colors in their pictures rise up and float between them. It was a memorable night and they felt so close, but after long hours of tripping, they started to tire of it and decided they needed help to come down. They took Thorazine and crashed.

From her flat downstairs, Little Linda heard Brittany crying.

Finally, Little Linda went upstairs. She saw no one so she called out, "Candy! Linda!" Suddenly she saw them sprawled out on the floor. I was in my pumpkin seat and Britt was in her crib, and both of us were screaming. By the time Linda, Donna, and Candy woke up, the whole day had gone by without anyone remembering to pick up Joanie from the airport.

Joanie was so pretty, with dark eyes, light brown hair, and a little curvy body. She was openhearted and gregarious, too, much less shy than Donna. Trouble, in a word, thought Duane. Joanie says Duane felt he had to keep an eye out for her, and asked everyone else to do the same. Once he saw her walking down the sidewalk smoking a cigarette.

He leaned out of his car window. "Ladies don't smoke in public!" he shouted.

Joanie became friends with Kim and Mike. She rode on the backs of their motorcycles and went with them to the Carousel Lounge, where the proprietor made chicken wings steeped to tenderness in fiery red-pepper sauce. She was seeing a side of Macon her sister didn't even know existed and she was having a great time.

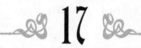

17

My cousin Rachael and I took a trip to Macon in 1987, when she was still in high school and I was in my first year of college. Neither of us had visited the town where we were born for years, and we'd never been there alone. It was storming as Rachael drove us from her home in Jacksonville to Macon in her Jeep. The sky was full of ominous clouds when we arrived, and small rain showers would start and stop with the wind.

We drove by every destination we could think of: the Central City Park band shell, the houses on College Street, Bond Street, and Orange Terrace, the scrap of grass where the band played cork ball, the H&H Restaurant (now with a mushroom logo on its sign). We took white roses to the cemetery.

I felt like an exile returning home to find everything unfamiliar. I experienced a kind of night blindness in Macon, an emotional narrowing of my vision. I was so busy searching for any remnant of 1969 that I could barely see the dense greenery and beautiful homes lining the streets. I was disappointed by how few signs of my father remained. The abandoned Capricorn Studios, a small bit of graffiti on a wall, "Remember Duane," a record store stocked almost entirely with bootlegged Allman paraphernalia, and a couple of boxes filled with photos and newspaper clippings marked "Allman Brothers Band Archive" at the public library downtown. I'm not sure what I expected—scorched earth, crying fans, "Elizabeth Reed" streaming out of car windows?

Macon felt so small and somehow unknowable, like it was withholding something from us, like there was something more to see that we didn't know how to find. I realized we were not yearning for this place at all; we wanted a portal back in time. Although my father wasn't anywhere, it seemed that he was most particularly not here, where I had most hoped to find him.

Rachael and I finished our pilgrimage at the grand home our parents and their friends called the Big House. Number 2321 Vineville Avenue is a massive house of brick and stucco, laced up with wood half-timbering in the Tudor style with twin peaked roofs and a deep porch. It was empty then, with a small FOR SALE sign in the dirty front window.

"Should we buy it?" I asked.

"Let's do it," Rachael said, climbing up onto the porch and peering into the windows. The walls of the entry were covered with busy floral wallpaper and dust powdered the worn floor. The staircase seemed familiar to me, probably from photographs. As a child, I would stare into the backgrounds of snapshots, trying to get a feeling for this house that was like a lost member of our family. I loved a shot of my mother stretched out on the bed she shared with my father, wearing his striped pants and smiling. Another photo shows me standing in my crib, goofy-faced under a psychedelic poster of my star sign, Virgo. I noted the small details: the deep crown moldings, high ceilings, and casement windows pouring sunlight over the wooden kitchen table, a fireplace almost big enough to stand in.

It felt right that the Big House was empty. It seemed to be protesting our absence and waiting for our return. The yard was thick with weeds, and through a tangle of wild lilies I could barely make out the edge of what was once a fountain. As I stepped over to it, a thin grass snake wriggled over my boot and I yelped.

Rachael and I had been talking about the band all day.

"I just want my small piece of the story. Not a big piece, just a piece of my own," Rachael said, her eyes searching the tall trees behind the house.

"You do have a piece. Your father was one of the first—" I started to say.

"I know, but no one knows about my father, or what he gave to the band."

"I do. I know," I said. "Everyone who matters knows. Did your father ever tell you about the night "Midnight Rider" was written? He walked up to Gregg and Kim while they were writing lyrics and said he had one dollar left and was going to get a bottle of wine. Your dad's dollar became "one more silver dollar.""

"I never knew that," Rachael said. She deserved to feel connected and acknowledged. Most of all by her father, Michael Callahan, the Allman Brothers soundman who was still alive but had little contact with her. Like me, Rachael favors her father so much, it's startling. She has his sweet smile, deep brown eyes, and tanned skin, inherited from his Cherokee ancestors. Her parents split up when she was a baby, and her dad was still living a crazy life then. There was no place in it for a child, and somehow, that never really changed. Eventually, Michael attended her wedding and met her kids, but Rachael never got to know him as well as she wanted to.

When she was about six years old and I was nine, Rachael said something to me that I will never forget. We were sitting on the carpeted steps of our grandparents' house in St. Louis. "You're lucky your daddy is dead. At least you can think he'd be with you if he could. My daddy is out there somewhere; he just doesn't want me."

I thought of the dozen apartments Rachael and I had shared with our mothers, the funky little rentals we shed like snakeskin every year or two to start again somewhere new.

It seemed impossible that this palace had ever been ours. What would we be like now if we had all stayed? The question was hanging in the air between us. What if we had stayed together in this big house?

In March 1970, as the first blush of a new spring was pinkening up the town's cheeks, Linda and Candy started looking for a new home for the Oakleys. They had checked out a few other places that left them cold when Linda noticed the ad for 2321 Vineville Avenue.

Candy drove Donna and Linda over to the house in the car she called Mehitable. (Candy had a knack for naming everything. She called her leather purse Wasted Moo.) They walked up the front steps onto the wide porch and unlocked the front door with the key they got from the rental office. The entryway opened to two large rooms, one on each side: a large parlor and a larger living room with a tall fireplace. The dining room at the back had hand-painted wallpaper with vines and birds, and a crystal chandelier. The kitchen opened onto a glassed-in sunroom with a view of the immense trees outside.

They climbed the curved staircase that led from the entry up to a small landing decorated with stained-glass panels of pink tulips with bright green stems. The second floor had a little central hallway lined with doors, like a scene from Alice in Wonderland.

They opened each door and wandered together from room to room. Interior doors connected every room on the floor. There were two bedrooms with fireplaces, and each bedroom had separate dressing rooms and bathrooms beside them, perfect for baby rooms.

"This could be Brittany's room, and that could be Galadrielle's!" Linda said.

A small balcony looked out onto the backyard.

"Romeo, wherefore art thou?" Donna called into the trees.

One bathroom had an enormous tiled shower, a small room with seven or eight showerheads mounted on the walls pointing in every direction.

"Oooooo!" they cried.

The last door they opened led to the third floor, an attic with vaulted ceilings, chandeliers, and small windows on two sides that illuminated the golden wood floors with sunshine.

"An attic? It's a ballroom!" Donna and Linda waltzed across the floor of the enormous open space. This house would bring everyone together, Brothers and Sisters. It was a real home.

The rent was a steep $225 a month, but if they shared the expense, it would be all right. They didn't know what the owner would make of them and their extended family, but they could try.

Candy, Linda, and Donna stood together in a tight circle and hugged one another.

"Let's do it!"

They moved in with very little: mattresses, baby beds, and their record player. Berry's grandmother gave them an antique sofa. Word was out that they needed furnishings. Someone found a few cable spools that could be used as tables, pretty when covered with India prints.

The small room between Linda and Berry's bedroom and Candy's room became known as "the Kasbah." They arranged pillows on the floor, draped tapestries on the walls, and set up their stereo. Many nights were spent there listening to records and smoking reefer, joints rolled and passed hand to hand until all eyes were glassy and they dreamed, together and apart. A pay phone was installed on the wall in the kitchen, Phil Walden's ingenious method of avoiding phone bills. A stack of dimes stayed piled on top. It was a big relief to no longer have to run over to Butch and Little Linda's apartment down the road to make a call.

They rented a refrigerator and cruised thrift stores and antiques shops, eventually scoring Oriental carpets and elaborately carved oak beds, a couple of rocking chairs and hurricane lamps that they fueled with scented oils from the five-and-dime. They draped lace curtains in the windows and filled jars with cut flowers pilfered from neighborhood gardens.

The upstairs rooms took on the auras of their inhabitants.

Candy's room was where the girls often gathered in the morning to plan their days when the band was on the road. Over her fireplace mantel hung a large art deco print. Her high-backed bed sat on a richly colored carpet. A large-leafed potted plant stretched out in the front window atop a heavy old steamer trunk. Colored beads were everywhere, in bottles and boxes and lidded jars. They lined the windowsills, where they sparkled like candy, tempting Brittany and me to eat them. Linda and Berry chose the sunroom, which was completely lined with windows and felt like a tree house nested in green. Duane and Donna's room was decorated with the huge valentine she made for him and a black velvet tapestry of two white swans; Duane had brought it home from New York.

One afternoon, the girls returned to the house to find an old upright piano in the parlor, which had become the music room. It was painted baby blue and most of the keys worked. Donna sat down and pretended to play, singing, "My old man, he's a singer in the park," doing her best Joni Mitchell.

Brittany was a year old, and I was four months behind her. Our mothers spent their days watching us play together like kittens, rolling and tumbling on the floor. We loved scooting up the carpeted staircase, then thumping down one stair at a time on our diapered butts. We both learned to walk and talk in the Big House. One night, we came back from Idlewild, and while our moms were bathing us, they noticed a change in Brittany.

"Leenda, look!" my mom said, running a washcloth down her tiny back. "Beebop has a neck!" Britt turned her big blue eyes to her mom with a huge cartoon smile and we all laughed together. After baths every evening, Donna stood in front of the mirror in the hall with a towel flopped over my head and let me look at myself. She would lay me down in my crib, and I would cry until I fell asleep, but I always woke up happy. You had to bounce Beebop to get her to sleep, so Linda would sit on the edge of her bed, plant her feet, and bounce with Brittany in her arms.

Every time Duane came home, it seemed, I would get a scratch or a bump right before he arrived. He would check out every little new thing about me, and he'd get to the scratch or bump and lower his chin and give Donna a questioning look. Duane sang "Dimples" to me, touching the four tiny dimples in my cheeks one by one. "You got dimples on your jaw! You my babe, I got my eyes on you!" Mom thought he made up the song for me, and was surprised when she heard Berry playing it in the music room one day.

Candy had a job at a boutique called Steven's selling clothes and fashion accessories. She was an independent woman with a car and money of her own. Donna and Linda spent afternoons on blankets in the garden, with babies and snacks, writing letters home or working together on craft projects. They made batiks with melted crayon, and knitted and embroidered blue jeans. My grandma Tommie came to visit the Big House. Mom was sitting on the floor rocking me in her arms, loving me so much, she didn't notice her mother standing there. Tommie quietly said, "And it never stops."

Ladies of the Canyon drifted out from the record player in the Kasbah, Joni Mitchell playing chords only her fingers could find on her acoustic guitar, her high, smooth voice floating down the stairs, full of longing and wisdom, warm and knowing. Duane and Berry came home from practice, stomping boots through the back door, shouting, "Turn that moaning bitch down!" Motorcycles roared down the road outside, up the side street into the dirt driveway at the back of the house. Red Dog and Kim would enter in midsentence, jiving about giving the cops the slip by ducking into the garages and closing the doors as they passed by, gunning their motors in frustration. The men moved through the cool, shady rooms like a blast of heat from the summer sun, laughing loud, trailing smoke from their cigarettes, leaving sweating beer cans on every surface, poking through the fridge, and drawling out their sweet southern accents in high parodies of the police.

They had a connection that was deepening by the day, built by the hour in their rehearsal space. Every free day they had was spent rehearsing. Their list of songs was growing, melodies strengthening with repetition. Bridges were lifted between parts that at first seemed unconnected, verse and chorus falling into place.

They were already beginning to tighten up material for their second album.

All Donna ever wanted was time alone with Duane; that was her happiness. Duane had a gift for slowing down time when he was by her side, and minutes moved like cold honey. The curving vowels in his voice were a warm current, and she wanted to be everywhere he had been, and asked him to tell her. His hands were gentle, but he was always hungry. To be able to give him anything he wanted was her joy. But their life was full of people, always coming and going. She would wake up in the pale light that filtered through their high bedroom window, the street's dim glow bouncing off the sky-blue walls. Heat rose off of Duane's body, his breathing deep and steady, and Donna could dip down into the deepest part of sleep, a different level of rest than she could ever find alone. She tried to stay up and consider his sleeping face, only hers to see. She adored his face, framed by his fine hair and thick, strong muttonchops, scratchy against her cheek. His cheekbones were sharp enough to cast shadows of their own. The tips of his teeth rested on his chapped lower lip, and his eyelids moved in strange dreamy circles, searching for something in a dream. She could make him jump by touching his bony knees with her cold feet. She inhaled his smell, part tobacco and sweet sweat, and tried to memorize the feeling of being tucked tightly against him, his spoon, and make it last forever.

Duane woke up from another dream of a new song. He picked up his acoustic guitar and played the riff, and was so excited he couldn't wait to record it. He made Jim Hawkins, one of Capricorn's engineers, get out of bed and meet him at the studio so he could record the tune before it got away. Twiggs met him there, too, and sat in the control room watching with Jim as Duane intently tore into a complex pattern, almost sounding like an elaborate madrigal from the Renaissance. Twiggs broke into a huge grin, turned to Jim, and said, "Which one of us is going to tell him that's 'Classical Gas'?"

Duane was unknowingly playing the song Donna had asked him if he knew when they first met.

When the band was home, the wives would gather and cook large meals and everyone would come. The men would play in the music room until the meal was served, then Berry would raise his glass of wine and stand up. Having everyone in his band and everyone they loved around a dining table felt like a significant accomplishment, and he acknowledged it with a toast.

The Big House and its many pleasures were difficult to leave, but the moment the big Winnebago merged onto the highway and picked up speed, it felt like something heavy lifted off everyone, and excitement would build. Duane called these days their study of the three R's: reds, Ripple, and Rahsaan Roland Kirk—downers, cheap wine, and experimental jazz, the crucial components of surviving the rough road. They had an eight-track player and a pile of Twiggs's tapes, a little taste of everything from the Carter Family to *Kind of Blue* by Miles Davis, which they kept on heavy rotation, fascinated by the interplay between Davis, Coltrane, and Cannonball Adderley. They strummed their acoustic guitars when they were lucid enough. They stoned themselves into a state of grace, the road pulsing beneath them.

Dates stacked up like money, and playing one gig after another, they fell into a deep groove. Everyone went through moods, manic ups and low downs, and whole days were blotted out with drugs to sleep on the drive. They paused in tiny towns for food at roadside diners and truck stops, telling jokes and smoking in parking lots, finally pulling up to venues in the late afternoons. They'd set up the gear and run through a sound check, then nap on the floor before playing all night. It was a grind and a gift. Nineteen seventy was dedicated to the road, and it took everything from them.

Touring was a relentless endurance test: the shitty food they could hardly eat, the desperate lack of sleep, the cycles of highs and hangovers. They lived in places stripped of any personal objects: dusty, depressing hotel rooms. The music was the only solace left, but it was total. Playing to crowds changed their chemistry with a flood of pure energy to the bloodstream. It was almost instantaneous; within the first moments of the first song they'd laugh at the joy of it, after the misery of the day. No one would believe what they went through, and how bad they'd felt just hours before.

The band often opened with "Statesboro Blues" taking off at a clip, and the audience would get to their feet. "Trouble No More" was a swaying hip shaker, Duane chasing Gregg, sounding every bit the big brother, following his Baybro's words with his own sassy back talk. Then Dickey's clean tone cut through like a blade. "Dreams" was a gentle groove building to Duane's lead, rolling out like an elaborate story in a voice as complex and full of yearning as his brother's. They knew how to build their set brick by brick, drawing people in and leading them through changes from emotional intensity to rocking fun. The songs created their own dimension. A song was started, became vast, and they wandered inside it. Time collapsed; the show felt endless one moment and was over the next.

The silence that followed a show felt shocking. Their ears would ring, blown out and buzzing. Their clothes would be soaked through with sweat; even their shoes were damp with effort. It took a while for verbal thoughts to return. To walk offstage and be approached wasn't always easy, hands to shake, questions to answer when they were still stripped down, illuminated and floating, under the spell of the music. Whatever they had drunk, smoked, or ingested earlier had burnt off and left them, but the music was its own high, strong enough to blow through anything, a feeling far past any other. After gigs, they got together with new friends and went to their hotel rooms to play some more. They forgot how to wind down.

They lived in an extreme state where time flowed differently. Long hours of waiting and traveling were eclipsed by brief bursts of playing, those few hours that were deep and seemed limitless, but were then fleeting. Night stood in for day, the most energized time, when the highs were waxing, waning only with the light of the rising sun. At dawn, they had to choose to keep going, try a new substance to maintain, or give in to a little sleep.

I gathered together a list of all the known concerts the Allman Brothers Band played from 1969 to 1971, consolidated from fan sites, tape traders' lists, and the notes in their road manager's date book, all in an effort to get my arms around the scope of my father's touring life. The list is absolutely staggering in its breadth and there are many other shows that cannot be accounted for because they left no paper trail or were free shows they played in parks all across the country. Duane spent many nights sitting in with other bands and recording in studios. He spent very few, if any, days without his guitar in hand.

Loading their gear in and out, the massive amps and road cases, the hours spent waiting to play and finally the playing—giving everything for hours, sweat dripping, ferocious amounts of energy burned—the thought of it exhausted me utterly. I felt each entry on my list as an effort, and I marveled at the days without rest, the distance between destinations, the Christmas away from home, the thousands and thousands of miles under their wheels. Then I think of my father, and I can feel his hand on my shoulder, smiling, bemused, shaking his head: *Little girl, don't you see?* This long list of shows is a string of pearls, each glowing stage a treasure savored. Every gig was a few precious hours of pleasure and danger, focus without struggle, and painless above all. The person you were when you stepped offstage hardly mattered. Your buzzing body, your dazzled and restless mind only wanted to get back there, a guitar in your hands and a crowd before you. Life was just waiting until you could play again, and there was never any question: Music is worth anything and everything it takes, and what it gives can never be measured. My father plants a phantom kiss on my forehead and I understand.

231

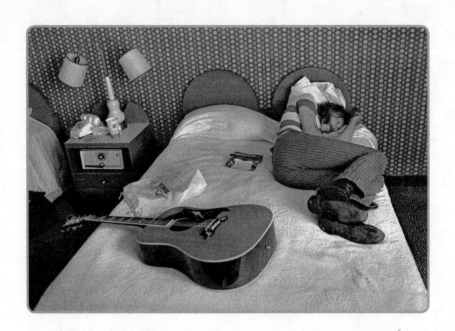

18

Delaney Bramlett wanted a slide player for the album he and Bonnie were recording for Atlantic Records, *To Bonnie from Delaney*. Ry Cooder was his first choice, but he wasn't free, so Jerry Wexler recommended Duane. As soon as he said it, Delaney wondered why he hadn't thought of Duane himself.

Tom Dowd brought Duane into Studio A at Criteria Studios in Miami, the largest of the two rooms at Criteria. It was an expansive space with wood floors and a high ceiling, vast enough to accommodate an entire orchestra. Duane sat down alone, facing the control room.

"Duane was out in the studio and Tommy and I were in the control room," Albhy Galuten, the engineer for the album, recalled. "With each song Tommy would get about a minute and a half in and Duane would go, 'I've got it.' We'd go back to the top, play it again, and he'd get it in one take. Unbelievable. I just sat there with my mouth open the whole time."

Duane felt as at home with Delaney and Bonnie as he did with their music. Delaney and Duane had a common passion for country blues, and for Robert Johnson in particular. Delaney was originally from Mississippi and came by it honest, as my granny would say. His southern heritage, his unshakable confidence and great talent made him a figure of integrity and inspiration for many other musicians, including Duane.

I drove myself from Johnny Sandlin's place in Alabama to Bonnie Bramlett's house on a hill in Nashville, not far from where the boys had lived as kids. As soon as my feet touched down in her dirt driveway, I was greeted by a couple of little dogs and had Bonnie's arms around my neck. We spent the better part of the next two days in Bonnie's car, driving around the city and talking. She pointed out the retirement home where Myrtle Allman had lived at the end of her life. Gregg had taken her there to visit his grandmother when Bonnie was playing with the Allman Brothers in the mid-seventies. We drove past the massive houses on Music Row. Back at her house in the evening, Bonnie sat in her easy chair and propped one foot against the wall, rocking herself constantly, searching for the motion of the highway moving under the tour bus, a remnant of years spent on the road. She began to speak about Duane.

"Delaney and he hit it off. They did, they did. He was like Duane's big brother. Duane had always been the big brother for everyone and he got tired of it. He'd say, 'No one loves that band more than me, but I need a break. Can I come with you?' And we'd say, 'Come on!' Duane would meet us wherever we were, and stay four or five nights, then he'd go back. He didn't like California, but he had to go there for work, beyond the Brothers. He had a lot of his own work going on. Truth is, he hardly talked about any of that. Maybe he did with Delaney. With me, Duane talked about music as a natural thing we both had. It was innate knowledge . . . knowing something that has never been taught to you. Having an automatic editing system so you know not to overdo or underdo. It's just a knowledge of where to begin and where to end. If you can take the leap of faith to start, then it's what you do in the middle until you land. You know you have to start at point A and end at point B. The recovery is the middle. Sometimes you free-fall in the middle for a minute. That to me is genius. How do you break out of free fall and come back? That's a hot lick! That's what a hot lick is. That's Duane's style of recovery. The way you do it when you make mistakes, how you clean it up—that is who you are. That's your voice.

"Duane, when he really hit a killer lick, he'd grin, like—'You hear that? How about that shit?' You're standing there, blowing your own freaking mind! The feeling that you get when you're really *on* is safety. . . . I am finally safe. This is my space. I now know what I'm doing. Nobody can ever say I'm not doing this right. I may have fucked up the rest of my life, can't balance a check-book, and everything else—but try to touch me here in this circle of light." Bonnie's dark eyes were fierce. We were listening to her most recent recording, a series of gospel songs. Her voice is strong and raw enough to bring tears to my eyes with a single note, and I swallowed hard to keep them down.

"I could fuck up my life, I could ruin everything around me," she said. "But that was always perfect."

I thought of the last time I saw Gregg at one of his solo shows, in San Rafael, California. Right before he stepped onstage, he held out his hand to me and it was shaking. "Isn't it crazy?" he said. "I'm nervous right now. This show is no big thing, and I'm shaking! You know, you can control it with your mind." He looked at his hand like a kid trying to bend a spoon with telepathy, but the shaking only shifted slightly. He stretched his fingers and slapped his palms together, and walked right onto the stage. When the white light hit him, he looked still and strong. His hands pressed down the keys of his Hammond organ and the song rolled out like water, just easy. With the music rolling, he was completely at ease.

Gregg is something of a changeling. He has always had the ability to pull his energy in and almost disappear in front of you. He can clear a room without a word or a gesture, and it never feels rude or mean. You don't even realize that your sudden decision to leave him alone is coming from him, but it is. Gregg could look right through you and make you disappear, too. You could only connect with him if he wanted you to. Other times he seems taller than everyone else in the room: funny, bright, and magnetic. I don't know if he is aware of his adaptability, but it's helped him survive his public life. I am learning that Duane was different, always direct, and present, grounded in the moment. He carried the confidence he had when he played at all times.

"Not to be ugly or arrogant about it. Not everybody has that little extra," Bonnie said. "It's an innate knowledge that you can be the best and you are the best. It's a knowledge you never want to say. Isn't that strange? That's humbleness. Geraldine taught them to be humble. Those Allman brothers were nice boys."

When Eric Clapton needed a reprieve from the rigors of a hectic tour with Blind Faith, his new project with Steve Winwood, he made his way to California to stay with Delaney and Bonnie. They were the opening act in the United States for the Blind Faith tour, and Clapton marveled at how much fun they seemed to be having every night. The intimate music of Blind Faith didn't seem particularly well suited to the massive halls they could fill due to their status as a "supergroup." Their first free show at London's Hyde Park on June 7, 1969, drew 150,000 fans. Exhausted and dissatisfied with the tour, Eric retreated to Delaney's ranch and began sitting in with their band in a low-key way. It was a nice change for him, to play for enjoyment, without pressure or hoopla.

"We were boot camp for a lot of players," Bonnie said. "Delaney was a rough customer. It was hard. Duane was pretty tough as well. Delaney and Duane had high expectations. The folks we played with knew the minute they left, they were better than when they came." Duane and Delaney had different styles of communicating with other players. "If Duane was playing twins with someone other than Dickey, he'd expect them to be right on, and if they

235

weren't there, he'd just step back. He'd just step away from them. That spoke volumes. Eric used to do that, too. If people wanted to turn playing into a contest, Eric would turn his guitar down and step back. Eric and Duane were a lot alike when it came to confrontation: Don't want it. Would prefer not to. It's like the communication when you're doing twin guitars. Delaney and I sang harmonies, twins, everything together. We breathed at the same time, everything. That's kind of what you have to do when you're playing twin guitars. One person has to take the other's style, which Dickey did to Duane and which I did to Delaney. When you're leading the style, if you're going to piss with the tall dogs you better make some foam in the sand. Don't be trying to take me somewhere: That's the understanding between you. So, Duane could understand us—what we were doing with our voices."

King Curtis, the masterful saxophone player, was such a frequent houseguest at Delaney and Bonnie's home, he had his own room. Duane and Curtis first met in January 1969 at an Aretha Franklin session in New York City. They had chemistry, personally and musically, and when the two of them joined Delaney Bramlett, they felt like the Three Musketeers. They sat in together in Manhattan nightclubs, taking over stages wherever they went for drinks. King Curtis knew everyone on the scene in the Village and up in Harlem. Curtis would come sit in with the Brothers when they played in New York, too.

Jaimoe remembers him sitting in on "Stormy Monday" once, and the Brothers had their own take on the tune. Duane didn't say anything to Curtis before they played; he liked to throw players curveballs now and then. Curtis was a master, and he could find his own way. Duane kept an amused eye on him, and as the change rolled around once, Curtis raised his eyes to Duane with a question in them. Duane gave him the walrus-whisker smile and winked. When it rolled around again, Curtis was on it inside and out and Duane was nodding and laughing. Look sharp and get ready.

King Curtis and his wife, Modine, joined Bonnie, Delaney, and

Duane for a few long weekends at Jerry Wexler's home in Montauk, New York, at the eastern end of Long Island, listening to his massive record collection and playing acoustic guitars on his porch in the dark. "We'd go out clam digging, listening to Jerry telling Billie Holiday stories," Bonnie recalled. Curtis brought a little motorcycle with them and Duane wanted to take Bonnie for a ride.

"Well, I don't know," Delaney says. "Don't go fast with her."

Jerry had a long driveway to the road, and as they started down it, Bonnie said, "Take me just a little fast, Duane."

Duane gunned the engine full tilt with Bonnie wrapped around his waist and screaming into the wind. When he reached the road, he pulled over and Bonnie hopped off. "You son of a bitch! You scared the hell out of me!"

"Oh my God, Bonnie. I promise, I never would have done that if I knew how upset you'd be," Duane said. "Please just get back on the bike. I promise, I'll be careful, just come on now." And she climbed behind him with a wary look.

"Oh, all right, but you better not—" As soon as she was settled, Duane took off, top speed, full out, Bonnie screaming and laughing all the way back to the house.

"Oh, he could look so sincere. Shit. Gave me whiplash all the way home!"

"We used to play a club in Long Island, a real trendy club, and once we were playing with the Allman Brothers, and we were all staying on the sixth floor of our hotel, the whole floor. Duane hung with us, that was just the way it was if we were around; he was with us. But the second night, Delaney and I got burnt-out and went to our room and went to sleep after the gig. Then we hear Duane out in the hallway, looking for us. 'Hey, you guys!' He starts knocking. 'Come on, you guys! It's only three o'clock!' Delaney whispers to me, 'Be quiet and he'll go away.' And then, about ten minutes later, we hear Duane slinging his boot over our balcony! He had shimmied over on the edge of three rooms' railings, on the sixth floor!

He slid open our balcony door and said, 'I knew you were in here! What are you doin'?'"

Duane had an easy time with them, playing and relaxing together, and it sometimes made it hard to return to his own life. Phil actually called him to remind him to come home once, afraid he was so caught up with the Bramletts he would miss a gig.

The Brothers had been touring steadily since the beginning of 1970, managing to get home for a week at the most each month from January to April, and the strain was starting to show on everyone, band and crew. They were completely tuned in to one another. The roadies would stand on either side of the stage and watch, responding when a string would break, a drum stand would shift, a cord would fritz out. They built up and tore down all the gear, day after day. It was hard work, and the crew didn't have the thrill of performing to boost their energy. What they did have was immense pride. They carried the weight of making it happen, every night.

As soon as Twiggs pulled the Winnie into the parking lot behind Aliotta's Lounge in Buffalo, New York, they all thought there must be some kind of mistake. It was just a little bar with a stage tucked in the back, a smaller venue than they usually played. Twiggs had gone twenty-two hours and counting without sleep and realized he hadn't eaten anything other than a couple of Dexamyls when they left Stony Brook, New York, around 5 A.M., and it was now after six in the evening. They were late and the club owner wasn't happy about it.

Twiggs figured that once he checked everyone into the Townhouse Motel, he might have time to catch an hour of sleep before the show started. He had arranged for three rooms, two adjoining for the band and one for him, Kim, Mike, and Red Dog to share. He needed to arrange a meal for everyone and make sure the gear was set up right. How it was all going to fit on that stage with room to play was a mystery, but they'd figure it out. Managing everything on the road was like trying to keep up on foot with a runaway train.

The show was just fine. It wasn't very well attended, but they played their asses off as always, and met a few nice girls. They didn't have to hit the road to Cincinnati for their next show until late the next afternoon, so they'd be able to catch a little sleep at the motel and eat a decent meal the next day. There was no sign of the owner, Angelo Aliotta, after they played, so Twiggs would go by the club in the morning and collect their five hundred dollars' pay.

Things started to go wrong first thing the next day. When Twiggs called the club, Aliotta said he wasn't happy with the gig and wanted the band to stay another night to make up for the small crowd and their late arrival. The band had been so loud, he said, people had left. Twiggs told Aliotta there was no way they could stay another night and he would be by to collect in a couple of hours. Twiggs called Jonny Podell, the band's agent in New York, and asked him to back him up if this guy tried to screw them out of their money. Podell could hear how incensed Twiggs was, and told him not to worry about it too much; it wasn't his fault if the guy dug in. They would get their money eventually. Twiggs was so very sick of these damn corrupt promoters and club owners trying to dick them around, especially once the music had been played. He wasn't about to walk away and leave it to Podell to sort out.

Twiggs was driven and methodical. He excelled in everything he attempted, and that was his blessing and his curse. Collecting money for the band was a task he took very seriously. He carried a metal Halliburton suitcase with their cash and protected it with his life. He wasn't going to walk away from a confrontation, if that was what it took to set things straight. The band had played, and they were owed. Right was right.

Twiggs tried to sleep in but he kept getting calls as soon as he'd drift off, from Walden, from Podell, from Bunky, so he gave up on sleeping. He was so tired his body ached, but he got up, dressed carefully, and combed his beard. The band went across the street to eat lunch at a joint called Gleason's. Before he headed to the restaurant, Duane told Twiggs not to worry about the guy. They would get theirs somehow. He could feel the tension in Twiggs, and he noticed Twiggs was wearing Duane's fishing knife in a leather sheath on his belt. Duane had looked for his knife the night before in the Winnebago, when he wanted to cut open an orange.

As Twiggs was about to leave for the club, Aliotta called again and said he had changed his mind; he would pay. Twiggs told him to give the money to Kim or Mike since they were already there packing up the gear. Within the hour, Kim called to say Aliotta wouldn't pay. Twiggs said he had had enough. He was going to straighten this fool out.

Soon afterward, Mike and Kim saw Twiggs at the far end of the bar talking intently to Aliotta. They continued loading gear until they heard a scuffle starting and ran over to back up Twiggs. Kim jumped over the bar and tried to grab Aliotta from behind, and Mike got ahold of Twiggs. He grabbed Twiggs's wrist and saw the knife buried up to its hilt in the bar owner's belly.

Twiggs slid the knife out. "Take it," he said, and Mike did. It was covered in blood. Aliotta staggered away from them and grabbed a bar towel to hold to his wound. Kim told a woman nearby to call a doctor. Aliotta held his belly and shouted for them to call the police. Twiggs sat calmly on a bar stool, saying, "Only God knows I'm sorry, but call the police."

Aliotta fell to the ground before he made it out from behind the bar. He was dead.

When the police arrived, Twiggs was sitting alone at a small table and motioned to them. "I'm the one you're looking for," he said. When the police tried to question him, he said, "I'm very tired. I don't want to talk right now. Can we go to jail so I can lay down?"

Twiggs had a volatile side everyone had seen, and there had been all sorts of small incidents, which rose up to the surface now that this horrible thing had happened. He has long been credited with being the first road manager to create a rider, the list of items the band needed to be present backstage at every venue as part of their contract, and his temper flared when the rider wasn't hon-

240

ored. He had the ability to stop the show for the pettiest infraction. He quit many times over small annoyances. Rahsaan Roland Kirk was playing a show near where the band was staying one night, and Twiggs wanted everyone to go see him play. It was important to him, but everyone was high and lazy and he couldn't get them out the door. He was furiously disappointed, so outraged that he quit for a day.

Twiggs called for constant meetings with the road crew. He planned everything, down to the minute, literally making schedules that started at 8 A.M. and spelled out how the night would go in half-hour increments. After a dozen or more meetings, Joe Dan Petty called a meeting of his own to say he couldn't take any more meetings.

When Red Dog told me any one of them would take a bullet for any other, he wasn't kidding. What happened in Buffalo in April 1970 was the most extreme example of dedication gone entirely too far. Twiggs would never have let himself quit his job, but he knew it was making him crazy.

Red Dog pulled the Winnie away from Aliotta's with tears in his eyes. Duane was sitting beside him in the front seat. He was surprised to see Red Dog so upset. Twiggs rode Red Dog harder than anyone. Red Dog wiped his face with the cuff of his denim jacket and turned to Duane. "I didn't know nothing but the hustle before I met Twiggs. He taught me everything I know about this gig. And you never leave a brother behind."

Duane couldn't afford to cry. He had to keep his head together. A man was dead, and it was his knife in his friend's hand, and his money his friend was fighting for. Duane couldn't wrap his mind around it. The silence in the camper over his shoulder was heavy and he knew he wasn't alone, trying to make sense of it.

Kim and Mike stayed in Buffalo with Twiggs. Everyone else went on to Cincinnati. Butch called in Willie Perkins, one of Twiggs's oldest friends, to replace him as road manager. Twiggs always said Willie was the man for the job if something should ever happen to him. Willie met them in Cincinnati without hesitation, even though this job was about as different from his current position at a Macon bank as could be imagined. When he opened Twiggs's suitcase to look through his paperwork for the tour, the total disarray shocked him. He had never known his meticulous friend to let things get so chaotic. It spoke volumes about the state Twiggs was in in Buffalo.

Berry called the Big House and told Linda the terrible news. No one was certain what would happen next. The band hired a masterful attorney named John Condon, who was recommended by Atlantic Records. A plan was in the works to have Condon interview the entire band a little farther down the road, in Washington, D.C. He would also travel to Macon to speak to Twiggs's family, and he asked Twiggs to spend a portion of his time writing an autobiography of sorts, including anything that might help them understand his mental state leading up to the crime.

Berry asked Linda to get everyone to write to Twiggs every day. It was crucial that Twiggs stay connected to the family. He suggested they send him books, drawings, photos: anything that would remind him of the world beyond the walls he was locked behind.

Twiggs wrote more than three hundred letters to friends and family from the Erie County Jail, and he seemed very upbeat, almost happy. He taught algebra to fellow inmates and negotiated TV privileges for them. He had learned needlepoint and carved small animals out of soap with a tool he made by grinding down a plastic toothbrush on the rough concrete floor of the jail's shower. Carving was his favorite diversion, until he heard the guards inspecting every cell for contraband and realized they might think of his tool as a weapon. He turned it in willingly, and wrote the warden directly afterward, asking for the tool back. He explained what it was for and assured him it was harmless, but he never got it back.

Not long after the incident in Buffalo, Duane once again retreated to Los Angeles to hang with Delaney and Bonnie. While he was there, he played on their new album, *Motel Shot*. The album was conceived as a loose jam in the spirit of the countless nights they had spent together in hotel rooms on the road, playing acoustic guitars and singing for fun with friends. In four or five hours at producer Bruce Botnick's home, the whole album was captured live off the floor. In addition to the members of their own band, the album featured Joe Cocker, Bobby Keys, Leon Russell, Stephen Stills, Gram Parsons, and many others. They all sat with their instruments in a wide circle on sofas and on the floor. They thumped a couple of suitcases for percussion and rolled through songs together in a free and easy way. The songs flow directly from their pumping and buoyant hearts, a pure expression of fellowship. It was just what Duane needed, and you can hear the love in every song, a little piece of church that greatly soothed him.

But when Donna picked Duane up at the airport in Macon, he was in a dark mood. She hadn't seen him since Twiggs's arrest. He looked like he might be on the verge of tears, and when she encouraged him to let it out he looked at her and exclaimed, "They will close the schools the day I cry." It wasn't only the pain of losing Twiggs, or the layer upon layer of exhaustion. King Curtis won a Grammy for Best R&B Instrumental Performance for "Games People Play," and no one thought to tell Duane. He knew his playing was an enormous part of what made the cut shine, and it hurt him not to hear it from Curtis. Much of his best playing put a feather in someone else's cap and he was getting a little tired of it. He was going to step back from session work. He felt he was beyond it now, and he didn't have the time.

There would be one major exception. Eric Clapton had recently joined forces with Delaney and Bonnie's band and claimed them for his own. He was planning to record an album with Tom Dowd in Miami at Criteria, using the name Derek and the Dominos.

19

The Allman Brothers Band album did not sell as well as everyone had hoped, but it was a critical success. *Rolling Stone* magazine's legendarily tough and irreverent Lester Bangs called it "consistently subtle, and honest, and moving." The band was utterly committed to playing; sales were not a serious consideration to them. They were already working on songs for their second album while playing more than three hundred shows in 1970. They were tireless.

On the road, the Brothers found parks to play for free on days between booked gigs. They traveled with a bin full of bright orange extension cords that connected into hundreds of feet of flowing current. They would find a willing neighbor who would let them plug in, and they'd find a hippie kid willing to stand by the point where the cords crossed the road and pay him a couple of joints in return. They were not always welcome to stretch out and play as long as they liked. Once in Audubon Park in New Orleans, the police came and unplugged Duane's amp to stop the band from going over the park's 7 P.M. curfew. Red Dog plugged him back in and ran like hell, to bait the cops into chasing him so the band could finish their set.

When they were home on a weekend, they'd go to Piedmont Park in Atlanta. The Piedmont Music Festival started out as a casual drop-in jam during the band's first months in Macon. Folks gathered naturally, until there were hundreds of people spread out in the grass around the musicians. It became a steady weekend gig during the band's first summer together in 1969, and the crowds swelled to the thousands. By the middle of 1970, it had grown into a proper festival with a stage, a generator, and dozens of other local bands.

To play with the sun on your shoulders, your friends sitting around, thousands of kids gathered peacefully together, was a beautiful thing. It was so chilled out, the police even seemed to enjoy it, and there were never any hassles. The wives and kids would come, too, and that was rare. Berry and Duane didn't really want Linda and Donna out at concerts, never on the road. They wanted them to stay safely tucked away in Macon, taking care of their babies. But when they played in Georgia, it was a different deal and the wives got to share in the music.

Duane liked to check out other local bands, and one that really caught his attention around this time was the Hampton Grease Band, fronted by Bruce Hampton, a young man everyone called the Colonel. They looked fairly clean-cut, with side-parted hair and suit jackets, but once they started cooking, it was a wild show. Bruce would raise his arms to the sky and preach, dance, and play guitar in completely unpredictable and accomplished improvisations. The music was jagged and jarring one moment, fluid and bluesy the next. Duane saw the bravery and the musicianship in it. He introduced Bruce to Alan Walden, Phil's brother, at Capricorn Records, and they inked a deal for a record. Duane didn't give anyone a choice about it. He told Walden to sign them and he did, even though he didn't have a clue where the Hampton Grease Band was coming from.

Duane was always keen to help musicians he believed in and he made good on his promises. "Duane made you want to give everything," Thom Doucette said. "When he laid it down, it stayed down, and he was seldom wrong. He was twenty-three going on fifty. The vistas were huge, and it was never about money. Duane wouldn't waste his energy on petty shit. If there was a problem, it was out in the open and over in a hot minute. Duane was right up in your face; there were no corners or dark spots. If there was a problem with Gregg, it could go on for years."

Rock festivals were a growing venture in the summer of 1970, and the Brothers played two back-to-back in July: the second annual Atlanta Pop Festival and the Love Valley Festival in North Carolina. The events felt like natural extensions of the free park concerts, and they were often so overwhelmed with crowds, they became free by default when the gates were crashed.

The second Atlanta Pop Festival took place July 3–5 in a soybean field beside the Middle Georgia Raceway in a little town called Byron, about ninety miles from Atlanta. The promoter, Alex Cooley, was hoping for a crowd of 100,000, about the size of the first festival he had promoted the year before, but estimates of the crowd went as high as 400,000 people, making the festival one of the largest gatherings in Georgia history. For fourteen dollars you could spend two days seeing B. B. King, Jimi Hendrix, Ravi Shankar, Procol Harum, and a dozen other bands, including the Hampton Grease Band. But soon the plywood fence that had been constructed to contain the festival was trampled as the crowd grew. From the stage, the crowd looked like a roiling, colorful sea. The summer sun was blazing, over one hundred degrees by late morning, and people wandered naked and jumped in the stream by the road to cool off. Tents were pitched under cover of a pecan grove beside the field.

By Friday morning the highway looked like a parking lot all the way back to Atlanta, and Duane was somewhere stranded in the middle of it an hour before he was supposed to be onstage. Willie Perkins was about to lose his mind when he saw Duane strut through the back gate and strap on his guitar moments before the music started. He had abandoned his Dogsled and convinced a guy on a motorcycle to ride the shoulder all the way to the gig. He barely had time to grin in Willie's direction before taking the stage. There was only one problem. He didn't have his Coricidin bottle. He must have left it in the car.

The announcer had a question for the crowd: "Does anyone got like a little finger-sized prescription bottle? A glass bottle? Like a pill bottle? Like a Coricidin bottle or something like that? A glass bottle we can slip on a guitarist's finger? Or a wine bottle with a long neck?" Ellen Hopkins remembers carefully dragging the broken neck of a wine bottle against concrete, trying to smooth the jagged edge. In the footage you can see the rough dark green cylinder on Duane's ring finger pressing against the strings of his goldtop Les Paul.

The Allman Brothers played two sets, one to open the festival on the afternoon of the third and one to close it on the night of the fifth, and while there may have been more famous musicians on the bill, they were the hometown heroes. Their performance was captured by a film crew, which was a very rare occurrence. Although legal wrangling has kept the footage under wraps for more than forty years, I have seen a small portion of the film and it is the most vivid documentation of the band at that time. It is electrifying. There is even a brief panning shot down a dusty path that shows Linda and Berry walking together hand in hand, smiling and waving to the camera. Linda saw it for the first time only recently and cried in shock and gratitude.

Then the announcer launches into a bizarre riff of his own to introduce them:

You know in *Life* magazine they had some pictures of the human egg being fertilized and when I was in school they used to give us this shuck that it's a big race, you know, and the sperm go out and as they race to the egg and the first one to get there goes into the egg. That isn't the way it happens. *Life* magazine . . . this Swedish nurse or Norwegian photographer took pictures of what happens and what really happens is the sperms surround the egg, the female ovum, and they twirl it with their tails at a rate of eight times per minute in this primordial dance, and this actually happens you know, eight times and, eight is the sign of infinity, right, it goes like this, you know, and that's where we all come from is this dance, so life isn't a race, it's not competing with anyone, it's playing together like all men play together, and these are the Allman Brothers and they play together, Allman Brothers . . . All Men!

Duane kicks into "Statesboro Blues," his knees bouncing, while Berry shifts his weight in a sexy shuffle, smiling like a kid. Dickey's head and shoulders dip, his cowboy hat shielding his face from the sun. The three of them dance with their axes, loose and limber, as comfortable in the flow as swimmers carried by a tide. Jaimoe holds his drumstick at an angle in the jazz style and bites his lower lip in concentration, while Butch looks straight out into the crowd, the smallest hint of anxiety in his eyes as he drives the band forward. You can see how they amazed one another when their faces bloom into smiles of wonder and encouragement.

Gregg sips from a can of Pabst Blue Ribbon and sings without lifting his eyes from his fingers. He looks so young it is startling. Deep into "Dreams," the crowd below dances in undulating patterns.

Donna was completely overwhelmed by the playing. Duane was on fire; she had never seen him play so freely. When he walked offstage toward her, she tried to find a way to express how the music made her feel but could only say, "You were so amazing."

Duane bent his head down to her and said quietly, "I'm glad you liked it."

He retreated to the comfort of a nearby camper and fell heavily asleep. When Donna tried to wake him to watch Jimi Hendrix play, he was too exhausted to move. As she walked back to her spot on the side of the stage, Jimi passed her in the dark with his guitar in his hand and said hello. Duane missed seeing Hendrix play "The Star-Spangled Banner" at midnight under a sky full of fireworks. Just a couple of months later, Jimi was gone.

Two months before, on May 4, a protest at Ohio's Kent State University against U.S. military operations in Cambodia ended in violence when members of the National Guard opened fire on student protesters, killing four and wounding nine. Kim Payne told me that the only time he ever saw my father completely unhinged with rage was after he read about the killings in the morning paper. To him it was the ultimate breach of trust. He paced and growled and told everyone they had to fight back, to arm themselves and go after them. A fundamental line had been crossed and now it was war. He was breathing fire, and everyone was a little stunned by his passion and menace. He wanted to round up whatever weapons they could find, get in the van, and drive to Washington, D.C. No one knew what to say to calm him back down. He paced and ranted until he wore himself out.

Even if the purpose was peaceful, any large crowd had a quiet undercurrent of tension after Kent State. The news from Vietnam loomed over these gatherings, too. Music was a galvanizing force against violence, and the South was changing because of it. Bands and their multiracial audiences were directly challenging the social conservatism of previous generations. It felt like a major accomplishment to pull off a concert of this size without incident. When Richie Havens played "Here Comes the Sun" to greet the dawn on the final morning, he seemed to be summoning hopefulness for everyone.

Less than two weeks after Atlanta Pop, the Brothers played the Love Valley Rock Festival in Statesville, North Carolina, a western-themed community of fewer than one hundred people in the foothills of the Brushy Mountains. The town was a single block of rustic wooden buildings linked by a wooden walkway and lined with hitching posts; it looked like a movie set, complete with a church and post office, a general store, and an arena where the festival was held. It was the dream of a young man named Andy Barker, who moved his wife and daughter from Charlotte to a country shack and slowly built the town of which he had always dreamed. The music festival attracted an estimated crowd of one hundred thousand people. The counterculture was spreading through the rural South, alarming many locals, and the events were getting national press.

The footage of that day begins with a hazy, sun-bleached moment. Duane leans into the camera for a kiss, and builds to a passionate and expansive rendition of "Mountain Jam." The camera stays with him, panning between his hands and his ecstatic face. Duane presses the base of his glass bottle high on the neck and the bright shock of birdsong rings out. He switches seamlessly between playing slide back to straight leads, and as the fever begins to break, the melody of "Will the Circle Be Unbroken" flows from his fingertips, all gentle sweetness. There are moments when you can see Gregg, Berry, and Butch all watching him as they play. They shift as he shifts and then, just as you think the song is ending, the band takes the melody into a fiery vamp, a country church service turned rocking roadhouse party. The thread never breaks, only weaves in countermelodies until somehow you are back in the psychedelic expanse of Donovan's pop song "There Is a Mountain." By the time they touch back down and the end approaches, Butch pounds a powerful pattern on timpani while Duane bows and rocks his guitar again and again, jumping and landing on the final note.

Linda and Donna traveled to North Carolina to join the band as a surprise, and Duane greeted Donna by asking her what she was doing there. The strain of traveling and playing full-out was showing on him and he was drinking heavily, culminating with him peeing in his sleep on their hotel room radiator in the middle of the night.

When things went dark with him, Donna thought Duane could just stop coming home altogether, or he could come home so changed she wouldn't want him there. She wasn't sure which would feel worse. This life she had built with him was so fragile.

From the beginning, Duane wanted to know what went on inside her. He wanted to see if he could open her up, and make her yield to him. She always did, but she also had a temper that could flare up in frustration. Duane didn't seem to understand how close to the bone they were living while the band was on the road. She and Linda would sometimes take the baby carriages and walk all the way across town to ask for money at the Capricorn office. When she tried to tell this to Duane, he cradled her face in his palms and said, "Oh darlin', the Ladies Auxiliary has gotten hold of you."

One night that summer, Duane came home from practice after midnight. Donna prepared him a late meal. He was leaving in the morning, just hours away, and she felt an urgency to connect with him. At the very least, she had to be sure she'd have money to buy what she needed while he was away. She asked for twenty dollars, and he scoffed at her. She would never talk back to Duane, or even raise her voice, but she slowly eased his plate across the table and let it fall into his lap. The hot, wet spaghetti dinner soaked his blue jeans, and she didn't wait to see how he would react. Her chair scraped the kitchen floor, and she quickly stalked upstairs. She positioned herself on the far edge of their bed so the mattress would be between them if he came into the room. She used to wait in the same position for her father to come pounding upstairs when she had done something wrong. She wasn't sure what Duane would do. He walked very slowly up the steps and stood in the doorway. "I want you out of here in the morning," he said, then left. *Yeah, right,* she thought as she listened to his car pull away. He was the one leaving, not her. His absence was just a different kind of slap.

Part of Donna was always waiting for the end to come. Every hard thing that happened seemed an unwelcome portent of his leaving. When she heard what Twiggs had done, her first thought was *This will do it. Duane will leave me.* It wasn't a logical thought, but it felt true. The more stress and pressure he was under, the further apart they grew.

The esteemed British producer Glyn Johns had written to Phil Walden to express his disappointment when Jerry Wexler vetoed the idea of the Allman Brothers recording their first album with him in England. "I am sure all will go well with Adrian Barber. In the same token, I still really want to do the second album. By then things should be a lot more straight on my end." Duane was still interested in working with him, but when the time came to record their next album, the band locked in Tom Dowd and headed for Criteria Studios in Miami in late August 1970.

Gregg wanted to know why they couldn't work at home. Capricorn was a state-of-the-art studio, right there in Macon. Duane said, "Dig it. This is Tommy Dowd's sandbox and his toys. Let's go give it a try."

The Allman Brothers recorded together in Studio B, the smaller of Criteria's two studios. They were arranged as they were onstage, Gregg stage right, Duane and Dickey beside him, and Berry stage left. Jaimoe's kit was behind Duane and Butch's was behind Berry. The only overdubs that were done separately were Gregg's vocals and the occasional corrected lead. Their year of heavy touring between albums was evident. They were able to work through songs quickly because they had aired them out live. This made for comparatively short work at Criteria Studios. Their touring schedule continued on. They divided their time working on the album into several sessions whenever they could find a few free days. They had worked up a portion of the new songs on the road, picking melodies on acoustic guitars in hotel rooms, but some things were still to be determined in the studio.

While they were down in Miami recording, they picked up as many Florida gigs as they could. Jo Jane still spent summers in Daytona with her aunt Jerry, and when the band came within a few hundred miles of Daytona Beach, they would spend hours in Jerry's tiny red Triumph convertible, just to give her the chance to hug the boys and spend a little time with them. The band and crew called Jerry "Mama A" and treated her like a queen.

Jerry and Jo Jane drove to Pensacola in the summer of 1970 for a couple of nights. The band started very late; they had been delayed by their equipment truck breaking down.

They had played only a few songs by the time the midnight curfew struck, and the promoter cut the power. Jo Jane felt an immediate tingle shoot up her spine, thinking, *You do not cut off Duane Allman while he's playing guitar!*

The sudden silence created a vacuum in the room, and people gasped, but Jaimoe and Butch kept playing. No longer tethered to the structure of song, they tapped into the oldest, deepest music used to move bodies and send signals, their drums rumbling in the darkness. The crowd stomped and howled while the rumbling drums built, driving tribal rhythm that moved through the room like a wave. It went on and on, as the rest of the band stood by clapping and stomping their feet, until the promoter had no choice but to turn on the juice and let them finish; the kids were going to tear the walls down if he didn't. The guitars flew back in like birds crying overhead, swooping in to reclaim their stage. Jo Jane and Jerry were amazed by it. The Allman Brothers were literally unstoppable.

(Years later, I asked Butchie if he remembered that night. "Oh, that used to happen all the time," he said.)

Kim's main job was maintaining what they called the Wall, the stack of amplifiers that loomed behind the drummers. For the most part, Duane and Dickey maintained their guitars on their own, without help from anyone on the crew, but occasionally something would go wrong and Kim would jump in. He once replaced one of Duane's broken strings without taking the guitar from him.

"Seriously, Kim? He kept playing while you changed his string?" I asked.

"Yeah, he kept right on playing. I just stayed away from his fingers best I could."

One night at the Warehouse in New Orleans, they were opening for Pink Floyd, and when they finished their set, the audience went completely nuts. The band played three encores, and still the crowd was cheering and calling for more. The crew cleared the stage, and Pink Floyd's crew set up their gear, but the crowd was still shouting for the Brothers to come back. Pink Floyd played a song or two, but the crowd would not let go, chanting for the band, so Pink Floyd walked off the stage to wait them out. Kim walked back to the dressing room and asked Duane what he wanted to do. Duane said, "Set it back up."

The roadies started to roll out the Brothers' gear, but the Pink Floyd crew asked them what in the hell they thought they were doing. Kim told them the crowd had spoken and the Brothers were going to play another set, but the other crew wouldn't back down. "Y'all aren't from around here, are ya?" Red Dog said, and punches started to fly. In the end, the Brothers took back the stage and played an entire second set, including a version of "Mountain Jam" that lasted more than two hours, until the drummers all but collapsed on their kits.

"We would like to keep playing, but we don't have any drummers," Duane said. "We're gonna go drink a beer, and if there's anybody still here, we'll play some more."

The band moved through towns like a storm system, gathering strength as their cool smacked against the heat of the crowd. Callahan sat at the mixing board in the crowd and received the flood of sound from the many mics onstage. He used his ears to bring them into perfect balance. He taped the shows at the soundboard most nights, for the band to listen to later and mark their progress. When the band fully opened up, he would crank up the volume so the music would be felt down to the bone. The players wouldn't know the difference from the stage, but for the crowd, it was total sensory immersion.

The year on the road had given the band a patina, a dusty, golden sheen. Nothing could shake their laid-back calm. Sometimes they'd sit on the edge of the stage and talk to people in the audience, shake hands, and make jokes; they remained accessible, engaging, charismatic. The Brothers now had a following they could depend on in a growing number of clubs across the country: at the Warehouse in New Orleans, the Boston Tea Party, Ludlow's Garage in Cincinnati, Fillmore East and West, and on many college campuses. They lived at the pace set by the road. They felt entitled to their fun, as hard as they worked. They fed girls on songs of love, so what did you expect? They were wanted.

The relationships between the women in the Big House were every bit as significant and satisfying as the Brothers' relationship to one another. Candy, Linda, and Donna worked hard to make a peaceful and lovely home. They cleaned and baked banana bread, and chased the baby girls around. The wonder of being mothers deeply bonded Linda and Donna. Candy was a working woman, out in the town at the boutique all day. Her thing with Gregg was long over; he had lived with her at the house for a time, but he didn't stay for long. She found a bundle of love letters from other girls tucked in with his clothes in her wardrobe, and that was it. She started seeing Kim. The women would pass a joint in the evening and confide in one another, describing the men's bodies and comparing their moves, the little things they liked, and they'd lie stretched out on the floor with the stereo turned up, playing the beautiful music the band sent home. The women felt like muses, hearing the love they shared reflected in the songs.

The Winnebago would roar up behind the house and men would pour out, dirty and tired, talking loud in the alley. Donna would hear them filling up the kitchen, and no one would come upstairs to her. Duane would still be out there somewhere, working. He'd have jumped in on a session or stayed in Atlanta. When he finally came home days later, there were no apologies or explanations. Sometimes he would sleep for days and then leave again. Donna knew what Duane expected of her; he wanted silence and stability. He told her to be "quiet as a mouse." He wanted to come home and find her waiting. When news came through friends that the band was close, she would dress up, clean the house, and cook. Her anticipation was stronger than any other feeling. When he didn't come home to her, the strain broke something inside her.

If Duane saw anyone in his band losing their way inside of sadness or stress, he would find words of encouragement to pull them out of it. Everyone had to move forward together. He was so adamant about taking care of everyone, in word and deed, that when the stress of his responsibilities showed on him, it was frightening. Even as the band promoted the importance of their families, the two halves of their lives were fitting together less easily all the time.

Duane's charm and intelligence were being pulled under a wave of arrogance, and dark moods. He would drink to drunkenness and smoke until he could barely keep his eyes open, repeating himself over and over, saying paranoid things that made no sense. Donna was scared. Listening to Robert Johnson in the music room, he said, "Never poison me," alluding to the story of the Delta blues master dying at the hand of a jealous man who poisoned his whisky after Johnson flirted with his wife. Duane cut his eyes at Donna over the neck of his wobbling guitar, as if she were the menacing one, picking and slurring out lyrics about no-good women and the evil they make men do.

Donna began to wonder how she had gotten here, so far from herself. Duane could be so crass and cold. After playing a show, he told Donna the concert hall had smelled like girls' wet panties as soon as he struck a chord. He joked that she was lucky I was born with red hair, or he would wonder if I was his, when he knew he was the only man she'd ever been with. Just mean for the sake of being mean.

In a moment of pure exhaustion, he tried to put the pressure he felt into words, saying, "What is this now? I have you and a baby? And I'm gonna die young."

Women and children were soft and sticky traps. A man would be wise to take to heart the warnings in his favorite blues songs about low-down women. But here is the rough stuff, bitter and strong: the small paper bindles of heroin, line upon line of cocaine, girlfriends in Atlanta and Los Angeles taken out on the road, teenage groupies used up and cast off. They were all so young, I tell myself. "It was a different time," Jaimoe says to me. The truth of the matter was, only one person was straying, and it wasn't my mother.

Red Dog said Duane pitched a bitch when he found a couple of needles hidden in the Winnebago, while they were parked somewhere in rural North Carolina between gigs. Duane paced the length of the caravan, holding the syringes by their empty bellies with fire in his eyes.

"Look, I ain't calling anyone out. I'm talking to everybody. I am gonna say this once. This shit will not fly. I don't care who is doing this." He paused and held a point in the air with his eyes resting on his brother's bent head. "If I see another needle, that's it. There will be no conversation, no hard feelings, but this shit is out of the question and you will be gone."

A little while down the road, he and Dickey were having an argument when Duane grabbed his arm, looking for track marks.

"You can say what you think we all ought to do, and I'll listen, but you're not going to check my arms," Dickey said.

Duane apologized the next day. Dickey told him he knew they were all taking things a little too far, and Duane was right to worry. But Dickey was his own man with his own choices to make, and Duane needed to understand that. He wasn't going to be dictated to that way.

.   .   .

Cocaine, marijuana, and MDA. Soma and sleeping pills and Robitussin AC, mescaline, LSD and mushrooms, whisky, wine, and heroin. You keep phone numbers scrawled on scraps of paper, but soon you don't have to call. They just come and wait by the back door when you come to town, and enter the backstage rooms smiling wide. You remember the face of the guy in Boston, in Philly, in New York City who knows how to get you what you want. Folded glassine paper sleeves and a tightly rolled bill, hidden needles and a blackened spoon. The ritual of preparation, the private moment with pills rolling loosely in your palm, the cold beer popped open, the warm, half-empty bottle of red wine, a razor tapping gently through a pile of powder, a little spoon or a long fingernail, a deep inhale, and soon you are restored to yourself. A pulsing energy belongs to you, shining from your eyes, and everything is easier. You see the same ease in the faces all around you. The music blooms in your hands and floats above the crowd, and builds to ferocious crescendos that rock your body. You are in it and of it, fed and freed by the music and the high.

Drugs were taking hold in a deeper way, no longer just a diversion or a way to escape the rigors of the road. Along with the inspirational sound of Coltrane and Bird came the darker story of the relationships between the players and heroin. Heroin stood like an unopened door that might lead more deeply into the songs, and soon Gregg and then Duane stepped through it, the entire band of Brothers behind him. Heroin was easily available and cheap, even in Macon. I asked Johnny Sandlin about the effects of heroin on the band and he said, honestly, at least in the beginning, it was mostly positive. Heroin could give you at once a deep feeling of privacy and an expansiveness, an absence of all discomfort, social and physical. All neurotic static cleared. Heroin was a direct channel into certainty. You felt you had what you needed. In the space it cleared, with each player relaxed and vigilant, they could conjure a pillar of fire. My father and all of the members of the band and crew, with the single exception of Butch Trucks, had fallen in love with heroin. The only thing Duane was more enthralled by was cocaine, and the way he was living, the two walked hand in hand, one taking over when the other trailed off. Cocaine was everywhere; they called it vitamin C. It was coming from sources both high and low, in the pockets of both the business moguls and the creeps who wanted a way in the stage door. Duane told Donna they were either up on it or up looking for more. While no one spelled it out explicitly, drugs were often part of the exchange for playing: payment for services rendered, especially in Miami, where the path to South America was worn smooth and easy.

When I first met Jim Marshall, the photographer who took the picture for the cover of *At Fillmore East,* he told me the familiar story about his great cover shot of the band laughing together. They were all moody and hard to loosen up, until a guy Duane recognized walked by and he ran after him. He returned with a little bag in his palm and a gleam in his eye. Everybody cracked up, and Jim caught the moment.

Jim grabbed my hand, looked into my eyes, and asked me if I'd ever done cocaine. Before I could answer he said in a conspiratorial tone, "Your daddy loved cocaine. He *loved* it." He said it like it was personal and important information. Maybe it is.

Donna says she didn't see any of it; they kept the hardest drugs out of the house. There was in fact a rule about leaving hard stuff in the garages out back. She wasn't aware of other girls gathering around Duane, either, until she found a love letter from a girl in Boston tucked into the small compartment of his guitar case that read "I'll never forget the night we spent together." She had been looking for the signed divorce papers that had finally arrived from Patti. She wanted to show them to Linda. When she confronted Duane, he said, "If you go looking for shit, you're going to find it."

Donna never heard the name Dixie, but everyone else did. Dixie and her friends lived in a house on Taft Street near Piedmont Park in Atlanta, and they notoriously welcomed bands that passed through town. They became known as the Taft Street Girls. When any of the Brothers stayed overnight in Atlanta for "business," it was clear the meetings were taking place in bed. All the girls the band met and enjoyed on the road were an open secret, rarely discussed. Groupies were part of another life entirely—a road perk like a good meal or pocket money, an irresistible comfort—but the proximity of the Taft Street Girls to Macon was troubling.

In what little time the band had when they weren't touring, they would retreat together to the cabin they called Idlewild South, named after the packed and frenetic New York City airport now known as JFK. People were in and out all the time; the name was apt. They were still at work on songs for their second album, which would be named after the cabin. Out in the country with no close neighbors to complain, they pulled their extension cords out into the yard and played under the blue sky. One afternoon they were running through a new tune while their wives and girlfriends cooked in the little kitchen. "People, can you feel it? Love is everywhere!" The girls couldn't help but see the irony. Love was getting starved out in Macon, Georgia, so they made up a chorus of their own: "Practice what you preach! Practice what you preach!"

Hard drugs and groupies were there from the first day. I had imagined an early innocence in 1969, when marijuana and marriage were all anyone wanted, but that's a child's fantasy. When everyone was living together at the hippie crash pad on College Street, the men used to go to the local colleges and check girls out of their dorms for the night like library books. If our mothers didn't know, it's partly because they didn't want to know.

I know the tale of a communal case of crabs that forced everyone to sit around a hotel room together with their cocks lathered, laughing, which seemed funny until it was mentioned they had gotten into this mess by "pulling a train," a poetic way to say a single girl took on all of them.

There was Twiggs's legendary carousel full of slides, each one a different teenage girl, naked and splayed, and his habit of passing around copies of the statutory rape laws in the different states they passed through. There were stories of girls who waited by the side of the road topless and climbed into the Winnebago ready to be the jackpot in a poker game. Blowjobs were given on the side stage, within sight of the crowd. They balled on moving motorcycles, on the hoods of cars still warm from a ride, in gas station restrooms during a quick refueling, in Rose Hill Cemetery on graves in the moonlight with other men's wives.

I was often told that my father wasn't the one who got up to this mischief, that he'd opt out by holding up the book he was reading, but he held his most private cards very close.

The crazy thing is, I wanted to know. Even as I felt a dark rage growing in me, I never shut down the storytellers.

I will always identify with the women, the ones at home and even the girls on the road. But I understand that the temptation for a pack of twenty-year-old rock stars was impossible to resist. If you were generating the kind of heat they were putting out onstage, it would have been impossible to go to bed and shiver alone. My question, though, is why did they marry and have babies so young? Did they need a different kind of life at home, a soft place to fall? Or did they get trapped when our mothers got pregnant? Did they really think of their families that way? Or did they just want it all? Well, they got it all, but it didn't come cheap.

After touring America with Blind Faith, a band that seemed to collapse under the weight of the musicians' collective fame, Eric Clapton was in a moment of transition. Immediately dubbed a "supergroup," convinced to rush their first album to market and play enormous venues rather than the intimate theaters they would have preferred, the band had to pad their set with hits from their previous bands, Cream and Traffic. The pressures of stardom were eclipsing the pleasure of playing. Meanwhile, the opening band on the Blind Faith tour, Delaney & Bonnie & Friends, played with great joy every night. After the tour, Blind Faith came apart, even with their album still on the British charts. Eric sought refuge at Delaney and Bonnie's home in Los Angeles and they became close friends. For the better part of the next year, he collaborated with the couple, an experience that culminated in a live album, *On Tour with Eric Clapton*. In the studio, Delaney helped produce Clapton's first, eponymous solo album, co-writing songs and famously encouraging him to sing. Shortly after bassist Carl Radle, drummer Jim Gordon, and keyboardist Bobby Whitlock parted ways with Delaney & Bonnie & Friends, they each returned to play with Clapton. Neither Delaney nor Bonnie took their exodus well.

While working with Eric in England, the band was christened Derek and the Dominos, in another bid for Clapton to remain somewhat anonymous. He wanted the music to speak for itself. They recorded behind Eric's close friend George Harrison on his first album after the dissolution of the Beatles, *All Things Must Pass*. It was during that project that Eric fell in love with Harrison's wife, Pattie, and the pain of that unrequited love fueled the writing of *Layla and Other Love Songs*. The album he wrote for the love he couldn't have won her in the end, and it reached far beyond her, into the wider culture, where it is revered as one of the great masterpieces of rock and roll.

I've pored over many books and magazines about the *Layla* sessions, trying to understand the connection between my father and Eric that was so evident in the songs. The most revealing insights came from an unlikely source. A London-based musician named Sam Hare interviewed Eric in 1997 for his dissertation. At the time, Sam was a photography student at Norwich School of Art and Design, where he was asked to pick any subject he was passionate about for his final project. He chose the Allman Brothers Band and their influence on popular music. Sam knew he needed a primary source for his paper and decided to take a chance and write to Eric Clapton. To his great surprise, Clapton responded and they had a remarkable conversation. While the interview was never intended for wider publication, it came to the attention of the then-president of *Hittin' the Note* magazine, who printed it, much to the surprise of Hare. The interview in its entirety has since been available to anyone willing to search for it online. The quotes contained here are from that interview.

"There were a lot of complications in my life. I'd fallen in love with someone else's wife, and all of this coming—that's what I was writing songs about. But there was also a tremendous bonding going on—the likes of which I've never known since," Eric said.

When they were ready to go into the studio to record, Eric thought of Tom Dowd, the producer he had first worked with on Cream's *Disraeli Gears*. Dowd was in the vanguard of music recording, an ingenious inventor who had found his calling as a producer. Many producers try to leave their stamp on the albums they cut, but Tom was an invisible guiding hand that enabled many artists to reach their full potential. At Atlantic Records he oversaw the creations of masterpieces by John Coltrane, Thelonious Monk, Charlie Parker, Ray Charles, Aretha Franklin, and a continuing list of artists in every conceivable genre of music. He was a happy and calm man, with a contagious smile and natural elegance. A technical innovator, he is credited as the first to record popular music in stereo. He invented faders, the sliding switches on recording consoles that could be raised and lowered smoothly. This single idea enabled him to play the soundboard as an instrument itself, using his ear to guide the mix. He had the mind and soul of an artist, and his ability to communicate with musicians and put them at ease was unparalleled.

Tom had great respect for Duane's talent and his ear, and he understood the range of influences the Allman Brothers were drawing from. He loved the band, and when they gave him a gold pendant of their mushroom logo, Tom wore it every day for the rest of his life. Duane and Tom had become close during their many shared Atlantic sessions, including *Idlewild South*, the Brothers' second album, which had been completed just before the Dominos arrived at Criteria. When Tom mentioned that Eric was on his way, Duane asked if he could come by the sessions. Duane had long admired and respected Clapton. The Yardbirds were one of his first inspirations; the Allman Joys covered their songs. Duane and Gregg had driven for hours to see Cream play when they lived in Los Angeles.

Tom invited Eric to see the Allman Brothers play; he was eager to introduce them. Eric had called Tom years before to ask who played the guitar solo on the back end of Wilson Pickett's "Hey Jude." Tom had a feeling Duane would push Eric and the Dominos in a new direction. Karl Richardson, an engineer on the sessions, remembered that Clapton had trepidations at the prospect of playing with Duane; he said he wasn't sure he could match him. Karl said, "He seemed scared to death."

Albhy Galuten, another engineer and keyboard player on the sessions, had a somewhat different take. "Eric was nervous that he might let Duane down by not being a good enough guitar player to pull his own weight. He wasn't nervous about what people would think, but he wanted to be up to snuff as a musician. After seeing the band play, you can see why he would be nervous."

It was a beautiful late August night for an outdoor concert in front of the Miami Beach Convention Center, and Tom had led Eric and the other members of the Dominos to a cordoned-off spot just in front of the stage where they had an excellent view of Duane. When he spotted Eric, Duane froze for a moment. Eric was moved by the power of the music. "There was like the perfect kind of weather," Eric said. "It was dark, it was balmy and hot and there was a strong breeze. They all had really, really long hair— right down to their waists almost; it was blowing back in the wind, and it was so picturesque. The music was unbelievable, because they were doing all of that harmony playing . . . it was fantastically worked out and very strong."

Tom couldn't wait to get them back to Criteria.

The Brothers and the Dominos went back to the studio after the show and they all stayed to jam. Only Jaimoe chose not to play. "I went in there, and I really wasn't knocked out about anything they were doing. I went back out to the Winnebago and did what we always did—listened to Sonny Williams, or Coltrane or Miles, or somebody. I was out there just smoking and listening to tapes. What we were doing was a hell of a lot more interesting than what Eric Clapton was doing in there." It was clear to him, too, that Duane was the only one Eric wanted. "He wanted Duane to play on his record and, shit, why not?" Jaimoe didn't perceive Clapton as a threat to the Brothers, but the rest of the band worried. Eric could offer Duane the wider world, and not someday soon, but right away.

The Dominos had been at work in the studio for about ten days and had completed three songs. "We didn't have very much material. I started recording anything I could think of," Eric remembered. "It almost started from the night of the concert, because they all came back to the studio after the show. We started right then and there and it was just . . . I think the best way to describe it is that up until the point that we connected with them, we were really firing blanks. We'd been in the studio for a couple of weeks and we were getting nothing done because really it was just about me trying to kind of stimulate myself with the guitar."

Duane walked into the studio, sat down with his guitar, and learned the fragmented beginnings of the songs Eric had written. His focus and precision impressed the most experienced producer in modern music and astounded the young engineers. Eric asked Duane to come back and play on the album. Duane agreed, and when he returned, he walked in with a whole new energy, clapping his hands together and saying, "Let's get this thing done."

The songs on *Layla* appear in the order in which they were recorded, with Duane's arrival on the fourth song, "Nobody Knows You When You're Down and Out," a cover of a Jimmy Cox tune made popular by Bessie Smith.

"We only had the quartet, and we were trying to write songs, but it just wasn't exciting," Eric said. "Then, when these guys came in—especially just me and Duane—we'd just keep thinking of things to do, songs to do from the past, that would make it possible for us to duet. We'd come up with 'Nobody Knows You When You're Down and Out,' 'Key to the Highway,' and 'Why Does Love Got to Be So Sad?' All these things were really vehicles so we could jam, and that ended up making up quite a deal of the bulk of the album—just excuses to jam with one another.

"For a start, Duane would play in straight tuning a lot of the time, I mean, I couldn't understand it. He would do—I really don't know how to describe it—but he would hit this seventh thing all the time, which I actually didn't approve of. . . . I mean every now and then we would argue about stuff like this because . . . I only believe that you should really play what had gone down before—which jived in a way with why I liked him, because I loved the fact that he was an improviser. He threw away tradition a lot of the time, but for me, that was really quite . . . sort of inappropriate! You know he was fantastically gifted."

In addition to engineering the sessions, Galuten played piano on the album as well.

"For Eric it was so powerful to have somebody who was an equal on guitar, because there are not many people as good as Eric. They did not do multiple takes. It was not the kind of recording session where you say, 'Let's try the bridge again. Let's work on this section.' Most records don't have that magic, spontaneous thing. When they were recording *Layla,* if the second take was still not great, they would just forget it and move on to another song." They didn't have to discuss what was needed; they played together until they found it. Richardson said that Duane became the de facto musical director on the session, and when someone would present an idea to Eric, he would say, "Run it by Duane." Duane met Eric where he was, and in some way almost stood in for the lover he wanted but could not have. "I'd kind of fallen in love with Duane," Eric said. "I mean I was even ignoring my own band, you know. We were just kind of having this musical affair in front of everybody.

"Duane was a very, very strong, driven, and aggressive man. I mean, he was very thin and wiry and not much to shout about in terms of being a tough guy or nothing, but he was very strong. There was a great deal of joy in our kind of dueling with one another because we came from almost a separate place. I mean, I was much more into Chicago stuff, and he was much more into the kind of southern, Georgian kind of country blues."

Galuten recalled, "On 'Key to the Highway,' when Duane did his solo, he started out with something so sweet and simple and straight, then about halfway through, he switched pickups and jumped to something that was incredibly aggressive, and yet absolutely right, and I remember everybody on the session was just like 'Oh my God!' It blew us all away. And in the mix, when you hear it back, it's pulled down. Tommy mixes it so it comes out kind of evenly, but at the time it was like he just owned the room."

"Those are notes that aren't on the instrument," Tom Dowd commented in *The Language of Music*, a documentary about his life, "Those are notes that are off the top of the instrument. That's what makes those people such magnificent guitar players. It's in the tips of their fingers. It's not in the knobs, it's not how loud they play—it's touch. It's touch. And both of them have exquisite technique and touch."

Duane played with delicate beauty on "I Am Yours," then played ferocious lead on "Why Does Love Got to Be So Sad?" He added a thundering lick to the beginning of the song "Layla," transforming a relaxed ballad into a passionate, rocking plea with one of the most recognizable riffs in modern music. Yet in all the interviews Duane gave about the record, he evaded questions that tried to differentiate his playing from Eric's. When asked what he played on *Layla,* he answered, "I played just enough." He also said, "I played the Gibson and he played the Fender, and if you know the difference, you can hear who played what." Duane valued his connection with Eric, and he wasn't going to be pitted against him, even in the subtlest way.

They repaired to the Thunderbird Hotel at Sunny Isles Beach at the end of their long days, which would start in the late afternoon and often continue into the early hours of morning. The hotel wasn't anything special, but it was on the beach and close to Criteria. It was also infamous for providing its guests with anything they might desire. Both Eric and Duane were still reveling in the peace and comfort heroin could bring, not yet at its mercy. Eric said, "Duane was like your archetypal Johnny Reb. I mean, he was really out there, and for a thin guy he had this very strong, very charismatic persona. You know, a lot of drinking was involved, and we were just getting into a lot of heavy drug taking, too, so to see him getting into that with me was . . . well, it's sad to look back on it. But Duane was very tough. The drugs when they took their toll, which was a little while later, kind of incapacitated us. I mean the Dominos broke up because of that—because we just couldn't function—but at the time of *Layla,* they really hadn't gotten a grip."

Cocaine was such a part of the culture of Miami, it was a given. Fellow Domino Bobby Whitlock has said that it was so abundant and strong that Duane and Eric ended up flushing a quantity of it down the toilet at the hotel, trying to release themselves from the excess of it. (The night he came home from the sessions, Little Linda watched Duane sit at the kitchen table in the Big House prying the silver disks off his Concho belt. "What are you doing? Don't take it apart; you'll never get it back together," she said. He smiled up at her like a little kid and slid a little bindle of powder from behind the silver decoration and held it up to her between two fingers with a wink.)

At the end of their time together, Duane agreed to return to Miami for overdubs, and Eric asked him if he would come out on the road with the band. Duane agreed. He wrote to Donna with the news.

··

September 5, 1970
Ramada Inn
Milwaukee, Wisconsin

Sunday

Dearest Spoon,
Thanks for the sweet secret message. Please try and have a little faith, honey, and everything will be alright.

Eric Clapton has asked me to join his band. I really don't know what to do, but don't mention a word of this to anyone at the house, or leave this letter where others might read it and do something foolish. It would mean about $5000 a week to us, as well as a home in England and a lot of things we'd like to have. We've cut a really super album together, and Eric plans a European as well as an American tour, and the receipts would be phenomenal on both. I'll be getting 20% of all of it, so I plan to do both of those tours with him.

I'll write more later when my thought is more stable. I'm really up in the air right now.

All my love to Gragri and everyone there.

Love Always,
Duane

P.S. Shhh!

Eric offered two tours, one in Europe and one in the United States, a high wage, and friendship with an equal. Duane told Donna with a kind of awe that he had seen an entire trunk full of beautiful boots and shoes in Eric's hotel room. He had fine silk shirts and velvet pants, the best of everything. Eric gave Duane a beautiful batik shirt, with abstract swirls that suggested peacocks in purple and deep blues on both sides of the placket. It was easily the most beautiful thing Duane had ever owned. In return, with humor, Duane gave Eric his red T-shirt that read "City Slicker." He knew Eric was offering him another kind of life.

After the *Layla* sessions were completed, Clapton returned to England with a rare left-handed Fender Stratocaster, a gift for Jimi Hendrix. He wanted him to hear the Dominos' recording of Hendrix's "Little Wing," a tribute he and Duane had recorded for him. They both greatly admired Hendrix, one of the few other rock guitarists who could stand toe-to-toe with them. Thom Doucette had planned to introduce Jimi and Duane when Jimi returned from Europe. But on the morning of September 18, 1970, Jimi Hendrix was found unconscious in a Notting Hill apartment in London. He died that afternoon at the hospital, having apparently suffocated while under the heavy sedation of sleeping pills. Eric never had the chance to see him.

Duane had an incredible dream about Jimi not long after he passed away, and he bounded out of bed late at night to share it with Donna.

Duane walked into a men's room in the lobby of a big hotel, like a Holiday Inn, and there was Jimi Hendrix, his wild corona of hair, his purple jacket covered in snaking gold cord and shiny buttons, a long red scarf around his neck. Duane had heard that Jimi died, and wondered if they were in Heaven and so he asked him, "Hey man, are you okay?"

But Jimi was excited and waved Duane over to the sink with a smile so big he could see every one of his teeth. "Man, come take a look at this! It's a groove!"

Jimi bent down toward the silver faucet, turned it gently, and kept teasing and turning, and as he did, a beautiful guitar riff came floating out and bounced off the white tile walls around them. Duane stood with his hands on his hips, and watched Jimi play the pretty little rambling tune by twisting the faucet.

Duane pulled his Dobro into bed with Donna and started picking out the riff. The melody Jimi gave him was the seed of the song "Little Martha."

Eric had a few American shows planned for the Dominos in December and Duane agreed to play as many as he could, given the Brothers' touring schedule. Duane had missed a few Brothers gigs in order to record Layla, but he didn't like doing that. He was going to have to decide very soon which band to commit to.

Tuffy Phillips is one of two remaining original roadies and he still lives in Macon. His van sits in his driveway decorated with dozens of bumper stickers honoring the military and telling Jane Fonda to fuck off. The skin of a bear, head and all, rides shotgun in the front seat. Tuffy wears wire-rimmed glasses with one eye covered by a rose-tinted lens with a small medallion glued in the center since he can't see out of that eye anyway. He is covered in tattoos and wears blue jeans, pale from hundreds of washings. His black leather vest is decorated with patches and long twin braids hang down over his shoulders. He wears earrings made of the claw of some small critter, and silver rings of his own making on every finger, their silver harvested from melted-down coins and old wedding rings. He gives me a necklace with a mountain lion tooth he pried from a skull beside a road in Wyoming. He talks with a thin cigar in his mouth and a handgun resting in front of him on the coffee table. As tough as he is, he is one of the kindest gentlemen I have ever known.

"Duane came in and asked which one of us was going to drive with him to Tampa to play with Eric Clapton," Tuffy said. "And everybody had an excuse why they couldn't carry him there. I was the only one who had nothing to do, and so we went. I was the driver for the band. I didn't know anything about taking care of Duane's guitars, but he trusted me. Well, he broke a string that first night, and I took his guitar from him, and then Eric's tech took it from me. He replaced the string and quick, cut the tops of the strings off at the headstock, and you know that's not what Duane liked. He liked to leave his strings long and curled up. He gave me such a look when I handed it back to him, like he could have killed me. Later, I told him it wasn't me that'd done it. Duane made a thousand dollars there, and he gave me five hundred of it. He told me I better not share one dollar of it with any of the guys. He said, they didn't earn it, but he told me to make sure they knew about it!"

After playing his second show with the Dominos the next night in Syracuse, New York, Eric approached Duane about his offer. "I said, 'You know, we really need you in the band now—I don't really want to go on as a quartet. Would you join us?' He said, 'I don't think I can do that,' and at that point, he went straight back to the Allman Brothers."

Joe Dan Petty picked up Duane at the airport, and he strutted up, pulled out a roll of bills, and said, "JD! I got Big Daddy bucks!" Once they were in the car, Duane said, "I'll tell you one thing, Clapton's got nothing on Dickey Betts."

· · ·

I wish my father could have known that *Layla* would be considered one of the landmark recordings in rock-and-roll history.

One of the most important and valued experiences of my father's life gave rise to a challenging and disillusioning experience in mine. True to the nature of the business at the time, the arrangement for compensating Duane for his work on *Layla* was handled very loosely, with a couple of phone calls rather than a negotiation or a signed contract. Duane was initially paid a couple of hundred dollars, a day rate for a studio musician, until it was clear Eric wanted him to stay and play on the entire album. At that point Phil Walden called Criteria and told Duane to stay out of the studio until a deal could be struck. Money was never a big consideration for Duane, and waiting for the deal to be made irritated him enough that he called Donna to complain about it. The lure of playing with a musician he greatly admired and respected was of the highest value to him, but within a few hours, a deal was struck to give Duane a small royalty.

When I turned eighteen, the responsibility for my father's estate fell to me, and I took it very seriously. My learning curve was steep. My grandfather Gil, the executor of Duane's estate until I came of age, noticed that royalty payments for *Layla* had stopped without explanation in 1983. My mother and I both wrote to Eric directly several times. When she went to see him play in 1972, after Duane's death, he had told Donna to get in touch with him if we ever needed anything. Lawyers answered our letters. It took me nearly twenty years to settle the dispute through legal mediation, which resulted in the original deal being reinstated going forward. Eric Clapton himself never weighed in on the matter.

Duane did not live long enough to receive either the accolades or fair compensation for *Layla*.

You can hear the fatigue and sadness in my father's voice when his playing with Clapton comes up in a 1971 interview on a Houston radio station. He is asked if he had heard of plans for a follow-up Dominos album, and whether he would participate in it. "I haven't heard from any of those guys since," Duane said.

21

In another hotel room late at night, blues harpist Thom Doucette and Duane sat on the edges of their beds, high and tired. Duane was on the telephone, his voice rising and falling, the edges hardening and sharpening. He forced air out of his lungs in a scoff, a sudden shout, sarcasm dripping as he swore and paced. Ace thought, *I wouldn't want to be Donna on the other end of that phone.*

Duane slammed down the phone and stormed over to his guitar, grabbed it by the neck for a beat-down, and played with ferocious power. Doucette felt like he shouldn't even be seeing it, it was so raw, but he watched and listened as Duane worked off his rage. His song shifted into lower gears until finally it was earthbound and calm. The tune wound down into something gentle and kept rolling for a while. It took more than an hour.

The Brothers toured constantly in September and October of 1970, fueling themselves with a diverse range of substances. They moved together through the phases of high, higher, unconscious, and hungover like the daily cycles of sun and moon.

After they played at Vanderbilt University on October 30, Red Dog was ready to hit the road for a night drive from Nashville to Atlanta, eager to be home. Everybody was exhausted, and getting them packed and out was like herding cats, but he was determined. Duane was the lone straggler, and he wasn't answering his door. They hadn't been back at the hotel long enough for him to go anywhere, and Red Dog started to panic. When the hotel manager unlocked the door, they found Duane unconscious.

Everybody had been tugging little pieces off a ball of opium and eating them all night, and Duane had ingested too much. His lips had turned a pale shade of blue, his hands were cold, and his breathing was shallow. There were blisters on his fingers from his cigarette burning down to the filter. An ambulance came. The tech told them not to get their hopes up too high; they would do what they could, but this guy was pretty far gone. Desperation rushed through everyone. They could not lose Duane. They could not even think about it.

They waited in the hospital for what felt like hours, until a doctor came to tell them Duane was conscious. He spent a couple of days recovering while the band and crew went on to Atlanta to play a gig at Emory University. Fans were not pleased with his unexplained absence and many asked for their money back.

Knowing the band was due home around Halloween and Big Linda's birthday, the women had started planning a feast. Linda, Candy, and Donna were so keyed up with all the anxious preparations, they each took a Valium and stood for a moment, hugging with their foreheads touching to catch a deep breath before the men arrived. The engines of the Winnie and Black Hearted Woman, the equipment truck, could be heard all the way down Vineville Avenue, and waiting for the sound could make you crazy. Everyone walked in, but Duane wasn't with them. When Kim came upstairs to put down his bag, Donna asked where Duane was. He said, "Didn't you hear what happened? Duane overdosed. He was DOA at the hospital."

"DOA?" Donna asked, her body going cold with shock.

"Dead on arrival, but he's okay. He came through it. He'll be home tomorrow."

As Doucette drove Duane home from Tennessee, he said to him, "You don't have to do this right away, man. Why don't you take a little time?"

"No, I have to do it and I have to do it right now," Duane answered.

He was talking through what he was going to say to Donna once he got home.

Everybody gathered at the house the next day for a celebratory meal. Donna was standing at the kitchen counter stirring a cracked egg into a bowl of Jiffy corn bread mix when Duane came in through the back door. He took her by her elbow and led her into the dining room at the back of the house, and before her welcoming smile had entirely faded from her face, she heard him say, "I'm leaving you. I love you, but I can't do this anymore."

All she could do was repeat what he said: "You love me but you can't do this anymore?"

"That's right. I'm leaving."

"You're leaving? You mean you're leaving me?"

"That's right."

He walked out of the house full of people primed for a party and drove to Atlanta to be with Dixie, one of the Taft Street Girls.

Donna went up to their room and lay down, stunned.

She stayed in a state of shock for days. Kim came into her room and sat on the edge of the bed to check on her. She asked him why Duane would leave her now, but his answer didn't make it any clearer. "Do you know what they do when a horse breaks its leg? They shoot her," he said.

My mother always mentions that she was in the middle of knitting Duane a scarf out of Aunt Lydia's multicolored rug yarn. She remembers the yarn because it was so heavy it continued to stretch under its own weight until the scarf became overwhelmingly long. She once made Duane a macramé guitar strap that stretched out, too. His guitar was hanging down to his knees before he knew it. He wore it as a belt instead. It was an important detail to her, that she kept knitting for him. She wanted him to see that she wasn't giving up. It was her quiet way of telling him she knew he would come home.

He did come back to her bed once in the weeks after their breakup, sick with a fever. She asked him again, "Duane, are you sure?" He didn't give her an answer.

He let her take care of him like a nurse, feeding him soup and resting her cool hand against his hot cheek. She was grateful to have him there, but once he was well, he left again. She learned that heartbreak was a real pulsing pain, her chest so sore she thought I might feel it through her skin when she held me. The hurting pinned her down and kept her still. She slept late and stopped helping around the house. Linda came into her darkened bedroom in the mornings, carrying me on her hip, and tried gently to rouse her.

One day Donna heard the sound of Duane's car turning into the driveway and walked out to meet him, carrying me in her arms, her lips pressed into my hair. She stopped short when both car doors opened. She couldn't believe he would bring her here. Donna stepped back through the back door and looked through the glass walls of the sunroom. Duane stood in the backyard with a short woman with short hair: Dixie. This girl wasn't taller or thinner than she was. She was not gorgeous or stylish or perfect. Donna hadn't consciously tried to picture her, but she had assumed she must be stunning in every way, and here was a perfectly ordinary girl—not better than her, just different. Donna suddenly felt that she had never really known Duane at all. If he could simply erase her, replace her, and let go of their child just to be with someone new, who was he? Who had he ever been?

She was spinning in a hellish swirl of feelings. Her home and loving family were a naïve dream. Duane was gone and it felt like he had never really been there at all. The walls around her seemed like paper, the light thin and sickly. Nothing was real there anymore. Then I cried a wet baby scream and the world firmed up under her feet.

There was laundry to fold, a baby to feed, warm baths to draw, damp diapers to change: a string of benign chores to fill her days and nights. My baby world was her safe home. There was always something more to do, and when she did something small for me, I would smile like she was made of sunshine. It was impossible to cry while looking at my dimpled cheeks and wide-open smile, which revealed tiny teeth poking through pink gums. *This is his baby,* she thought. *We are his family. Someday he will come back.*

How cruel that *Layla and Other Love Songs* was released just after their breakup. Duane had assured her that this album contained the seed of their future; with it would come all the things they both wanted. The songs were so full of pathos and longing, it seemed Duane was playing her pain. His crying guitar and the beautiful lyrics said all she wished she could find a way to say to him: *You've got me on my knees. . . . Why does love got to be so sad?*

Mom tells me that whenever I heard "Layla," I would dance from the first note until the last. I was two years old, tiny with serious dark eyes and bright orange hair. At the clarion call of my father's guitar I would begin spinning with my hands raised over my head. I closed my eyes and swayed slowing to the piano coda, my hands fluttering around me. My mother was mesmerized.

Donna served Duane with divorce papers. Her lawyer said the length of their relationship and the fact that he asked her to use the name Allman qualified them as married under common law. She hired the lawyer when Phil Walden presented her with papers of his own, laying out an arrangement that seemed neither clear nor fair. Walden wanted to move us to an apartment in town so Duane could still see me. Donna went to look at a couple of places, but standing in an empty second-floor duplex, looking out into a silent street with bare winter trees, she broke down. She didn't want to live alone after living with her closest friends. The Big House was home, and it was too much to lose all at once: the house and friends, her love and her identity. She couldn't stay close enough to watch it go on without her. How could she start all over again across town by herself? She decided to go back to St. Louis to her parents, as hard as that seemed; at least it was far away from everything she was losing.

Duane wouldn't sign the divorce papers. He gave them back covered with handwritten changes. He disputed the amount of money she was asking for—saying it was too much. He refused to get the life insurance her lawyer recommended, saying no one was going to bet that he was going to die before them.

He said, "I'll give Galadrielle money for whatever she needs, but I am not gonna give you roller-skating money!"

Big Linda suggested to Donna that he was stalling because Duane didn't really want to lose us, and Donna still held on to hope even as she moved forward. The papers went back and forth a half dozen times. Donna finally asked Duane to come to the house and talk it through with her. They sat at the table in the sunroom. She explained that it was important to her to have time with me. She didn't want to get a job and let a stranger take care of me all day. She just wanted a little support so she could raise me right. He understood, and he finally signed the papers.

Soon after, Michael Callahan, the band's soundman and roadie, was diagnosed with hepatitis and everyone had to go down to the clinic and get a shot. Donna and Duane ran into each other in the parking lot behind the doctor's office. She set me down and they stood together on the grass and watched me toddle around. Donna saw Duane tear up watching me. "I just can't do it," he said. "I love you, but I can't be a husband. I can't be a father."

There was nothing else to say. Duane wasn't going to change, and it wasn't because of Dixie. It wasn't that Donna wasn't good enough or pretty enough. What kept him away from her was something more difficult to see.

A white sport coat and a pink carnation
I'm all alone in romance

In a drunken radio interview recorded at WABC in New York on December 9, 1970, Duane described Donna as "a white sport coat and a pink carnation," a line from a Marty Robbins song, an opaque indictment of her innocence and apparent unsuitability for a man like him. His manic monologue is one of only a few recordings of him talking at any length. The velocity of his delivery is wild. Rolling with a thought, his voice drawls out into near nonsense. He sounds so high, you can practically join him on his bender by listening to him shucking and jiving. He puts on a cruel high-pitched voice to mock her, while telling a wholly made-up story of meeting Donna backstage at a concert. He makes it sound like he lost his freedom to a girl who was part savvy man-eater, part naïve child. All of this came spilling out of him when the DJ asked him if he lived in Atlanta:

"I live in Macon, Georgia, right now. I've got a house, man. . . . Berry and his old lady and kid live there, and me and my old lady and kid live there and Gregg and his chick which is Berry's sister live there and make it nice and so, anyhow, I got rid of my old lady and my kid. I said, no old ladies and no kids, just guitars, man. She's a teenage queen. . . ."

"Who's a teenage queen? Your kid?"

"My old lady. My kid's a kid, man. She's mine, man. She's part of me. You can see me in her. Man, I look at her and say, 'Hey, me! How you doin'?' It's good, man. It's good. Children are good, man, if you love 'em. If you got time to do it. It's not good if the old lady ain't nowhere, man. And my old lady is a white sport coat and a pink carnation. She's just, 'Do you love me, son?' And I said, 'No, I don't love you, I just seen you, man.' You come by the gig and ask me if I'd ball ya and I said okay, yeah. And then ten months later, 'I'm pregnant! What'll I do? What'll I do?' I said, 'I don't know what to do.' So she comes down and she gets a crib see, gets an apartment and says, 'Duane! Here's your home! Here's your home!' and I said, 'Well, I've been lookin' for a home. This must be it!' and I'm in the door, man, and right away I start getting pulled at and shoved at. I don't want none of that, man. I don't want none of that. So I said, 'Okay, here's your bucks. Here's your car. Here's your trip. Hit the road.' So, it's me and my old guitar, which is a Jimmie Rodgers song, 'Me and My Old Guitar.' It's a beaut. Y'all should play some of him! He's good!"

My mom never heard that interview, and it was only recently that I found it on the Internet for the first time. It took me a long time to bring myself to listen to it; friends warned me that it was rough. I didn't recognize their relationship in anything he said—not how they met or how they parted. It was close to the time of their breakup, and he was raging. Still, I wish I had listened sooner. As mean as he gets, his sweet words for me are tucked in there, too. For the first time I considered that he and I might have had our own bond, separate from theirs. I was always so close to my mother, and felt the impact of the pain he caused her; it had never occurred to me that he might have felt differently about her than he did about me . . . a horribly disloyal thought. Even before I listened to the interview I felt caught in the loyalty bind created by my love for her and my love for him.

Mom and I left for St. Louis just before Christmas 1970, on a bitterly cold and damp morning. As she prepared to walk out of the Big House for the last time, Donna was shocked to find Duane sleeping in the living room with the rug from the floor pulled over him for warmth. She stood above him and watched him for a moment, but didn't wake him to say goodbye.

Why didn't he come upstairs? Why did he come so close and not take the final step? What would have happened if she had woken him up? I asked her to picture the moment she saw Duane sleeping there.

"Did he know we were leaving?" I asked.

"I don't know. Maybe he did."

"He must have, right? Was he sleeping on the floor? Or a couch? Under a rug? The rug from the floor?"

"Yes, a rug. He must have gotten very cold. I don't know if he was on the floor. . . ."

"Can you try to picture it?"

"I pulled it up over him, and that was it."

"Was he up on a piece of furniture, or did you have to bend down to the floor?"

"I don't know, I was so shocked to see him there."

"Mom, try."

"Galadrielle. I don't know. Does your memory work that way? Can you remember details from your first love by trying?"

"I think I can."

"Well, good for you. I can't."

We were sitting in an empty restaurant over a wine-stained tablecloth and empty coffee cups. She had told me this story many times before, but I had never been so merciless about details. We left the restaurant in opposite directions to our waiting cars, barely saying goodbye. It took me a while to realize how cruel I had been. She was telling me about the very last time she saw my father alive.

Some men seem able to sever ties in ways that women can't fathom. They can box things up—love, pain, the past—shelving the things that might weigh them down. They know how to get free and keep moving forward. I have seen how completely women's lives are changed by the decisions that men make. My mother could no more decide to stop loving my father than she could have decided to stop loving me; he was her family. He is her family. The strange twin virtues of freedom and control that everyone so admired in him, did they draw him away?

"Some people have satellites. They create their own gravity," my mom said. "When you have that strength, people see it in you

282

and they are drawn in. You develop your talent, and then you can generate anything: money, sex, music. People adore you for it. But that music, it's like wind through the trees. It's just going through them. It is not them." The distance between Duane and his loving presence in songs felt immense after their breakup.

Forty years later, she is still trying to find answers, still wondering if she could have fought him and made him stay. What if she had yelled, "We are your family! You are not going!" She marvels at her own paralysis and weakness, but I think it was closer to pride. How can you make a man stay when what he has loved best in you is your gentleness, and the likeliness that you would never fight?

"He was disappointing himself. He was disappointing me. I was tangled up in it, and it was easier to walk away and feel changed by it. I felt like Duane. I was just as bad as he was. I was just as angry and just as broken. I couldn't feel a separation between him and me. I felt how strong I really was and I decided to push through and live. Duane had lived, and I had witnessed him living, and I carried him within me. That is how real it was. I thought, *Now I am him.*"

Saying goodbye to Candy and Linda was incredibly hard. They were so angry and sad, but there was nothing to be done. Candy drove us to the airport in Atlanta, and when she came home, she stood in front of Linda in the kitchen, threw up her hands, and said, "All gone!"

"Why is Duane doing this?" Linda asked Berry.

"When he looks at Donna he feels guilty. She's pure of heart and she really loves him so much. He doesn't feel guilty when he looks at Dixie. She'll be his little puppy and follow him around and he can do whatever he wants." Berry was upset about it, too. Duane was breaking up their family. Brittany and I had never been apart. "Baby, the *root* is the root of all evil," he concluded with a sad smile.

Linda saw this breach in our family as the first and knew it would lead to other cracks in the foundation, and she was right. Before too long, she was contending with a girlfriend of Berry's, too. "I know what was between Donna and Duane," Linda told me years later. "I was there. He always treated her so special. If you would have told me what was coming with Dixie, I never would have believed it."

In Duane's case, Linda thought it was more than sex. She thought Duane wanted to protect us from the crazy life he was leading. It must have shocked Duane to feel death standing beside him. I know he felt an acute responsibility for the band and he must have known how frightened everyone was of losing him. Did the overdose shake him? Maybe he imagined it would be easier for us to survive if we were away from him, should something tragic take him.

I asked Ace, the one person I knew who might have been close enough to know what was in my father's mind. "Did he ask us to go as a way of protecting us?"

He answered without a moment's hesitation. "Absolutely. That is absolutely why."

I realized that what I told myself lightly all along was the whole truth: My father fell in love with music. Music woke Duane up in the morning with fragments of songs rescued from his dreams. Melodies coursed through his blood all day. He played every hour he could, stopping to eat, to walk from one place to another, to sleep, only grudgingly setting his guitar aside. Every other moment, he wrapped his hands around his guitar like a ravenous lover, pushing her golden body to cries of ecstasy, never letting her rest. I hadn't considered what that love meant for us, the ones who loved him most.

Music sustained my father, and he would follow it wherever it led. He didn't need us the way we needed him. To be complete, he needed only to play. He was tapped into a higher source, and we were tapped into him, which wasn't fair to any of us. I was something that happened to him, not something he craved or created out of a need. He handled my arrival with grace and warmth, and my mother always insists that I was the one thing they always agreed on, but he continued down his path. When the road became dark and dangerous, he told us to go.

We stayed at my grandparents' house for several months, in a guest bedroom downstairs from Donna's teenage bedroom. It was the hardest time for Mom. With a word, Duane had stripped her of everything that had come to her so magically, and she was back where she started.

By Easter, I was running with abandon. Grandpa took pictures of me in the yard, hunting for eggs with a basket on my arm. I carried a tiny red chair around and sat on it proudly, dressed in a pale green dress with a petticoat. Donna mailed prints to Linda, Candy, and Joanie, and when they arrived, they asked Duane if he'd like to see them.

He said no. "Has she married a floorwalker at Belk's yet?" he asked Joanie bitterly.

But Joanie saw him ease open the drawer of the sideboard in the dining room where she left the pictures of me when he thought he was alone. He kept them all.

Duane tosses out a little slide riff and says into the mic, "Test one . . . I hope this comes out pretty good. We're cutting our third album here tonight!"

It wasn't an easy sell, convincing Atlantic Records to give a band with two underperforming albums behind them the chance to record a live album. Live albums were usually released to satisfy eager fans waiting for new studio albums from highly successful artists, but capturing the power of the Allman Brothers Band in front of a crowd had become the band's ultimate ambition. With Phil Walden's help, they were able to convince Atlantic Records that it was an important next step. When they were cooking in front of a crowd, no one could deny them. It might be just the thing they needed to really break through commercially.

The first thought was that they would record at the Warehouse in New Orleans, one of their favorite places to play, but the

Fillmore East remained the crown jewel of the Brothers' touring schedule, and New York City won out. The theater had fantastic acoustics, the audience was always passionate, and Bill Graham had assembled an incredible crew of people who worked with skill and devotion. Dickey called the Fillmore East the Carnegie Hall of rock and roll. The room was a little rough and dusty but still beautiful, with elaborate murals and gold-painted plaster flourishes. A velvet curtain was raised when performances began and the rows of seats encouraged the crowd to sit and listen rather than wandering the floor and socializing.

In 1926, the theater at 105 Second Avenue was called the Commodore, part of a stretch of venues called the Jewish Rialto, where vaudeville, burlesque, and plays were performed in both Yiddish and English, drawing crowds from the Lower East Side. Then Loews purchased the theater in the forties and films were screened there until the popularity of Hollywood movies demanded larger venues. In the early sixties, it once again became a live music venue called the Village Theater. Jaimoe first played the Village Theater with Otis Redding in 1966. He said it felt like the spirits of players from the past hung out there, looking for bodies to play through. In 1968, Bill Graham decided to expand on the phenomenal success of his theater in San Francisco's Fillmore district and bring all he had learned to Manhattan.

Graham made sure the place was run with a great deal of love and care, even arranging for small touches like flowers in the dressing rooms provided by a local florist in exchange for an ad in the programs. Graham was passionate about supporting musicians and wanted to expose audiences to a variety of artists they might not find on their own. The shows were often eclectic: Laura Nyro paired with Miles Davis, or Albert King with the Flying Burrito Brothers.

There were two shows a night on Fridays and Saturdays, plus shows midweek for auditions, special events, and benefits. Because there wasn't a curfew, the late show often went until dawn. With Ratner's, the legendary Jewish dairy restaurant, open twenty-four hours next door, Second Avenue and Sixth Street in New York City was a hot spot all night long.

Graham went to great lengths to provide innovative solutions to some basic challenges. Rolling platforms and risers were built to speed equipment changes between bands. A system of closed-circuit TVs were set up to monitor the stage, and the crew communicated via headsets. The sound system was built for the space and customized to address the challenges loud rock bands created. The sound crew set up a dozen open mics onstage, and used a multichannel mixing board equipped with faders that rivaled some recording studios. The speakers were specially built to withstand high volume without losing detail in the upper registers. These kinds of considerations seem obvious, but Bill Graham was the first to implement them.

The psychedelic light show was as important to the vibe as the music, even getting top billing on the marquee outside. Overseen by Joshua White, the pioneering lighting crew were performers, creating a visual accompaniment in tandem with the music. Four people worked together on a two-level scaffold and two others worked as soloists from the box seats above the exits in front of the house. The scaffold was built against the brick back wall of the theater behind the stage, and the projections were cast onto the back of a special scrim using the only lights powerful enough to show clearly: the giant bulbs used in landing lights on airport runways. Color oils they tinted themselves were swirled in convex glass dishes taken from the faces of large clocks, and the layers of wild undulating shapes approximated the psychedelic visions of a hallucinating mind. They took cameras out into the city and filmed trains and traffic, used vintage cartoon reels, color wheels made from bicycle spokes covered in transparent gels, and pieces of broken mirror to bounce light around. The crew of six was led by a master mixer at his own control board. The Fillmore East was a community, and the audience was so committed, they would sleep on the street outside to get tickets to see popular acts.

On March 12, 1971, the Allman Brothers Band rolled through the East Village like kings, passing out packs of cigarettes and jugs of cheap wine to the tramps on Bowery from the open door of the Winnebago—Berry's idea—to spread the love. Tom Dowd arranged for a fully equipped, multitrack studio built inside a truck to be parked beside the theater, and ran cables through the back door and onto the stage.

The Fillmore East record is a jubilant and vital document of what made the Allman Brothers such special live performers. The album retains the spontaneity of the playing as it happened; it feels like it is unfolding as you listen. The songs are so complex, so varied, that you can hear new moments with every listen. One of my favorite games, started before I was aware I was doing it, is listening to one instrument at a time. Follow Berry from his solo in "Whipping Post" through the rest of the song. Just stay with him, pushing the guitars into the periphery. You can do it with each man, and it reveals the truth that they were all soloists in shifting moments, surprisingly creative and varied. Duane's solo in the center of "You Don't Love Me," played without accompaniment, ends in a long, drawn-out note, stretched to its tense extreme, then another that resolves perfectly. When Twiggs heard the album, he said, "Those were the two finest notes Duane ever played."

As Duane starts to take off again, a man's voice calls out, "Play all night!" and he winds his way through "Joy to the World" before landing with complete satisfaction and precision on the final note, a completed thought.

The album has been one of the places I find my father when I need him. My favorite way to listen is through headphones late at night, ideally on vinyl, my mother's copy from 1971. I have fallen asleep to the album hundreds of times; even the most rocking and intense moments soothe me; I imagine it is close to the feeling of hearing one's parents talking together in another room while falling asleep as a child. My father sounds so close, it brings me deep comfort.

The next best way to listen is while walking through New York City. The street life is a great counterpoint to the propulsive power of the songs, the faces and bodies ducking and weaving by like the tumbling notes in my ears. I feel Duane strutting beside me, and I broaden my stride to keep pace with him, speeding and slowing with the rhythms of the songs.

The album gives as much as you are willing to take from it— a blasting party, light and fun, or an exploration of your own yearnings and desires. It is a perfect trigger, a way in to your dreams, and I swear as many times as I have listened, I still hear new things. It is never the same twice, unfolding like a feast before me every time.

After the shows, the band grabbed some takeout and headed for Broadway and Sixtieth Street, to Atlantic Studios to listen to show tapes with Tom Dowd over a few beers. They decided which version of each song was best and made the set list for the next night to cover all the bases. The quality of the recordings and the experience of listening with Tom together after playing was really fantastic. While you were in it, you didn't stop to reflect on what you were doing, and when it was over, there was no way to recall everywhere you'd been, so they were blowing their own minds a bit. It sounded damn good.

The band played at the high level captured by the album five and six days a week, as Duane reminded an interviewer. The album was a document of two shows among hundreds. Tom pieced together a song or two, notably marrying two versions of "You Don't Love Me" to keep the best solos from each night together, but it was basically untouched, captured as played.

They soon realized it would take four album sides to do the shows justice, and editing the songs was never discussed by the band and Tom. But Atlantic wasn't thrilled with the idea of releasing a double album. Jerry Wexler thought a few of the jams were excessive, and he suggested they be shaved down for radio play. Berry insisted it be sold at a special low price to keep it within their fans' reach. Walden and the band fought for it and won; it would be a double album, priced as a single album.

Johnny Sandlin explained that the players were mixed in the positions they stood in onstage, something I can hear clearly but never consciously thought about, and it really gives a listener the feeling of standing in front of them. It also creates a spatial separation between the two guitars that allows you to appreciate their interplay.

It was also a shining accomplishment for Gregg. Jaimoe said it best: "Gregg is every bit the genius that Duane was." His phrasing, his raw honesty is the hook, the way in for everyone. Tom Dowd mixed in the sounds from the crowd between songs, and you can feel the intimacy of the space, and the excitement builds as the show goes on. Members of the audience call out songs they want to hear, and whistle and shout.

Jaimoe once described the experience this way: The moment you think you know all there is to know is the moment things get interesting. What you thought was the solid ground beneath your feet was the still surface of a deep sea. Playing wasn't just a matter of mastery. Duane had learned the lesson of the Delta blues, how a single naked melody could be completely captivating if a musician was willing to infuse each note with emotion. There was nowhere to hide, and if you weren't feeling it, no one else would, either. When that kind of stripped down soulfulness is where each player begins, when their direct and emotionally honest playing is electrified and laid over driving rhythms, the music becomes vital, a torrent, a force of nature.

On one night of the run, Duane invited Jaimoe's friend from home, Juicy Carter, a saxophone player, to sit in with the band. When Tom heard the warbling horn bleeding into his mics, atonal jazz riffs sliding in between the guitars sounding like a damn traffic accident, he put a stop to it. Duane thought they were smoking hot. He didn't want Juicy to go, but the playback didn't lie. It was one too many cooks in the kitchen, and the whole third night was essentially unusable.

When the album was released in July, the buzz about it soon turned into a roar. Friends shared the experience, passing joints while stretched out on floors in front of stereo speakers, sitting in parked cars, listening to all four sides play out on late-night radio.

Albhy Galuten said, "During this period, young people really cared about music and really listened to it. If a new album came out, you would take it home and sit down in front of the speakers and you would do nothing else except listening to it. So, you could believe then that you could write a song to end world hunger. There was this sense that there was so much power in music because it was in the zeitgeist, and that's part of what made the music great. You were making it for people thinking, *They are going to get this.* And it's going to mean something to them, and it did mean something to them. So you were stimulated in the creative process by your audience. It was so incredible and so dynamic."

Young guitarists started approaching the licks like they were cracking codes, sharing their breakthroughs with one another as they learned. The record was a spark that lit fires in generations of young players, including each guitarist who would later grow up to become members of later incarnations of the Allman Brothers Band. *At Fillmore East* carved a path for itself out in the world and it was paved with gold. The Brothers were awarded their first gold record in September 1971.

"Dickey said something interesting one time, a cool analogy," Jaimoe told me. "We were in the Winnebago, maybe we'd been drinking, and he said, 'If this was 1850 and we was running around the country like this, we'd be Jesse James and the Cole Younger boys.' What a good analogy. They were the baddest cats at what they were doing whether it was right, wrong, or indifferent, and so were we." The analogy would soon prove prophetic; they became outlaws.

A little over a week after their triumphant run at the Fillmore, the Brothers took a wrong turn in the Winnie on a night drive from Baton Rouge, Louisiana, to Jackson, Mississippi, that landed them in a rural Alabama jail. To be honest about it, Red Dog took the bad turn, which made sense when you factored in the mescaline. One minute he was driving, trying to maintain while the white line was waving back at him, and the next he was rousing from a nap in the backseat of a rental car in the parking lot of a little diner in broad daylight. Well, shit. He was worn-out and he could see through the window that everyone was accounted for, no harm done. Except Dickey, where was he? He was doubled over puking behind the Winnie within sight of a table full of country cops. Red Dog lay back down and closed his eyes.

Ironically, it wasn't the half dozen bedraggled hippies ordering breakfast in the middle of the day or the sick young man ruining everyone else's meal in the parking lot that caused the hassle. It was Jaimoe simply walking in the door that made them decide to shake these boys down. One of the waitresses said in a loud voice that she wasn't going to serve the nigger, and the guys knew it was time to go.

They had been through this shit before. In fact, many small clubs made them sign race riders before they unloaded their gear, a legal declaration that they were responsible for bringing a black man on the premises and would be responsible for any damage that ensued.

Red Dog woke up choking on the fatty underside of a sweaty cop's arm reaching over his neck to pull his stash out of his pocket. He was holding some pot and a bottle of penicillin for the drip, a hazard of the road and his deep and abiding love of the ladies.

While Red Dog and Dickey were being frisked and put into the police car, the rest of the band quietly repaired to a rental car that was parked out of view of the diner and tried to get away. Gregg had a case filled with contraband and began tossing small bags of drugs out the window as they drove. As soon as the police realized the men had taken off, they sent another police cruiser after them, and everyone reunited in the Grove Hill, Alabama, jail. The band and crew were put in four cells, except Jaimoe, who was held in a separate cell, segregated out. The mood was jovial at first, as they took up singing every prison tune they could think of at the tops of their voices. They drew a crowd of local kids to the windows, and Red Dog decided to give them a real show. He stripped naked and did his most uncanny impression of a wild gorilla in a cage. He was still tripping his balls off.

The little jail decided to move them over to the county jail in Jackson, Alabama; they would be better equipped to deal with such freakishness.

It took three days and a few grand to liberate the band, with the help of John Condon, the same lawyer they had called on to defend Twiggs. All in all, it wasn't such a bad scene. For some reason, the Winnie and their suitcases were never searched, and the small amounts of contraband they had squirreled away in their pockets didn't amount to much. Luckily, they had money to spread around, since road manager Willie Perkins refused to turn over the briefcase with the band's earnings inside. He wore it handcuffed to his wrist and wouldn't give up the key to Christ himself. They were kept in the black side of the segregated jail and they made friends with the help of a couple of cartons of cigarettes and some candy. They played cards and told tall tales. They talked their way out of a few scuffles, and were back on the road and on to the next gig as soon as they were free.

By the end of June, forty or so shows later, they were called back to the Fillmore East. Bill Graham had decided to close the theater and he wanted to give it a proper send-off. Music was being corporatized. In Graham's mind, Woodstock had changed the game significantly, showing the kind of power rock and roll had to draw people by the hundreds of thousands. Many musicians and their labels set their sights on big paydays, and priced themselves out of reach of small places like the Fillmores East and West. Graham saw the writing on the wall, and decided to get out of the business of owning venues. He wrote a detailed goodbye letter, explaining his thinking, published in *The Village Voice*. In it, he decried greedy artists, managers, and promoters, apathetic audiences, and the press for portraying so negatively his high standards and toughness. It's a remarkable and principled statement that says a lot about Graham's values. He ended by saying he was tired and needed a rest. He then wrote:

> The rock scene in this country was created by a need felt by the people, expressed by the musicians, and, I hope, aided to some degree by the efforts of the Fillmores. But whatever has become of that scene, wherever it turned into—the music industry of festivals, 20,000-seat halls, miserable production quality, and second-rate promoters—however it went wrong—please, each of you, stop and think whether or not you allowed it, whether or not you supported it regardless of how little you received in return.

"That's all Folks" was spelled out on the marquee and the final show was scheduled for June 27, 1971.

Jonny Podell told me the twenty-nine people who worked the Fillmore East voted for the bands they wanted to play. They chose the Allman Brothers Band to be the final act, Bill's absolute favorite band. "Bill loved three things: money, music and the Allman Brothers Band, and not in that order," Jonny said. "He might have put the Brothers first."

The band played for two nights leading up to the final night, and by all accounts, the second night was stunning. Graham turned the house lights down, put a spotlight on the mirrored ball hanging from the high ceiling, and filled the room with spinning starlight. The band played for hours, lulling the audience into a waking dream. It was almost four hours before the band finally touched back down. When the theater's heavy doors were at last pushed open by the silent, awestruck audience, a single shaft of pale light broke through. Bill Graham stood beside Duane and they marveled at the beam of morning sunlight swirling with dust motes, coming in through the out door.

"It's like church," Duane said.

The epic final night included sets by the Beach Boys, Country Joe, Mountain, Albert King, J. Geils Band, and Edgar Winter. It was broadcast live on WNEW radio. A red rose was pinned to each seat, and admission was by invitation only. Jo Jane witnessed Duane negotiating with the Beach Boys and Bill Graham over who would play last, and Duane wasn't budging. She could see how strong and direct he still was, the way he held his shoulders square with his hands on his hips and met people's eyes. He could be surrounded by men twice his weight and a foot taller than him, and he never backed down. He was the same tough kid he'd always been, and she saw his young self shining through him, his essential energy still so strong. He prevailed; the Beach Boys played first.

Graham introduced the Brothers on the next and final night of music at the Fillmore East:

> In the years we've been doing this, the introductions have been short, and this one is going to be short but a little longer than usual. The last few days we've had the privilege of working with this particular group, and in the past year or so we've had them on both coasts a number of times, in all that time, I've never heard the kind of music that this group plays. And last night, we had the good fortune of having them get on stage at about 2:30 or 3 o'clock and they walked out of here at 7 o'clock in the morning, and it's not just that they played quantity, from my amateur ears, in all my life I've never heard the kind of music that this group plays . . . the finest contemporary music. We are going to round it off with the best of them all, the Allman Brothers Band.

The band kicked into "Statesboro Blues."

. . .

Joanie stayed in Macon long after we left, and Duane kept an eye out for her. He made sure she was included in the group of friends and family invited to New York for the closing shows at the Fillmore. It was her first time in the big city. She even had her own room at One Fifth Avenue, the hotel where everyone stayed. When Duane saw her walking up the stairs backstage in her short skirt and tall boots, he called her into the dressing room and scolded her. "Hey! What are you sniffing around for? If you want something, you ask us for it. Don't you take anything from anybody you don't know, hear me?" He waved her toward a little pile of brown powder on a mirror.

"I wasn't looking for anything!" she insisted. "I was just walking around!"

Heroin was showing in their playing. At the Fillmore shows, the first night was great, the second night was stupendous, and the third night was a sweaty mess; they sounded like shit, as far as Big Linda was concerned. "I mean, they were always good, don't get me wrong . . . better than good, but they were exhausted and they were starting to get sick. Drug sick. We all knew how incredible they could be, and that wasn't it."

Back at the hotel after the gig, Jo Jane sat sideways with her legs draped over the arm of a chair facing Duane, who was leaning against the headboard with his acoustic guitar in his lap. He played a lilting, delicate tune that rambled on for a while. "A song I wrote for my daughter," he told her.

When Jo Jane shared this story with me years later, I immediately asked, "Was it 'Little Martha'?" I knew that Duane had dedicated it to Dixie, but Linda and my mom always told me the tune was around long before he and Dixie met. The song moved me so much, I wanted it to be for me.

"No, it wasn't. It was sweeter and lighter than that. Almost classical sounding. I wish I could remember it to hum it for you. I wonder if it would come to me under hypnosis. It's still in my mind somewhere," Jo Jane said.

Duane had a session at Atlantic the day after the Fillmore

closing, with jazz flutist Herbie Mann. Mann had an apartment overlooking Central Park, and when Delaney and Bonnie played an outdoor concert there, he was lured across the avenue by the sound.

"Herbie Mann came up onstage to jam, along with Mitch Mitchell, King Curtis, and Duane," Bonnie said. "Dave Mason was there and some unbelievable Afro-Cuban percussionist. But what I remember most about the show was Delaney. It started to rain a little bit. He gets up out there with his guitar on his shoulder and he started to invoke himself to the sky and throws his arms up and says, 'Oh Lord, take this rain away, we need to do a concert.' The rain stopped. He stopped the rain! Then I thought, *I can never live with this man! He thinks he is Moses! He stopped the freakin' rain!*"

Duane and Mann made a connection that day that resulted in an invitation to play on Mann's album *Push Push.*

In the stripped-down beginning of "Spirit in the Dark," Duane explores melody lines like a storyteller slowly building a narrative. He slips right into a fluid interplay with flute and horns. Much is made of the fact that Herbie Mann was a jazz artist, and this was Duane's foray into a new genre of music, but his approach is his own. The Brothers improvised in a jazz mode and Duane didn't have to stretch very far to find his way into the music Mann was serving, a funky collection of songs elevated by the unlikely inclusion of Duane's electric guitar. In the control room, listening to playbacks, Duane told Herbie that one of his dreams was about to come true. In a few days, his band was going to play the legendary Newport Jazz Festival on the Fourth of July, and what's more, they were on a bill with Aretha Franklin, B. B. King, and Ray Charles . . . not to mention Rahsaan Roland Kirk! He could not wait!

At Newport, the day before the Brothers were supposed to play, the gates were rushed by a huge crowd wanting to get in for free. They overwhelmed the stage and destroyed equipment while Dionne Warwick was performing "What the World Needs Now Is Love." The rest of the festival was canceled.

On July 5, the band traveled to Atlantic City to play a week of shows on the Steel Pier. It was pitched to them as a sort of working vacation. Everyone hoped staying in one spot by the ocean for a week would be conducive to a little healing and relaxation. There was talk of kicking drugs there. But Atlantic City was depressing even as they approached. The pier stretched way out into the ocean, covered with concession stands and arcade games that had seen better days. Half-drunk parents milled around with their sticky-faced, whiny kids. This wasn't a crowd that gave two shits about music. By the first morning, Duane and Gregg were fighting over the last bag of dope. It was a bad trip.

A single day of drug sickness in the heat was enough to crush their collective spirits. Duane soon sent Red Dog and Kim to procure a little comfort in town.

The stage where the band set up was just one stop along the boardwalk, sandwiched between rides and games. The highlight of the Steel Pier was a tower fifty feet high set in front of a huge pool of water. The crowd was waiting for a girl in a bathing suit and goggles to climb on the back of her fearless horse and dive.

"You have got to be shitting me," Duane said.

"No, sir. Come and see," answered Red Dog.

Red Dog and Duane stood with their arms crossed and their heads tipped back, staring up at the little chute that jutted over the edge of the scaffold.

"She's a pretty little thing," Red Dog said. "How did she end up here doing this?"

"The horse or the chick?" Duane asked. Red Dog laughed.

"The question is, how the hell did we end up here?" Duane said.

The girl and her pony went down a short slide into thin air. It was strangely beautiful, the horse and rider hanging in the blue sky for a moment. Then there was a horrible splash.

"Sure as shit ain't Newport," Red Dog said with a grin.

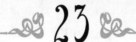

23

The Brothers were at the peak of their power now, as pure and searing as fire onstage. They only had one rule—play hard, bringing all of your strength, intuition, and knowledge to every performance. You can hear the quantum leap they took musically by listening to a song like "Dreams," first from 1969 on their studio album, and then a later live version, like their show at the State University of New York at Stony Brook on September 19, 1971. The song, which was ambitious and haunting in the studio, has a new expansiveness two years later. It is the difference between a photograph and an action movie.

Jaimoe says their story was in the songs' development over time. "What Ornette Coleman was doing in 1959 with Ed Blackwell was basically what we were doing and still do to this day," he said. "A good example is, Twiggs came up with this thing, a Donovan song, 'There Is a Mountain.' Twiggs and Duane played it, then Dickey and Duane played it. He took the melody to 'Mama's Little Baby

Loves Short'nin' Bread,' and Dickey's melody answered and made statements to Duane's melody. It's very, very simple. It's like Ping-Pong. Which way is the ball going? That ball is going to go a lot of different places until you learn how to control it. Every which direction the ball is going is where you go; the ball controls the game. You have to learn how to control it. You have to learn how to know where you're going. When you learn how to do it, that's when things get really interesting. Well, you think you know how to do it, and you have a pretty good idea but it becomes more and more interesting the more you know." We were sitting in his hotel room after a show at the Beacon Theatre in New York in 2013, talking and listening to jazz. I watched him arrange a pile of magazines on the coffee table in front of him, piling two and then three on top of one another, then placing a single one off to the side. He began playing a complex little riff with his drumsticks, hitting the different magazines and the edge of the table, and each surface made a slightly different tone. He said, "I've been working on this pattern for forty years."

Playing live for two solid years was one source of their power, and the other was listening. The band listened to music all day every day, and drew from the most challenging and innovative players across the board. Listening to masterful musicians fed their imaginations and recharged their spirits when the road wore them down.

In August, word came that one of the great players who had inspired Duane and became his true friend had been killed. Curtis Ousley, the legendary saxophone player known as King Curtis, was stabbed to death in New York City when he tried to run off a couple of drug dealers on his stoop. Duane attended his funeral. Aretha Franklin sang and Stevie Wonder played. Jesse Jackson performed the service at St. Peter's Lutheran Church in Manhattan.

A week or so after the funeral, Duane stepped up to the microphone, "About King Curtis, that was one of the finest cats there ever was. He was just right on top of getting next to the young people, you know. It's a shame. If y'all get a chance to listen to that album he made out at Fillmore West, boy, it was incredible. It's unbelievable, the power of that and the emotional stature that man had. He was an incredible human being. I hope that whoever it was that did it knows what they did, it's a terrible thing."

They played "You Don't Love Me," and during the solo Duane played unaccompanied, slowly building a lovely, subtle bridge into "Soul Serenade." The band joined him in a tribute to King Curtis while the audience cheered, clapping along. They lingered inside the song Duane had recorded with his friend, the optimistic, sunny melody flowing out of him, then Dickey turned a phrase around and pulled them smoothly back into "You Don't Love Me." They created a heartbreaking, spontaneous tribute for a man they all admired in a way he would have loved.

The band had strong songs for the new album, but they felt a new kind of pressure, now that their live album was such a success. With Tom Dowd's help, they wanted to record a studio album that could stand toe-to-toe with *At Fillmore East,* and they felt they were on the right track.

Dickey wanted Gregg to sing "Blue Sky," the love song Dickey had written for his new wife, Sandy Wabegijig. Duane wouldn't hear it. He told Dickey his voice would suit the song perfectly, and the beauty of the sentiment was all his to share. It was the first recording the Brothers released with Dickey singing lead, a taste of things to come.

"Stand Back" was a real barnburner with funky swagger to spare, and Duane loved it. It felt like something of a new direction for the Brothers, a tight groove they could easily imagine on the radio. As soon as he got back to Macon, Duane took it to the studio to play it for Johnny Sandlin. He stood by Johnny's chair with his head bent and listened in the control room. They sat there, tapping their feet and listening with their eyes closed, so proud. This new album was going to be huge. They could feel it.

Albhy Galuten, who once again worked as an engineer on the

album, regretted that they hadn't kept the outtakes of these *Eat a Peach* sessions. "In those days they didn't keep outtakes because tape was expensive, and so they would roll back over previous takes. I remember on 'Blue Sky,' there were three takes, and the reason we chose the take we did was because it had Dickey's best solo and it was Dickey's song. That was not official, it's not like we said that, it was just an unspoken thing between me and Tommy: Hey wow, Dickey is really beginning to come into his own, because everybody was in Duane's shadow. Clearly Duane was so much the leader of the band. 'Stand Back' was originally called 'Calico' before the words were written, and we did three takes on that, and every one of Duane's solos were entirely different. Not like most musicians, who would improvise a little for a couple bars. Of course the All-man Brothers did that for all their orchestrated parts. Duane and Dickey would do harmonies, but Duane would just play stuff that was totally different every time."

In late August, Duane returned to Muscle Shoals to record with Cowboy, a band that Scott Boyer, a member of the 31st of February, had formed with Tommy Talton, and which Duane had brought to Phil Walden's attention.

"He played great on 'Please Be with Me,'" Scott Boyer said. "There were jaws dropping all over the studio on Jackson Highway. Session players had to build a track and it would take hours and Duane didn't have the patience to sit through all that. He wanted to come in and lay something on top of it. He was like, 'Play the track and I'll put something on it and then I'm out, I've got places to go.'" He wanted to play on something brand-new.

Duane told Scott, "I don't want to add to a track you already have worked out, because you already have three guitars, and I'll never find a place to play, so let's start with a brand-new song."

They tossed out four or five tunes before Scott said, "Well, I've got this one I wrote last night."

Scott had stayed behind at the motel while the band went out to dinner the night before. He picked up his notebook.

"I wrote stream of thought. In about fifteen minutes I had

eleven stanzas that didn't rhyme and didn't make sense, and it was like a puzzle. I threw the pad on the floor and went to bed." Scott played Duane what he had worked out, and Duane thought it was a beautiful song.

"I thought it was stupid, the line 'I sit here lying in my bed'? How can you sit and lie in bed at the same time?" Scott said.

Johnny Sandlin, who produced the session, said, "I thought it meant I'm sitting in my bed, lying to myself about the way things are."

"Wow! That's deep! That's good! I like that!" Scott said.

"Duane and I sat side by side and played together, both facing Johnny. George [Clark] played upright bass, which he never did before, and he did it pretty well. We recorded that night, the night that Duane came into town. They overdubbed my vocal, along with Tommy and George Clark singing harmonies, and it was done."

Duane's Dobro was buzzing; the bridge was out of alignment or something and Johnny had someone come in and fix it. They recorded another take in the morning with it fixed. Scott didn't think the new take was as good and he told Johnny he wanted to use the take from the night before.

"It's buzzin'," Johnny said.

"I don't care. The buzzing doesn't bother me. He played great on it," Scott said, so they used the first version. (Years later, Johnny asked Scott if he could use the second take of "Please Be with Me" on the first Duane Allman anthology. "Fine. I'm over it," Scott said.)

"I tried to get him to play on 'All My Friends,'" Scott recalled. "The way I did it on the Cowboy album, there were seven-beat measures in the verse, and there were seven-beat measures in the solo, and Duane did that solo until he got so mad, he took his guitar off and threw it down on the floor and he stormed out of the studio. Then Eddie Hinton couldn't do it and Tommy couldn't either, so I finally put a violin part on it, and it wasn't very good, but I had to put something there. They couldn't get that extra beat to recycle in their heads. They kept losing the time. Duane was playing great stuff, but he couldn't get from point A to point B. Somewhere along the way he'd mentally trip and it was hard to watch it.

"You never saw Duane unable to play. It was the only time I ever saw it.

"He was an emotional guy. He wore his feelings on his sleeve. He'd get excited about stuff, but not mad. Oh my God, I wished to God I never wrote that song, I felt so bad."

The pace of the Allman Brothers' touring didn't let up for anything, not even the completion of their album. They were traveling to Miami whenever they had a few free days in a row. Duane, Dickey, and Berry recorded a little instrumental tune at Criteria. The melody had been growing inside Duane since they had first started playing together, little traces recognizable from a hundred nights spent with their acoustic guitars, Dickey with his Martin, Berry with his Hummingbird, and Duane with his Dobro. They had perched together on the edge of narrow hotel room beds, sat at the edge of the water at Idlewild, and rested on their amps in the music room at the Big House. Many of their songs had been born that way, letting a simple tune lead wherever it wanted to go. At first they cut a version with Berry playing bass, but they agreed that the little tune didn't need the weight. "Little Martha" had a peaceful, rambling quality that only wanted the two guitars lightly rolling through.

It was the first song Duane had ever written for the Allman Brothers and it was the last song he ever recorded in a studio.

Twiggs had been in jail in Buffalo for a few months when John Condon decided to bring in Andrew Watson, a Michigan law professor, medical doctor, and psychiatrist. He felt they needed Watson to be there for the trial, but it would be a year before he had time in his calendar. They agreed to delay the trial for a year. The jail was rougher than prison. It operated on a shoestring and had no real facilities. Twiggs told his family the New York state prison at Attica would be better when he got there. All in all, Twiggs spent almost eighteen months in jail awaiting trial. The Brothers stayed in contact with his legal team and with Twiggs through letters. Twiggs's brother Skoots brought him a copy of *At Fillmore East*. On the back cover, above the heads of the roadies who posed all together on the road cases was a picture of Twiggs. There was no way they would leave him out of their family portrait.

When Watson was free, he and Condon got to work putting a defense together. They wanted to trace Twiggs's behavior and personality from birth until the night at Aliotta's Lounge. They had Twiggs write a personal chronology, and interviewed his family, the band, and many of his friends. In the end, they felt confident that they could show he had no option but to commit the crime.

When Condon came to Macon to visit the Lyndon family home, he began by stating that his hourly rate began from the moment he left his office until he returned there, travel time included. As far as the Lyndons understood, Phil Walden was paying Twiggs's legal fees, but most likely he was billing the band.

The trial was slated to begin in September 1971. Condon said it would likely take two weeks, because he had waived a jury trial. Watson suggested that the two state psychiatrists jointly interview Twiggs. They agreed that he had had a psychotic episode brought on by the stress of life on the road with the band. Berry Oakley was assigned the task of testifying personally to the effects of life on the road.

As soon as Berry and Kim landed in Buffalo, they asked a friend there to help them find drugs. He took them to a local pharmacy. They were dope sick because they knew better than to risk flying while holding. After a ridiculous negotiation, with the pharmacist telling them he could only give them drugs if they said it was for pain, Berry said, "Fuck Payne, the dope is for me!" Kim says they were only given enough to feed their enormous tolerance and the week they spent there was fraught with sickness.

On the stand, Berry paused for long moments to process his thoughts before answering. The state's attorney was getting frustrated. He asked Berry how many times he had taken LSD: more than twenty-five, fifty, one hundred times? Finally Berry said, "Lots more than a hundred times."

While he talked and spaced out, Berry kept pulling out a roll of tablets and popping them in his mouth. Finally, the prosecutor demanded to know what drug he was taking, in plain view of the court.

Berry smiled and said, "Tums, for my tummy."

Twiggs was found not guilty by reason of insanity and was sentenced to six additional months in a state mental hospital.

The Brothers played two nights at Winterland in San Francisco on October 8 and 9, and after the second night's encore, Duane snatched his strap off and turned his back on the crowd, quickly walking into the wings, wound up and ready for running. It was hard to find a place to put the immense energy that surged through him when the band built to such intensity and then stopped. It could feel like a free fall, and the only stable place was inside another song. It hadn't felt right all night. It didn't get off the ground. He felt alone, out on a limb, and no one followed where he was pointing. Butch brushed by him as he left the stage and Duane grabbed his arm and said, "I need to talk to you!"

"Okay, man, let's go back to the hotel and we'll talk," Butch said.

An hour later, Duane was pounding on his door. "When Dickey gets up to play, y'all are pounding away, backing him up, and when I get up there you're laying back and not pushing at all!" Duane shouted as he shouldered his way into Butch's room.

Butch met Duane's angry eyes and raised his voice, something he had never done before. "Duane, you're so fucked up you're not giving us anything."

Duane looked down at his hands. They were shaking. He knew Butch was telling him the truth. They sat together in silence for a minute or two.

"This shit has got to stop," Duane said quietly, and put a hand on Butch's back as he walked out the door. "Thanks, brother."

Heroin had gained the upper hand, in ways I'm not sure Duane believed it could. He had fallen prey to the idea that snorting it was safe and his abhorrence for needles would protect him from serious addiction, but the lie of that was starting to show.

Jerry Wexler and his partner Ahmet Ertegun took Duane and Gregg into a back room at a party in New York and told them they needed to talk. They didn't waste a moment with polite chat. They told the brothers they had seen this bullshit all before and they were not going to sit by and watch two young, talented men kill themselves. They were squandering their talent and their opportunities. They had watched helplessly while Ray Charles struggled with heroin. It had killed Charlie Parker. They would be no different. The shit had to stop. Wexler and Ertegun were self-made millionaires who had launched the careers of an astounding number of artists. To be scolded like a couple of kids deeply embarrassed the brothers. Gregg felt sure all they really cared about was Duane, because of the way they spoke directly to him. He felt invisible next to his big brother, and guilty that he had been the first one to bring dope around.

Duane was resolved. The next time he spoke to either of these men, he would be clear-eyed and sober. And he would make sure everyone in his band was clean, too.

He was the bridge between the band and the businessmen. He was the one who started the train rolling and he was responsible for all of them.

It bothered him that he hadn't seen clearly the moment when heroin started working against him, beaching him on the other side of the warm wave where there was only cold grit and need. Around this time, he told Jonny Podell, "I'm not doing heroin anymore, heroin is doing me." He had called Podell to ask him to sort out rehab beds for everyone. He arranged for Duane, Berry, Gregg, Kim, and Red Dog to enter Linwood-Bryant Hospital, in Buffalo, to undergo medically supervised detox. The bill is marked October

20, 1971. Dickey agreed to clean up and would take care of it himself. I believe Jaimoe and Butch did the same.

Gregg told me very simply that drugs would have come between him and his brother eventually. Drugs were the thing that would have driven them apart, he said. It made me consider how different their personalities were. Gregg was the dreamer, private, shy, and comfort-seeking, while Duane turned toward the world; he wanted to engage with it and sought a sense of purpose. Gregg could retreat into himself and his high, with a woman and a bottle, and become completely unreachable. As heavily as Duane was into drugs, he wasn't an escapist, and when it began to interfere with his music, he knew enough to put an end to it.

Gregg didn't show up to fly to Buffalo, and Duane called him from the airport, furious. Bunky Odom, who was traveling with them, overheard Duane say, "You are not fit to fry fish for my band."

Red Dog went to visit Twiggs in the mental hospital while they were all in Buffalo for rehab. He and Twiggs were left alone and they had a nice visit. Twiggs told him an incredible story about a man who hadn't said a word inside for more than twenty years, until Twiggs convinced him it would be a gas to surprise everyone by simply saying hello the next day, and the man agreed.

Duane didn't go to see Twiggs. He couldn't handle it.

When Duane got out of rehab, he went to Manhattan and called Ace and told him he wanted to take him fishing when he got back to Macon to tell him about it. He said he had learned a lot and wanted to share it. Ace was into meditation and yoga, and he could go deep in conversation. Duane was looking forward to a good long talk. They had plans to make.

He also called John Hammond and invited him to come hang out at his friend's place on Fifth Avenue, where he was staying for a couple of days.

"It wasn't often that I got to hang out with him," John recalled, "but when I did it was just terrific because we talked music and blues and he knew the guys that I knew and I hipped him to some guys, he hipped me to some guys. . . . It was just terrific. I was about to go to play these shows in Canada," John said. He had a loft downtown on Broadway and they headed over to jam together and keep talking.

Duane was in a good space. During his week in Buffalo, he had let the last year sink in. He had never felt stronger or sharper. With *Layla, At Fillmore East,* and the new songs, he was doing the best work of his life and he didn't want to waste any more time chasing a high.

Having friends like John, musicians he admired, there was really no limit to the projects he could envision for the coming year. Money was starting to come in, and that would help buy a little downtime.

"He was talking about producing a record for me, and I was so excited," John said. "What a fantastic deal that was. He was beginning to talk percentages and stuff, which I didn't know anything about, but it all sounded really real and exciting. I had to leave early the next morning for Newfoundland and he was on his way home to Macon."

Still, they couldn't resist the chance to play together, and Duane had carried the Dobro over. They sat knee to knee and started rolling through tunes they both loved. The city was quiet in the time between night and earliest dawn, the sky still dark, but shifting every moment toward pale blue morning, only the momentary hiss of a passing taxi now and then, and soon enough the sound of the first steel gate being raised on a distant market. Duane loved the way John played. He had been living and breathing the blues, watching and learning from the best, a direct line from Charley Patton to Howlin' Wolf to John. He was holding down stages alone with his guitar the way the original masters did it. His deep, gravelly voice, the sound of his boot heel on the floor, and the wide resonance of his National. He loved it, the interplay between them.

"We jammed, and had ideas for songs . . . country blues, slide, Robert Johnson stuff: That was my inspiration. I had played with

Howlin' Wolf and Muddy Waters, and all these guys he admired so much, and he'd ask me about them. Duane would have been a great producer. He knew how to deal with sidemen, with players and producers, instinctively, I guess. He headed back to Macon, and that's the last time I saw him. He was a great person and I often think about him and wonder, what if? I feel richer for having known him. He was a cut above everybody else. He had such a vision of what he wanted to do, how to make songs work. He could really play anything. He had the facility to play and I admired him so much."

The next day was Linda Oakley's birthday, October 29, 1971, and Duane wanted to be home for her party.

Can you feel it?

The road is waiting and his wheels have started to roll. I can't stop them.

I stopped working. For months, I refused to write it, but it stayed there, just waiting for me. The road was laid under the first sentence I wrote about him years before. I idly picked up a good bottle of whisky at the grocery store and was walking out into the parking lot with the small brown paper bag before I realized what I'd done. I stood like my grandmother by my kitchen sink and swallowed a hot shot of the amber liquid like medicine for pain, and then another. If I couldn't slow down the story, I could slow my mind and numb my heart. I think of the recording of Duane's drunken voice, talking to a DJ, saying his grandfather soaked his feet in Jack Daniel's. I drink and then I sleep. When I wake up, the white page is still on the screen, the cursor blinking like a traffic light. The road is waiting and my father is moving now, picking up speed. I am reckless with rage. There is nowhere to turn.

You learn how to stay suspended in a moment when someone you love is taken from you. You imagine the moment just before the thing happens, and part of you lives there.

You camp out, pinning down the moment in time when everything was still okay, and hold it still with the weight of your body and the force of your will.

Part of me lives on Broadway, staring up at John Paul Hammond's lit window from the street. In the stillness when the wind shifts, I can hear the sound of them playing—two moans, one low and one high, threading through each other like smoke.

Anything is possible from where I stand. Duane will walk out the door soon.

He could turn right instead of left. He could miss his plane. Or decide to fly to Canada with John. Some small choice could change now, and everything would be different. Everything.

24

Linda Oakley, at my request, wrote me an account of October 29, 1971.

> They had just returned from Buffalo, N.Y. and the craziness of "getting clean" . . . getting together . . . and, at last turning over a new leaf. We'd been through a baptism of fire, reborn and renewed. The path before us was clear. We were headed for higher ground.
>
> It was so so good to be back home . . . "all in our places with sunshiny faces." . . . We had gotten a big orange pumpkin to celebrate the season. Berry and I took the Beebop out to the garden. In the warm afternoon we spread ourselves next to the fishpond and set to work scooping out the squishy pulp. Brittany clutched her Crayola pens, ready to draw a face for Daddy to carve.

We heard a car and a motorcycle pull into the back drive-way. Visitors! Peering over the hedges, I saw a huge bouquet of flowers held aloft by brother Duane. He graciously presented them with a big hug and a "Happy Birthday!" He and Dixie had just returned from a stopover in The Big Apple to see John Hammond. I was so touched and thrilled that they'd taken the time to come over and wish me well.

"Ah, a Jack-o-lantern I see! Can I cut out the eye, nose, and mouth?" That was typical Duane. We later wandered into the house as he rhapsodized about the great time they had with John Hammond.

". . . up all night with our acoustics, just riffin'. Such a righteous cat, man!" He was glowing.

Berry wanted me to show off my new patchwork knee high boots. He'd had them custom made for me at "Granny Takes a Trip" in New York and they'd just arrived via the post.

"You look so good in them boots it's enough to make my old pecker hard!" Again typical Duane: bold as brass! I took it as a great compliment. So did BO of course. "I hear you're takin' your old lady out jukin' tonight!" We were supposed to go to dinner while Aunt Candy entertained the Beebop.

Duane and Dixie headed home to recover from their travels and Candy left to run some errands. We started getting ready for our big date; just waiting for Candy to get back. That's when the phone rang.

They were all headed to Duane's place; him on his bike, Dixie behind him in the car, Candy following in Mehitable. The bike spun out and slid after glancing off the back of a truck. Dixie screeched to a halt and ran over to where he lay. Yes, Candy was right there. I can only imagine how surreal it was for them. She told us he'd been taken to the ER . . . they were there waiting to hear. . . . Berry and I just looked at each other. . . . He was just here. . . . How could this happen? NOT DUANE!

Promising to call as soon as he knew anything, Berry raced to join the gathering of brothers and sisters keeping vigil at Middle Georgia Hospital.

I went through the motions of fixing dinner for Brittany, music playing, I think it was Cowboy, as I sent out my prayers. Time slows down when you are waiting, waiting and wondering, worrying and wishing and hoping. At last I heard the back doors opening and closing. I ran to the stairs. As I stood on the landing, Berry was dragging up the stairs. The look on his face just pierced my heart. Candy came in right behind him and said,

"He's gone!"

Heartbreak. Broken. Devastation. Disbelief. We were the walking wounded, sometimes not even able to walk. Joanie and I talked about this yesterday. That night, she and Callahan and Berry and countless others filled Grant's Lounge to celebrate Duane . . . many toasts of tequila. I think they were expecting him to show up and tell them it was all a bad dream. When the bar shut down, Joan and Michael managed to walk to their apartment. Berry had driven his Z car. He almost made it safely home but he missed the turn into the driveway and hit the wall instead. The car was totaled but Berry was able to extricate himself. Luckily Willie was there and got him into the house by the time the police came. The rest of the night is a blur . . . thankfully.

I don't recall who spilled the beans about the surprise birthday party they had planned. Berry? Candy? That's what they were up to. Showing me the love again. More than that it was a time to get us all together again, celebrating the mission of the music. Drawing the family in . . . the circle. Well the circle had been broken.

Strangely it came together because we all loved Duane so much. You and Donna came back to Macon. Sisters had been apart too long. We had shared a lifetime in the blink of an eye. That was the most amazing funeral I have even been to. It was Glory Gospel Hour, a real revival. The roster of musicians and dignitaries alone would have made you think the King had died. "Long Live the King!"

We put on our finest frocks and danced and sang and clapped and cried our eyes out. The band and guests played for all they were worth, enough to wake the dead? I think Duane would have been pleased that it was a celebration of his life. Oh but the sight of that guitar, like a quiet sentinel on its stand . . .

My beautiful birthday bouquet was joined by a multitude of floral displays. Most impressive were the ones arranged in the image of his Les Paul. There were flowers all over the front porch of the Big House, spilling out into the front yard for all to see. Do you know, when those blossoms began to fade and dry, we made candles. We pinned the flowers around the surface of each one, then dipped them in the hot wax until they were firmly attached. We gave them as Christmas gifts. Tuffy's sister still has one.

Those Cowboys sang us through our grief with their angel harmonies . . . and lending his voice as only he could, there was Duane with us still.

I love you,
Linda

A flatbed truck began to make a wide turn in the middle of the intersection ahead. For a moment, it seemed that Duane could easily make it around the back end of the truck, but when it stopped short, he was forced under the hot, spinning body of his Harley and knocked unconscious. Candy and Dixie leaped from their cars and ran to him, calling out for help. Candy banged on the doors of several houses on the street, pleading for someone to call an ambulance. She pulled the covers off the seats of her car to cover him while they waited for help to come. He had a scratch on his face, but the worst of his injuries did not show. It took forever for the ambulance to come, its siren blaring.

Friends gathered at the hospital as word spread, and they were taken to a small waiting room. As Duane was wheeled down the corridor, Berry grasped his hand and bent down to kiss his cheek.

After a couple of hours, a male nurse came in and said Duane had a broken arm and bumped his head, so he might not play guitar for a while, but he would recover.

Butch went out to get a bottle of wine to celebrate, and Gregg and Chank, one of his closest friends in Macon, went back to his apartment on Orange Terrace to hang.

In fact, the golden time everyone had shared for the last two and a half years was narrowing down to a single golden hour, the small window of time when it still seemed possible that Duane would live. He was losing his battle in the operating room, and after three hours of attempts to repair the internal damage done, my father died.

When the surgeon walked into the waiting room, he was visibly shaken to find everyone in a lighthearted mood. He told them Duane hadn't made it through the surgery, and everything stopped. No one could move or speak for a moment, and then panic set in. Pacing, crying, holding one another. Red Dog stepped outside just as Butch was returning with his wine, and the moment Butch saw the tears in his friend's eyes, he dropped the bottle and it shattered at their feet.

Allman Brothers fans pore over photographs of the site of the accident on websites, discussing how fast he might have been going, whether or not his bike caught air on the incline of the hill, whether he hit the back of the truck or merely slipped under it. There are video tours taken from a handheld video camera that circle around the road filming the site and describing the accident. Apocryphal stories circulated about the truck having a huge ball hanging from a crane, or a hook, or a pile of pipes, and all of these things were said to have struck him. Was there a fire hydrant and did he hit it? Was he on drugs or drunk? Did the truck stop before or after he was hit?

When I was in second grade, a boy taunted me by saying my father was killed by a peach truck, and that was why the band's next record was called *Eat a Peach*. I didn't know if it was true or not, but I threw a pinecone at him hard enough to make his forehead bleed.

Of course it wasn't true. The whole scene is dissected at great length, to what end?

My father was killed in an accident, a meaningless, blameless moment that could never be changed. What else is there to know?

At Gregory's house, I had been treading lightly for a week or more, easing into the slow pace of life in Savannah, enjoying being with him. His home sits beside a wide river and is surrounded by giant oak trees covered in dusty gray Spanish moss. His little dogs bound through the house barking at every distant sound from the road; otherwise there is sweet silence and peace. My uncle has lived in many houses in many towns, but this place is the first that feels like a real home. I had so little time with him, it felt wrong to me to be there with any kind of agenda, even one as personal as wanting to talk about my father, so I waited for Duane to find his way into our talks naturally, and in time, he did amble through. One night, we watched a brutal action movie about a dirty cop with a drug habit and afterward, while Gregory put on a pot of coffee, he said, "You know, I died the night my brother died."

We stood in silence for a long moment before he went on. "I don't know if I want to tell you about that. I'd hate to hurt the way you think of me."

"You won't," I said quickly, but he didn't say any more.

The thing was, I already knew the story he was hesitating to tell. I read it in a book about the band, and Red Dog had told me, too.

Gregg and Chank left the hospital together, thinking Duane was in the clear. They went to get high. After he fixed, Gregg slumped to the floor and Chank knew he had taken too much. He tried shooting salt water into Gregg's arm, and then he tried milk.

"Milk?" I asked.

"Yeah, baby. Sometimes that could work," Red Dog said. Chank held Gregg under his arms and lifted him into his bathtub. He ran icy water over him, but he was out. He slapped his face and talked to him. He tried another shot of salt water.

"Nothing was working, and Chank knew he had to go," Red Dog said.

"He was going to leave him?" I asked.

"Baby girl, that was the way it had to be. We all knew, if somebody was gone, you had to haul ass. No point in going to jail on top of everything else, dig?"

Chank propped Gregg up at the edge of the tub and was about to leave him to die when Red Dog knocked on the door. He stood in the doorway with his mouth opening in a silent cry.

Chank said, "Don't tell me."

Gregg's small voice called out behind them, "Don't tell me what?"

In a single moment, Chank knew that Gregg was alive and Duane was dead; both feelings arrived at once, hot and cold.

Red Dog made a quick gesture with his thumb, squeezing an invisible syringe into the crook of his bent arm, and said, "We cried and shot and cried some more, and sat up together until dawn." This new loss was too huge to see all at once from so close-up.

They hid out in that high for years.

No one called to tell Twiggs that night, and he heard the news of Duane's death on the radio in the mental hospital. Twiggs told his mother not to be sad, because Duane had lived more in his twenty-four years than most people ever do. Twiggs was denied a day pass to go to Duane's funeral.

Dickey was home with his folks in Florida. His stepfather came to the club where he was playing with a friend's band to give him the news. Dickey rushed back to Macon in pure shock. Phil Walden was vacationing in Bimini when he got the call. His first thought was that the last time Phil saw him, Duane had wondered aloud if he could ever play any better than he was playing then.

Joanie walked the hospital halls trying to calm herself enough to call her parents. They had to find her sister and tell her. She called my grandmother and noticed halfway through the awful call that she was in the same wooden booth she had called her parents from when I was born. Grandma tried to track us down, but the night Duane died, Mom and I were camping next to a reservoir in Missouri with her friends Maureen and Frank, and a medical student Mom had just begun to date. The night passed without word from the outside world.

Donna's friends had brought along some mushrooms to take, and Donna finally took the hit of LSD that Duane had given her when she left Macon, a parting gift she never understood. She said he never gave her drugs; it was out of character, but he said he thought she might like it.

Donna wandered down along the water's edge, wanting to feel herself in the world as her high was blooming. Distant trees waved their arms through a blur of wood smoke and the afternoon sky took on an odd, ghostly sheen. Donna felt the pulse of the breeze that rippled the indigo water rising up through her legs and watched the sky turn gray. Then the wind kicked up all at once, no longer gentle, and the sky and water became one menacing mass. A horrible knowledge suddenly spread through her, carried by the approaching storm. She felt Duane move through her and she knew she had lost his love. Their breakup suddenly seemed permanent and fixed in place, and she knew there was no way back to him. Fear gathered around her, like a heavy woolen cloak that weighed down her slender shoulders, and the sky pulled back into itself and turned away.

Something was very wrong.

Donna's parents found a friend who was willing to drive to the campsite. When he arrived, he was told Donna was tripping and everyone decided to wait. Donna wandered back to the camp and found her friends sitting in a strange silence. Tension was in the air that she didn't understand, and no one explained. They told her it was time to head home, before the rains moved in. The wind was becoming wild; the fabric walls of the tents flapped so hard it sounded like shrieking. They packed up in the dark and loaded the cars, and reached the closest friend's house very late. My mom put me down to sleep in an unfamiliar bedroom.

Her friend Skip came to her and said, "Duane has been in an accident."

"Is he all right?"

"He's dead . . . I think," he said, trying to soften the blow.

"I cried like an animal until I had nothing left inside," my mother told me. "You slept through it all, I don't know how. I watched you sleeping and all I could think was, *Someday I will have to tell her.*"

Donna told herself I would not suffer because I would not remember him, and it relieved her. How can you lose what you never had?

The first time I heard my mother tell the story of this night, we were at a fancy restaurant celebrating New Year's Eve of 2004. She was telling two of my oldest friends simply because one of them had asked. The wind, the water, the feeling coming before the news: My two friends sat in rapt attention while Mom talked, tears shining in her eyes. Donna was wearing a party hat she had made, a pleated tin foil crown topped with an orange ostrich plume. The festive room fell away from us, leaving only black water as she described the weight of my sleeping body being lifted out of our tent.

I wanted to hear the story, but not like this. I kept eating quietly and didn't look at her. I felt she was performing for my friends, and a silent rage tightened my chest. I stood up suddenly before she was finished and went to the restroom. When I returned, I asked primly if we could move on to a lighter topic. My mother wiped her wet cheeks with her napkin and said she was sorry, smiling gently at me and at my friends.

Last year, at Thanksgiving, the day came up again. Mom and I looked through a box of photographs over pie, passing each other snapshots from Jacksonville and St. Louis, my grade school portraits mixed in with her baby pictures, shots of the ocean, pets long since passed, friends with forgotten names. Mom paused over a black-and-white image of our backs huddled together beside a body of water.

"That's where we went camping," she said. I knew exactly what she meant but still I asked.

"When?" She didn't answer. I said, "There's a picture from that day?"

"I guess so," she said.

We looked at the photograph together, a single frame, her head bent down over mine, simple, a throwaway shot that suddenly seemed like the saddest picture I had ever seen.

The night before Duane's funeral, there was a private viewing arranged at the chapel inside the funeral home. Donna, her mother, and I had flown from St. Louis. Tommie Jean was being so strong for her daughter, carrying me and keeping me occupied while Donna did what she needed to do. All Donna wanted was to see him. She walked alone down the aisle between rows of chairs to the open coffin, and as soon as she was close enough to see his face, she knew it was not him. He was not in his body anymore. His fire, his beauty, his strength were gone.

Kim came to her, gently took her by the elbow, and steered her outside. She was crying, and her knees were buckling. Someone came to them, it may have been Chank, and said they were gathering things to place in Duane's coffin before it was closed, if there was something she wanted to add. She borrowed Kim's knife and cut a lock of her hair from the nape of her neck, and gave it to him.

A huge guitar made of hundreds of fluffy flower heads stood in the front yard at the Big House beside a wheel with a broken spoke made of roses, the circle broken. The funeral happened somehow. No one remembers it quite clearly, and for that they are grateful. I have a cassette of the service. I listened to it once when I was about sixteen and never again. Delaney Bramlett and Mac Reben-nack (Dr. John) joined the band to play songs Duane loved: "The Sky Is Crying." "Melissa." "Will the Circle Be Unbroken."

Jerry was very strong and silent. Her heart was shattered, her vision narrowed down to a tunnel that ended only in the sight of her youngest son. She resolved not to let her despair show. She kept a close eye on Gregg, hoping to help him get through the day.

The Brothers played and sang beside Duane's coffin, now draped in a blanket of white roses. Jerry Wexler gave a eulogy, as he had for Otis Redding:

It was at King Curtis's funeral that I last saw Duane All-man, and Duane with tears in his eyes told me that Curtis's encouragement and praise was valuable to him in the pur-suit of his music and career. They were both gifted natural musicians with an unlimited ability for truly melodic impro-visation. They were both born in the South and they both learned their music from great black musicians and blues singers. They were both utterly dedicated to their music, and both intolerant of the false and the meretricious and they would never permit the incorporation of the commer-cial compromise to their music—not for love or money.

I remember a magic summer night of music when Duane and Delaney sat on an outdoor patio overlooking the water both playing acoustic guitars as softly as they possibly could and both of them singing—Blind Willie Johnson, Rob-ert Johnson, Jimmie Rodgers, and an unforgettable Jimmy Davis song called "Shackled and Chained." The music was incredibly pure—completely free of affect—and almost avoided personality as each of them gave himself over to

323

the ineffable beauty of southern gospel, country, and blues music as only southern musicians can.

Those of us who were privileged to know Duane will remember him from all the studios, backstage dressing rooms, the Downtowners, the Holiday Inns, the Sheratons, the late nights, relaxing after the sessions, the whisky and the music talk, playing back cassettes until night gave way to dawn, the meals and the pool games, and fishing in Miami and Long Island, this young beautiful man who we love so dearly but who is not lost to us, because we have his music, and the music is imperishable.

Dixie spoke to Donna for the first time. "He was ornery, wasn't he?" she said.

Donna thought it was a strangely perfect thing to say.

Gregg wanted to arrange for a mausoleum to be built for Duane on a plot in Rose Hill.

Phil took Donna into his office and told her he had paid the considerable amount of $6,600 for Duane's funeral, and that he would forgive Duane's debts to Capricorn. Donna realized what he was saying; he wanted her to know no further money would come from him, other than royalties as they were earned.

Donna told Jerry that I would be eligible to receive a survivor's benefit from Social Security. She wanted Granny to know that I would be provided for, but her timing felt very wrong. Jerry and Gregg were upset that she had raised the subject of money at all. Within weeks of Duane's death, rumors circulated that Donna was going to sue the band for money. Nothing could have been less true. She had met with the lawyer who had handled her divorce while she was in Macon, and he had advised her to file an action against the trucking company on my behalf, and she did. He also told her that since I was Duane's only heir, she had the right to take any of his possessions she thought I should have. The lawyer

324

said that all of Duane's possessions would be seized and put into storage. They would go through probate and it could take years to sort out. Dixie had left town, and no one else had a key to the house they shared. Donna's lawyer drove her over and when they could not find another way in, he broke a pane of glass in the back door.

It was a terrible feeling to be inside the home Duane shared with another woman. It felt wrong to look at their things and try to choose what to take. The only things that seemed familiar to her were his shirts and two guitars, and that is what she left with. Her lawyer suggested she take his car, and she said, "Are you sure?" He said it was fine.

A week or so after she left, her lawyer called her and said the probate judge needed her to bring back Duane's car, so she did.

Donna went to the Big House and left the folded pile of shirts on Berry and Linda's bed, except for the silk shirt Eric Clapton gave Duane; she took that one to Gregg.

When she returned to St. Louis, Donna gave his 1959 cherry-burst Les Paul to Joey Marshall, the friend who first introduced her to Duane. She asked him to return it to me when I turned twenty-one, and he agreed. She kept his 1959 Gibson 335 sunburst until several years later, when Tommy Talton mentioned that he did not have a guitar and she loaned it to him. Later, it was stolen from him while he was out on the road, totally breaking his heart.

The next time she heard from her lawyer, he reported that Dixie had filed her own claim against the trucking company, as Duane's common-law wife. She was asking for $2 million. But Joanie overheard Dixie talking to a friend on the telephone, saying she was still married to someone else. Joanie told Donna, and Dixie's claim was withdrawn. In the end, the company paid $16,000 in damages to Duane's estate, and the lawyer kept $8,000. Mom put the money in the bank and couldn't bring herself to use it for years.

The Brothers were scheduled to play Carnegie Hall on November 25, 1971, less than a month after Duane's death, and just five days after what would have been his twenty-fifth birthday. It was

325

one of Duane's dreams to play there with his band, and it was devastating to everyone to contemplate playing without him. The only thing worse would be not playing at all. They knew they had come too far to let their band die with Duane. He would be the first to demand that they continue. In the end, it wasn't a choice. They had to play to survive the pain.

They brought Duane's treasured Les Paul guitar with them and rested it on a stand beside Gregg onstage. They brought friends and family with them to New York for the concert. It was a solemn show at first, the band looking at one another uncertainly. Eventually, they settled into the songs they knew so well, relaxing and opening up as the night went on. The audience was with them, their hearts aching.

There were other plans in the works that Duane had looked forward to eagerly.

Claude Nobs, who was then the assistant director of the Montreux Jazz Festival, had extended an invitation to him, via Frank Fenter at Capricorn. His letter read in part:

> The idea is to have an evening devoted entirely to blues, bringing together such bluesmen as Howlin' Wolf, Chuck Berry, Freddy Below, the Myers Brothers, Hubert Sumlin, Memphis Slim and singer Koko Taylor, together with English musicians like Peter Green, John Paul Jones and Mick Taylor.
>
> I know you can help a lot. This project would, in addition, give the name of Allman a lot of publicity before the group itself comes to Europe this summer.

The world was on the cusp of opening up for the band on a huge scale. There was still the matter of completing their third album, and they returned to Criteria. They rose to the occasion in a remarkable way. Dickey wrote a beautiful new instrumental piece called "Les Brers in A Minor" and Gregg wrote "Ain't Wastin' Time No More." Both songs were rallying cries and tributes, representing their commitment to walking forward together. They also revisited "Melissa," the lovely song Duane and Gregg had brought to Butch's previous band, the 31st of February, and the lyrics and melancholy tone of the song seemed to take on new meaning now.

Crossroads, will you ever let him go?
Will you hide the dead man's ghost,
Or will he lie, beneath the clay,
Or will his spirit roll away?

The album was rounded out by the best remaining tracks from their concerts at the Fillmore East and dedicated to Brother Duane. Butch suggested it be titled *Eat a Peach* when he saw the artwork Phil had found of a peach truck taken from an old post-card. It was based on a brilliant, smart-ass quip Duane made to a reporter who asked him how he did his part for the revolution. He answered, "There is no revolution, it's evolution . . . but whenever I'm in Georgia I eat a peach for peace . . . the two-legged Georgia variety."

Twiggs was finally released from the mental hospital in December 1971. He immediately joined the Brothers down in Miami while they finished *Eat a Peach*. He became the keyboard roadie and ran the roost. There were problems to help solve; that's what he lived for. He slipped right back into it, in a less pressured role.

The last time I saw Twiggs, I was maybe five years old, visiting Macon with my mother. I have a clear memory of being held on my mother's hip, eye to eye with Twiggs. His eyes were very blue and happy. I loved him right away. He very quietly pulled up the sleeve of his T-shirt to reveal a tattoo on his shoulder.

"That's my daddy," I said.

"That's right! I love him very much, and he loved you," he said, and kissed my head.

Twiggs died in 1979 parachuting out of a plane over a New York State town called Duanesburg. Twiggs was a skillful and experienced skydiver, and it isn't known whether his chute malfunctioned or if he had decided to end his life doing something he loved. While it is almost impossible to imagine the meticulous Twiggs making a mistake with his gear, it is also hard to imagine him wanting to die at that point in his life. He was in a good place, and he was thirty-seven years old.

In the aftermath of Duane's death, Atlantic Records dropped the Allman Brothers Band. It felt like a coldhearted decision; the company clearly had no faith in the band without Duane. The Brothers had the ultimate satisfaction when *Eat a Peach* became a huge success for their new label, Warner Bros. Records.

Just before the first anniversary of Duane's death, my mother got a call from a reporter at *Newsweek* magazine asking why Duane had not been buried. His body was still in the common mausoleum at Rose Hill, and it was becoming clear that something needed to happen. Gregg had wanted to have a special crypt built of Italian marble and stained glass, but it was a hard thing to face doing. Donna thought she should probably go to Macon and talk to Gregg about it. Within the week, Joanie gave birth to her daughter, Rachael Zeff Callahan, so we went to visit. Michael and Joanie were just starting their relationship when Duane's accident happened, and they grew closer, grieving together. Michael was the smartest man Joanie had ever met, and strong enough to lean on through the most tragic of events. She was only nineteen.

For me and Rachael, it was love at first sight. She was my first real baby, a living doll. Brittany and I begged to give her a bath, push her stroller, and carry her outside—Joanie said no, no, and no, but she let me hold her on my lap if I sat very still on the sofa and was gentle. Rachael gripped my finger with her tiny hand.

On that visit, Brittany and I had a big reunion. We were chasing each other around in the front yard of the Big House when Berry came home in a stranger's car. Donna watched the driver walking up the steps, a conservatively dressed woman who looked very upset. Berry came up behind her, pale and disoriented, and went straight to bed. The woman had witnessed Berry crash his motorcycle into the side of a city bus. Kim was riding with him but couldn't convince him to go to the hospital; Berry insisted he was fine.

Linda tried to ask him what had happened, but Berry told her not to harsh his mellow. He just wanted to sleep. When Kim arrived at the Big House several minutes later, he said they should try to get Berry to the hospital.

Berry was in a dark place after Duane's death. Loss showed on him more than anyone. He said there were only three things he wanted: "I want to get high, I want to be high, and I want to stay high." Heroin and alcohol had a tight grip on him.

By the time Candy and Linda finally convinced him to go to the hospital, Berry was incoherent and in terrible pain. His helmet had struck the base of his skull and although it didn't show, he was bleeding internally. Berry died at the hospital shortly after he arrived.

The doctor assured them that they could not have saved him even if he had come in right away. His internal injuries were too grave. Still, those three wasted hours haunted everyone, especially Kim. The trauma of the accident effectively ended his love affair with Candy, loss piled upon loss. She didn't have to say she blamed Kim for not keeping her brother safe; it was clear. All of the Brothers had been charged with protecting BO from himself, and they had failed.

When Linda came home from the hospital, she knelt down beside Brittany on the porch and wrapped her arms around her. Donna held me and watched them quietly. She knew that Linda and Beebop were on the first steps of a long, dark road, the same one we had been lost on for a year.

Linda looked over her shoulder into Donna's eyes, and more than they could have expressed passed wordlessly between them.

The wide covered porch was the first thing that made them fall in love with this house. Living together with their lovers and their daughters was a perfect dream. Now, just three years later, it had all slipped away. They were about to relive everything they had been through: the guitar made of hundreds of carnations, the friends in shock, drugged to numb their pain, and the impossible task of facing Berry's parents. The Oakleys were a beautiful family, close and affectionate, whip-smart and funny. Candy and Berry were best friends. Their parents adored them.

There is a strange and undeniable symmetry in the deaths of Duane and Berry. Their accidents were so similar, only three blocks and one year apart. The uncanny similarities fed superstition and legend. The southern gothic idea that the devil was at work took root in the popular imagination. Our family was living under some kind of curse and paying a price for a deal made in the dark, where the Southern crossed the Yella Dog, as the old blues songs described the crossroads.

No one who knew Berry and Duane could stand that kind of talk, and yet their fates were undeniably entwined. "When Duane died, they should have made the box they buried him in twice as wide, because Berry was gone, too," Tuffy said.

I found a tape in Granny's garage, a radio interview with Gregory from 1974. He told a local Daytona DJ that it wasn't until Berry died that he realized that Duane was really gone. It was easier to imagine his brother out "sailing the seven seas," living an adventure. When Berry was gone, there was no way to deny that they were living in a terrible and devouring darkness, and each of the Brothers wondered if death might come for them next.

Berry Oakley deserves to be honored and mourned in his own right, separate from his lost bandmate. Like the elaborate and powerful melodies he conjured on bass, layered beneath the wild twin guitars, he is too often obscured. He was a unique and remarkable man with his own journey, his own family, and his own life. Duane's loss hurt Berry in terrible ways, and he hurt himself while mourning his brother. He felt pressure to step into the void, to be a leader and be strong. Everyone hoped time would heal him.

Within a few short weeks of Berry's death, the band began discussing who they could find to play bass with them. They had just asked a talented young piano player named Chuck Leavell to join the Brothers, rather than filling Duane's spot with another guitar player, but they needed a bass player to anchor them. They never discussed quitting. Jaimoe suggested Lamar Williams, one of his closest friends from Mississippi, who was recently home from Vietnam. Lamar started right away, a calm and anchoring presence.

"Ramblin' Man," the song that would bring the band its most wide-reaching fame, was recorded just before Berry passed.

Another startling event was entangled with the sadness of Berry's loss: He was leaving behind another child. His secret girlfriend from California was pregnant. His son, Berry Duane Oakley, was born in March 1973.

Linda, Candy, and Donna sat together in the music room at the Big House and talked about what kind of graves Berry and Duane should have. While they shared ideas, Linda sketched. It was a strangely familiar feeling, being together in the house and being creative, a dark mirroring of their carefree afternoons making art. When they were happy with the plans, they went to Gregg's apartment to show him. Donna was nervous to broach the subject with him, but he was very cool about it, relaxed and easy. Duane's headstone would be engraved with a small phoenix, his name and dates wrapped in the musical notations of "Little Martha." His Les Paul would be carved across the length of the crypt, with his diary entry from New Year's Day, 1969, inscribed beneath it:

> This year I will be more thoughtful of my fellow man, exert more effort in each of my endeavors professionally as well as personally, take love wherever I find it, and offer it to everyone who will take it. In this coming year I will seek knowledge from those wiser than me and try to teach those who wish to learn from me. I love being alive and I will be the best man I possibly can—

For Berry, Linda and Candy chose a scarab and a Hindu proverb, "Help thy brother's boat across, and Lo! Thine own has reached the shore," and a carving of his bass. Duane and Berry share a beautiful spot in beloved Rose Hill, under tall trees overlooking the train tracks and the Ocmulgee River. It became a place that fans visited by the thousands over the years, a blessing and a curse, as the graves were vandalized and laid upon. Candy took up the fight to restrict the site for private family use, and spent many years on patrol, cleaning chalk and ink from the stones, gathering guitar picks and glass slides left beside them, along with empty beer cans and partially smoked joints. It made her so unhappy, we all finally agreed to fence them in.

Back in St. Louis, after our long stay in Macon, Donna sat on the edge of the tub and ran a soapy washcloth over my back. We were finally settled back into our quiet life. Cat Stevens's "Moonshadow" was playing in the next room, and she was smoking a joint. As she held the roach up to her lips, the glowing cherry tip fell onto the cold tile floor.

I looked at her and said, "Maybe it won't ever go out." Donna thought I had learned that everything dies and I was trying to find an exception to the rule. We had all lost our innocence; even those of us too young to understand could feel the weight of the pain all around us, narrowing our own futures and making them finite. Death was inevitable and no one can choose when or how it comes. I swear I can tell on sight who has learned this lesson and who hasn't; the knowledge shows in our eyes.

When a family is broken by death, there is no clear way forward out of despair. It is easy to mistake grief for proof of love, and so refuse to relinquish it. For the first year or longer, there is a constant, grinding question that hangs over you: Stay or go? You fixate on the fantasy of willing time to roll backward. You find the precise moment before they were taken, and plant your flag there. Death becomes the territory where our love lives, a dangerous place for the living to stay for very long.

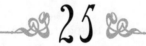

In 1974, Donna was twenty-three years old, a mother and a widow. She didn't take time to mourn, she just kept moving. Her lawyer in Macon had tried to inspire her with all the possibilities life could offer: greener pastures, a broader horizon, a larger world waiting for her. None of it came into focus until he mentioned traveling to Europe. The seed of the idea had stayed with her and taken root.

The day we left St. Louis, Donna wore an outfit she had carefully chosen for the occasion. It seemed important to look like the woman she wanted to be. She wore a forest-green felt hat with a wide floppy brim, snakeskin pumps, and a vintage dress from the 1940s. She was so thin you could see her hip bones clearly through the fabric. She carried a sweater with a plush fox fur collar that had belonged to her grandmother, Zeff. Tommie Jean gave her an art deco ring with a tiny emerald set in the center of two silver waves speckled with diamonds. She presented the ring to Donna in a quiet moment over dinner the night before we left, and told her daughter she was living the kind of adventurous life she herself had always dreamed of. Donna was surprised by how supportive her mother was of her plan, which wasn't much of a plan at all, just a place: Paris.

In the airport, I was trailing slightly behind my mom, tugging on my droopy purple tights and occasionally dropping my bulky princess coat with the fur collar and cuffs. Before long I was whining loudly, begging to be carried. I was five, and far too tall to be toted, but my mom hiked me up on her hip and gave a little groan every time my feet in their dirty white Buster Browns hit her in the thigh as she walked.

Once in Paris, we stayed in a *pension de famille,* or boarding house, on the rue d'Alsace, across the street from the Jardin du Luxembourg, where my mom took me to puppet shows and carousel rides. She wrote letters to Linda Oakley about taking French classes and walking through museums. Linda wanted to come and join us.

It rained almost every day that autumn. At first it was very beautiful and romantic, the darkened cobblestones, the rippling surface of the Seine, but Donna was starving for sunshine on her skin. We hit the road with a touring band called Gong, in hopes of seeing a little of the countryside. Giorgio Gomelsky, the esteemed rock promoter, was one of Donna's contacts in Paris, and he had arranged for her to travel with the band, thinking it would be fun for us to be out with people. When the grim weather did not subside, Donna told Linda plans were changing. "Meet me in Casablanca!" she wrote, and Linda and Brittany did just that.

We traveled all over Morocco together in the White Elephant, a Volkswagen van. We stayed in North Africa for ten months, until Brittany and I had to start first grade. Our mothers were fearless, driving through the desert, listening to Om Kalsoum on a tape deck, smoking hash, taking pictures, and shopping in the Medinas. They found they only needed one crucial phrase to explain their situation, to answer the only question everyone asked, "Where is your husband?" They learned to say, "Mon mari est mort."

I am back in Daytona now, driving Granny's bright red Cadillac over the Silver Beach drawbridge. The V-8 engine has a badass growl that I will miss when I return to my silent Volvo. I'm headed toward the ocean.

Small wooden houses sit half eaten by the wet salty air and it feels like home to me, like Jacksonville in the seventies. The air and the light here are gentle and infused with the sea. I imagine my father as a teen looking at the blue-green water, the Intracoastal Waterway flowing below the curving concrete bridge; he's riding his first motorcycle, buzzing up over the water until he can see the ocean ahead of him.

I park the car in Granny's garage and notice the cool, dusty smell of it. In the corner is the Radio Flyer wagon Granny had painted a sparkly blue at my whim. I walk through into the kitchen and watch Granny quietly crocheting in her chair before she notices me standing there. She is very methodical and careful with herself now. She neatly folds and stacks her newspaper while she reads it, then recycles it as soon as she's done. She works through two crossword puzzles a day and says she feels no need to succeed at them, just enjoys the attempt. She radiates a relaxed wisdom, telling stories punctuated by her own laughter. When I am settled in across from her on the couch, she recounts a conversation she once had with a young woman at a rock concert. Jerry was sitting alone in the crowd, waiting for Gregg to play. A girl in the row ahead of her kept turning around to stare. She finally leaned over the back of her seat and shouted in Granny's face, "I know you're somebody! I can tell. Who are you?"

"Of course I'm somebody," Jerry replied. "Aren't you?" She has told me this quip many times and it always makes both of us laugh.

She says she doesn't worry about anything now. Sure, she has her concerns, but she knows how destructive it is to "chew on a thing." She makes it seem like a simple choice, and what else would it be? She says she can't change "a feather of it." I never want to forget the way she talks. I try to pay close attention to her rhythms

335

and her sayings, and I take notes before I go to bed. We fall into easy silence. I mimic her stillness until it becomes my own. I link my breaths to hers, steadily in and out, and I am calmed. I find a spaciousness within myself, a peaceful kingdom to dwell within, like meditating. So many things she casually expresses to me feel like life lessons, sought by all, taught by Buddhists and therapists. She naturally knows how to live in the moment. She appreciates sitting and breathing and being. The loud blast of air from the air conditioner mutes her high voice. She looks good, fit and strong. I can't believe she is ninety-five years old. She is so sweet to me. Holding her, saying good night, I feel connected to her. I always have been. I am so glad we have a week to spend together.

A little bronze statue that Ellen Hopkins, Duane's friend from Jacksonville, made of my father stands under a glass bell on the top of Granny's bookshelf. In the shape of him, the curve of his back, his hands in his pocket, the slight tilt of his head, you can see that Ellen loved him and memorized him. The statue looks like a smaller version of the Three Musketeers sculptures hanging just above him, the figures I have been looking at all my life and he looked at all of his. I don't know if Duane ever found this kind of simple peace. I don't know if he was ever satisfied or knew what he was worth to us, and to everyone who ever listened to him play. I will always wonder what age and experience would have brought him, and what the songs played into his old age would have sounded like. Most of all, I wonder what kind of a father he would have been.

Suddenly, Granny looks up from her crocheting—another pair of slippers for Gregory—and asks me if she has ever told me about the night Duane died. She was home alone when she got the call, in this very room. She was in such deep shock when she hung up the phone, she had to sit down. The nearest chair was pulled up to the dining table, so she gathered up her knees close to her body and sat there for a while. Then she heard Duane's unmistakable approach.

"I was sitting with my knees up and my head down at that table there, and I heard his boots on the driveway. I could always tell my boys by the sound of their walk as soon as they hit that driveway. Duane popped through the door and said, 'Mama, you're crying.' I said, 'They told me you were dead.' He said 'Look at me. Now, who would have told you a thing like that?' I know he was telling me that his spirit is here and always will be, and I wasn't the least bit afraid. He came to comfort me. When it's happening, and they're here, you know it's them. Without a doubt."

Jerry stayed with Jo Jane and her husband, Penn, and daughter Eden after Duane's death. She grieved deeply with the numbing aid of whisky. It took her many years to return to herself, but once she did, she got sober and seemed truly healed. I have always wondered how she found the strength to weather so many losses, but I see she keeps them close and it helps her.

She says Duane came that night to tell her he was not dead and would never be. Whatever work he was here to do was still undone. I will put the Allman Brothers Band on my headphones and sleep in my father's bedroom tonight, breathing the same air as his mother in the room down the hall. I will imagine him sitting up late in the living room playing along, his boot heel tapping out Jaimoe's eccentric patterns, smiling in the dark. Let this house flip back and forth through layers of time so we can share this roof tonight.

"Duane is still here around us in spirit, because he's not finished with what he came to do," Granny says. "Maybe he's here to protect you, or maybe he's here to inspire Gregg to write more music, or we don't know what it is. He's inspiring people in the world, all over the world." She stands up and hugs me tightly before going to bed. I press my cheek against hers and try to memorize its softness and warmth. "I love you and I always have," she says.

"I love you, too, Granny."

I fall deeply asleep and have an incredible dream.

I am standing at the foot of a staircase with my father and I am really looking at him. His eyes look tired, his left eye slightly off center, drifting. He is delicate somehow, or refined, like he took great care in dressing. His buttoned dress shirt is very white and pressed; his black pants break over his boots and barely graze the floor. He is warm and solid and his shoulders are relaxed and even. We stand between the closed front door and the empty stairs and talk. I tell him I am in love with a young man, and I ask if it is ever possible to know if someone is truthful. I notice his hair is cut the same way as mine, softly framing his face. He says it's nothing he doesn't understand, this situation I am in . . . young love and its games. He doesn't say anything more, not dismissive exactly, but strong. His presence and the way he is looking at me draw my confusion out of me and I relax. I feel how well he knows me.

Then, we walk through the door and into the night. It has rained and the city street is slick and shining with bright red blurs from reflected taillights. I look down and see a sturdy black guitar case balanced at the handle, resting naturally in my father's hand. I hadn't noticed it before. He says it's his good guitar and he needs to lock it in the trunk of his car and points up the street. I wait for him, watching as he walks up the block to a white car. He unlocks the trunk and lays his case inside.

A yellow taxi is idling right in front of me, beyond the parked cars at the curb, and it seems it is waiting for us. The driver gets impatient, rolls down the window, and whistles loudly after Duane. Under his breath, he calls my father a lowlife.

We slide quickly into the slippery vinyl seat of the cab, closely tucked together. It suddenly feels that a spell has been broken and the formal mood we were in is gone. Sitting close, we are very happy, laughing in the middle of a funny conversation. His eyes are shining and looking right into mine. His cheeks are high and rosy, his red whiskers like curtains pulled back from a stage, revealing the main show—his crooked and beautiful smile. He says he is so happy to be looking at me. We hug and I feel the raindrops warming on his back, the cloth soft and damp under my palms. I grip him so tightly, I start to cry.

"I can't live without you. I won't," I say.

He tells me again how good it is to be here with me right now, *and tips my chin up to look into my eyes. He says if it had been the way it was before—if he was dead and we were apart—it would be impossible for both of us.*

I see then that we are saying goodbye. Panic starts to fill me like static rising to the surface of my skin. I feel my back against the bed and hear my pulse quicken. My face is wet and my heart is desperate. I push my feet against the covers and raise myself up until I am leaning against the bedroom wall, awake now. I have wrapped both arms around myself while sleeping, gripping my own ribs tightly, an echo of his arms around me, but they are only my hands, and he is gone.

A bit of wisdom comes into my mind, like a song breaking through static on a radio, and I know it came from him:

Do what you love and own who you are.

Time is precious and death is real.

So is Art: It defies them both.

Outro

If you have ghosts then you have everything.

—Roky Erikson

There is something in this night's quiet and the way my hair feels against my face when I sit up in bed that brings you to me. The blood in my veins sings and our story feels alive in me now. I no longer feel ennobled by my reluctance to let you go.

The tone of your guitar is the voice you use to call out to me: warm, round, and resonant. It is my substitute for you standing in the street calling me in to dinner. It is your half of the argument we would have had about bad boys and what they want. It is how you would have sounded saying, *No you cannot, you will not, this is my house and these are my rules*. It is the voice you would have used to soothe my fears when dark dreams shook me at night. It is the sound of your praise when I do something well and it is your wisdom handed down to me. The sound of your guitar tells me all I will ever know of your love.

In the force of your intention and the perfection of your tone I can hear everything that ever happened to you, good or bad, the raw and ragged edge and the center worn so smooth and kind by the tireless efforts of your hands. Your fingers pulling, floating, teasing each note, sound as direct as your eye trained on me. Listening to you, knowledge is gained, and help is received.

Before I could speak the words your brother sang, I knew the spaces the music created intimately. You built me a house of familiar rooms and I marveled at the distant rafters, the dark corners, the vines curling and blooming up the high walls. You wander beside me here as long as the songs play on. If I could I would ask you: Do musicians know what they give us? Do they know where they take us, only to leave us to find our own ways home, back from the depths of their dream?

Before there was a fence around your grave, I sat beside you, and now I can only stare through the black bars, down at the inscribed marble slab and the little carved angel, replaced, after being repeatedly stolen, with money raised by your fans. My name is carved on the marble pedestal under her feet. The angel is my tiny proxy, invoking my love. An identical angel stands over Brittany's name at the foot of Berry's grave beside you. When we were little, we lay on the white marble slabs above you, Brittany and I making beds of our fathers' graves. I pictured you inside like Snow White in her glass coffin, your heart still but visible, a red bloom in a cage of bone, your face perfect and calm like a prince, asleep.

I have carved out a place inside me where I keep everything I know about you, each detail a colored piece of glass in the window of a chapel built for dreaming. This is the closest we can be, when I'm on my knees, felled by the pain, trying to find you down in the flood of feelings. I go to this temple in my mind when I don't know where else to go.

Did you light a candle for your father and sit in a worn wooden pew where children like us carved their names with secret pocket-knives? When you were sick with fever, did you ever feel the weight of his warm palm resting on your forehead, relief passing through you whether you imagined it or not? Did you give his love to your-self and call it grace?

I wonder. Maybe you were always stronger than me, and turned outward instead of in. Maybe your father lived in the clouds, a god of distant thunder, a keeper of cold stars who inspired only inde-pendence in you. Maybe you never imagined Bill at all, and used every part of your body and mind only for music, speeding away from the pain on your motorcycle.

I know you would not approve of the uncountable days I have spent in bed, curled toward the wall whispering to you, picturing your hand reaching out to me while hot tears roll from my eyes. I used to believe the pain of losing you would kill me with my own hand. I want to be where you are and I am so tired of waiting. You would say just what your mama said when I told her how much sadness I carry around. She fairly shouted, "Get rid of it!" There is no bringing you back here. You won't come down again, not even for me. There's no use in crying.

I feel like the window is closing now; the breeze blowing you back to me is flagging. The writing, the traveling, the daily consid-eration of your life will wind down and I will be alone again, with-out the shadow of you resting beside me. I want to believe you will stay close to me. I tell myself you live in my blood and bones and you will come when I need you. I will stop seeking you constantly now. I will know you are in me and not out in the world. I know there is more than being left behind.

We are tied together as surely as a string is wound tightly through the tuning peg of a guitar. The connection between us is physical, actual, real.

I want you to know I understand you better than I used to. There is detail to my longing now. There are moments fully imagined in places where questions used to be. I have walked down streets where you walked, and I carried you with me as I traveled. Instead of feeling the weight of you in the center of my chest like the echo of a punch, a new sensation has bloomed in me. It is a longing I do not recognize, for a life of my own. I suddenly want the speed of life to pull me forward; I want to live unafraid. I missed the lesson you played so clear and strong every night of your own grown life, the lilting line from "Joy to the World" winding wild through your hands in the middle of your song. You tried to tell me from where you are to live my life. I am sorry it took me so long to hear you.

Acknowledgments

Every detail found in these pages was given to me by a person who loved my father. The moments that we shared enriched my sense of who Duane was, and for that I am grateful. I am humbled by their generosity, openness, and honesty.

Thanks to my family, in all of its permutations. I love you all so much.

Granny A, your wit and grace inspire me every day. This book and this family would not exist without your strength and love.

Mama Donna, thank you for allowing me to trample through your delicate garden of memories in my dirty boots. You are beautiful, fierce, and talented beyond measure. We made it through together.

Jo Jane Pitt, your memories, letters, journals, and photographs are the life's blood of this book. It would not exist without your love and support.

Joanie Callahan, you are the one I could always count on to talk to me about my father. I am so grateful for that and for your constant belief in me. And yes, I know, you used to kiss my butt.

Tommie Jean, Grandma, thank you for all of your support and love. Your belief in me means more than you know. I see your heart.

Linda Miller, you were a maternal force in my life before memory. Your words and insights carried me through the darkest moments. I feel I know Berry because of you. Thank you for always being there.

Candy Oakley, thank you for our walks and talks through Rose Hill. I carry some of your strength and determination with me always.

Brittany Oakley, my sister, we have shared so much on this long hard road. You understand in ways no one else ever will.

Linda Trucks, thank you for sharing your stories with absolute honesty.

Rachael Interdonato, my girl. You live in my heart, sun-kissed and running down the beach. Thanks for sharing your beautiful family with me. You are my home.

Gregory, you are beautiful inside and out. Thank you for sharing your love for my pop with me, and for answering my many questions during a time of healing. You handle everything with such kindness, humor, and strength. Your voice is the sound I carry in my heart every day.

Jaimoe, you are wise and full of love. More than anyone, you brought the process of making music into focus for me. I am so thankful for you—the backbeat and the backbone of this whole circus.

Butchie, you are always first in line to tell the world about what made Duane so special and powerful. Thank you for reminding me I am still Gragrie, the same kid who asked you, "What are *you* lookin' at?"

Dickey, I tried to do justice to the love and respect you and my father had for each other, always. The sound of your guitars together carried me through this journey and taught me so much.

Bonnie Bramlett, beautiful and fiery woman, you stood toe-to-toe with these talented men and sang your song. I treasure you. Thank you for sharing with me.

Johnny Sandlin, the sweetest of them all, you and Ann opened your home, your family, and your memories to me. You were the first one I came to, and I am so lucky I did. Thank you for introducing me to the legendary gentlemen of Muscle Shoals: David Hood, Jimmy Johnson, and Spooner Oldham. I thank each of you for your memories, your time, and for playing the soundtrack of my life.

Rick Hall, thank you for my enjoyable time at FAME, and for sharing your memories in such a vivid and exciting way. And thank you for giving Duane his shot.

Pete Carr, thank you for sharing your memories and the only picture of my parents together.

Paul Hornsby, thank you for your insights and the songs you played me on your piano.

Bill Connell, thank you for bringing the Allman Joys to life for me with your stories.

John McEuen, thank you for sharing your memories about the wild L.A. days.

Rob McNeish, the letter my father wrote your mother, Holly, is a perfectly captured moment in time. Thank you so much for sharing it with me.

Thom Doucette, thank you for your honesty. I could truly see my father through your eyes and I am so grateful for that.

Thank you to Twiggs Lyndon's brothers—John, Skoots, and A.J.—for your incredible act of love: giving me my father's guitar. Thank you for sharing your memories and Twiggs's remarkable photos. Twiggs's jacket protected and inspired me while I wrote.

Scott Boyer, thank you for the long talk and for graciously allowing me to use "Please Be with Me," the title of your beautiful song, as the title of this book. It's a song I've always relied on to find my father's heart. It works every time.

Jerry Jemmott, thank you for teaching me to chant "Nam myoho renge kyo" in front of a huge golden Buddha. That was quite a day.

Mac Rebennack, you said, "Your daddy went to heaven on the back of a red-tailed hawk. Never forget that. Light a candle for him and be proud of your ancestry." I won't, I will, and I am. Thank you for your friendship and your music.

Floyd Miles, thank you for your constant love and support of Gregory and Granny, and your generous time spent with me.

Boz Scaggs, thank you for telling me such a great story, in the same warm voice you sing in. A vivid tale.

George Gruhn, thank you for the fascinating conversations. I hope to meet you and the snakes someday.

Charlie and Richie Ingui, thank you for sharing your memories with me.

Ronnie Hawkins, thanks for the talk, and for telling me I am "as sweet as a mother's love." So are you.

John Paul Hammond, thank you for sharing your story and your music with me. You are the real deal.

Thank you to Albhy Galuten, Karl Richardson, and Sam Hare for bringing the *Layla* sessions to life. It was a real challenge, and you three saved the day.

Warren Haynes and Derek Trucks, watching you both play has been an education and a gift. Thank you for answering my questions and being true friends. You are living proof that Duane continues to inspire. He would be so proud of you.

Oteil Burbridge, thank you for telling me I already know what it feels like to play music: like giving a gift to someone you love. Thank you for your friendship.

Marc Quinones, thank you for being a brother to me and to the band.

Colonel Bruce Hampton, you are a remarkable man and I thank you for sharing your memories of Duane and for teachin' the young'uns how to fly.

Brian Farmer, just 'cuz. Thank you for all the support and love, brother.

Chank Middleton, you gave me the biggest laugh of all when you told me what Mama A said to you about life on the road: "It's like going in the asshole of everywhere and seeing the front of nothing." True!

Kim Payne, you are the salt in my soup. You gave this book the kick in the pants it needed. Thank you for your love, your humor, and your honesty.

Tuffy Phillips, sitting with you was one of the great highlights of my journey. You are all heart, but I won't tell anybody.

Judi Petty, thank you for your loving memories of Twiggs and Joe Dan. You're a peach.

Ellen Hopkins, thank you for the stories and the flight with dragons.

John Rosenberg, thank you for years of support and sage advice. You are a true friend.

Bert Holman, thank you for your friendship and for sharing your knowledge with me. You keep the wheels rolling.

Jonny Podell, you are the original badass with a big heart. I can't wait to read your book.

Vaylor Trucks, thank you for sharing your remarkable understanding of how Duane and Dickey played together so harmoniously. You have a brilliant mind.

Michael Lehman, thank you for your tireless support of my uncle and your kindness to me.

E. J. Devokaitis, thank you for your constant support, your encyclopedic knowledge of all things ABB, and your tireless enthusiasm. You are my brother.

Thanks to Jared Wright, Andrea Adgie, Scott Bergin, Richard Brent, and Jeromy Haines for assisting E.J.

John Lynskey, thank you for your friendship and your belief in this book.

Amalie R. Rothschild, thank you for your beautiful photographs, your insights into the Fillmore East, and your warm friendship.

John Gellman, what a gift to find such beautiful shots of my father after all this time! Thank you for sharing them so graciously.

Stephen Paley, thank you for the incredible photographs and for sharing your memories.

Salli Jo Doud, thank you for the great picture. What a treasure.

Maggie Olive, thank you for sharing your father Jim Higgins's photos with me.

Sydney Smith, Albert J. Sullivan, and Jeff Albertson, thank you for the use of your remarkable photographs. They bring him home to me.

To Duane and Gregg's childhood friends in Daytona: Albert Teebagy, Penny Vernon, and Mina Sue Kelly. Thank you for your stories and your kindness.

Jim Carter, thank you for sharing memories and for being my Granny's guardian angel.

Joanne Patten, thank you for sharing Larry Beck's tapes with me. I couldn't have given him his rightful place in my father's story without your help.

Rob Hosier, thank you for telling me about the world of Castle Heights, and sending the yearbooks, pictures, and mementos of that time.

Thanks to my father's first champions in the music business, Phil Walden and Jerry Wexler, for their passionate and eloquent conversations over the years. I am so grateful I spoke to both of them before they left us. May they rest in peace.

Jim Marshall, another friend I lost along the way—you were one of the most unique and talented people I have ever known, with a huge heart and a mouth to match. I miss you. And thank you to Jay Blakesberg for enabling me to share Jim's beautiful photographs.

In memory of Joseph "Red Dog" Campbell: You showed your love for me and my father every single time I saw you. There will never be another like you.

We also lost Joe Dan Petty and Michael Callahan during the years I was writing, and they are both so loved and so missed.

To my nearest and dearest friends, who walked beside me while I carried this book on my back. I could not have made it without your love, insight, humor, and chutzpah. I love each of you so much.

Barbara Herman, you held my hand and kicked my ass, and you

knew precisely which I needed in tough moments. I never would have started without your push, and I never would have finished without your love. You are a will in heels.

Catherine Zimmer, thank you for thirty years of friendship. Your keen mind, immense strength, and ridiculous humor help me survive.

Dana Landis, you are my sister. You see things more clearly than anyone and you are stronger than you know. I am thankful for you every day.

Noah Landis, thank you for sharing this lifelong love with me. There are no words, only songs for you.

Zeena Meurer, thank you for your constant love and belief in me. Our friendship is one of my life's great gifts. Your careful reading did this book so much good.

Matt Friedson, my fellow writer and romantic, thank you for your careful readings, pep talks, and cutting wit.

Aya de Leon, another woman who picked up a pen and found her way, you are my spiritual bandmate. Walking with you keeps my feet on the ground.

Thank you to my sweet friends Katie Danielson, Christine Rotolo, and Greg Dale, who read my drafts, fed me beautiful meals, played me songs, and let me cry on their shoulders.

Sasha Voynow, every important thing I know about living like a grownup I learned with you or from you. Thank you for the many years of love and support.

Karinne Dotinga Quinn, thank you for your careful guidance and friendship. You've helped me become stronger than I have ever been before.

Madeline Feingold, I could not have done this without your wisdom and constant support. I don't know how I feel about anything until I tell you.

Thanks to my publisher and editor, Julie Grau. Your patience and understanding through the often difficult gestation and birth of this book meant everything to me. You made this book stronger in every way. Thank you for your trust and your understanding.

351

Thanks to the kind, focused, and organized Laura Van der Veer. I am grateful for all of your help.

Thanks to my agent, Richard Pine of Inkwell Management. The way we met was the most magical moment of this entire process. I have no doubt he led me to you. You saw the potential in me and in this project from the first paragraph of the first letter. I am so lucky to have you in my corner. You are my champion.

I share this story with all of the Allman Brothers' kids. I hope this book returns a piece of our shared history to you and to your children. Nothing would make me prouder. With love to Michael Allman, Devon Allman, Elijah Blue Allman, Delilah Island Allman, Layla Brooklyn Allman, Kimberly Betts, Christie Betts, Jessica Betts, Duane Betts, Jahonie Johnson, Cajai Johnson, Brittany Oakley, Berry Duane Oakley, Vaylor Trucks, Melody Trucks, Seth Trucks, and Elise Trucks, and the children of the crew: Rachael Callahan, Hope Phillips, Michael Phillips, Jody Petty, J. J. Petty, and Clark Bush.

Letters

What follows are selected letters that appear or are referenced in the body of the book and are reprinted here as facsimiles.

This year I will be more thoughtful of my fellow man, exert more effort in each of my endeavors professionally as well as personally, take love wherever I find it, and offer it to everyone who will take it. In this coming year I will seek knowledge from those wiser than me and try to teach those who wish to learn from me. I love being alive and I will be the best man I possibly can —

Duane Allman

Duane's first entry in the appointment calendar Rick Hall gave him, January 1, 1969

RECORDING AND
PUBLISHING COMPANY, INC.

603 E. AVALON
P. O. BOX 2238
MUSCLE SHOALS, ALA.

PHONE 381-0801

Skinny Gorilla Girl That I Love,

you've been gone three hours now, and I'm nice and drunk trying not to remember that you're gone. I thought about cutting my house in half and sending half to you so at least we'd be under the same roof, but my old heart's aching so bad I don't think I could pull a saw to do it. Jai Johnny took two of those blackbirds and he's really flying and doesn't know it: what a groove. He's sure a fine friend. I sure do love you and miss you and I just wish that this pen ~~pen~~ would say what I want to say. Oh mama, I need you so bad this minute I could bust. Don't ever make me watch you leave me again, I don't think I could handle it at all. I'd better quit this before I get in my car and come after you.

I'll Love You Till There's No Till,

Duane

From Duane to Donna, Muscle Shoals, Alabama, February 4, 1969

355

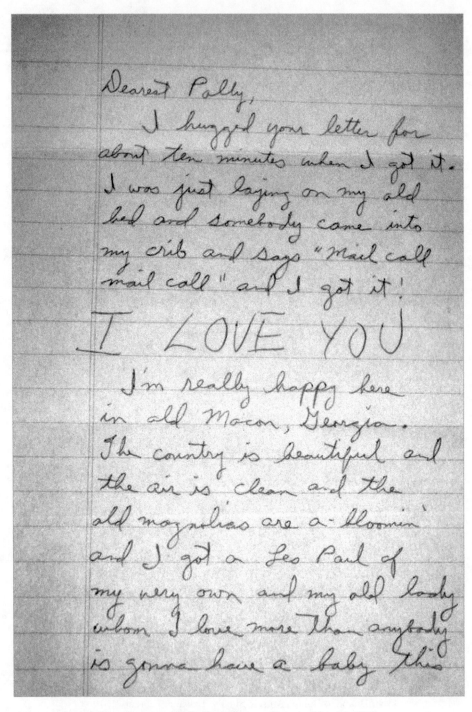

Dearest Patty,

I hugged your letter for about ten minutes when I got it. I was just laying on my old bed and somebody came into my crib and says "Mail call mail call" and I got it!

I LOVE YOU

I'm really happy here in old Macon, Georgia. The country is beautiful and the air is clean and the old magnolias are a-bloomin' and I got a Les Paul of my very own and my old lady whom I love more than anybody is gonna have a baby this

From Duane to Holly Barr, Macon, Georgia, May 16, 1969

356

coming November ❦ and Gregg's here
gigging with me and I got about
the greatest band I ever did hear
together and a Marshall amp and
two drummers and I quit taking
speed and I been going swimming
nekkid in the creek.

I quit my session job to get
into this group thing again and we'll
probably be moseying on out to
California in a month or so. I
even bought a car and a box guitar
a Gibson Heritage and it sounds real
pretty but I can't do those things
ya'll do with it. The name of the
band is the Allman Bros. and we
mostly play music to fuck by and
it's too loud but it's sure fun.
My old eyelids are drooping down

357

so I'm gonna go to bed, but
write to me real soon and God
bless you and yours. My address is
309B College St.
Macon, Georgia
Oh yeah! I got to take Zelma
Redding (Otis's widow) motorcycle
riding last weekend. She's really
great.

Love Always,
Duane

I had a picture of me I was
gonna send you but I can't
find it. I'll send it next time.
My best to lucky old Ralph Barr →

358

Deer Leenda,

What you doin? Nuthin, probably, you so lazee. How is little Peeglet doin? Is she bein good? I sure do miss her. You take good care of her but don't spoil her to bad so she be a brat like you. Of B.O. what you say? Co you steens? As you might be able to tell B.O. ees flipping out up here. We are ending up paying more dues than we figured on before getting off the ground and we still don't have a definate date set for the album.

We were supposed to have a job in New York this weekend + next week but that fell through and the thought of just hanging till next weeks gig is a drag but there doesn't seem to be anything I can do about it or anything else and that is

From Berry to Linda, Boston, Massachusetts, June 12, 1969

fucking my mind up to. Fuck!?

I am writing by candle light
so I can't see very good but I'm
trying. You know what a fine writer
I am. Boston is really a coockoo
place, its different, really different
everybody here is a freak + nobody
gives a shit its nuts, and boy
do they talk funny, kind of like
New Yawkas. It is also very
funny, at least most of the places
were been. The place were been staying
in for the last week is er hammered
as the Pick Wick without furniture.
yeack ☻

We've been practicing every day
but not getting much done. the
lethargy rate is too high.

Tomorrow Johnny Winter is playing
here for the whole weekend I guess
we'll be around the club getting
drunk watching him. The guy
that owns the club has about four

cases of beer and some wine in the big old band room each night when there's a gig so we go there and drink it all up ha ha
There was a great band there last weekend Delaney & Bonnie & Friends and the Serfs to we sat around and got drunk with them and rapped.
Tell everybody I said Hi. Sure wish we could play down there I miss it.

I thought of a new lick today for a song so I'm going to go get the gitar and see if I can remember it.

Be good and take care of little one

Love B.O.

We left South Carolina not long after I wrote you Fri. and finally got here Sat. about 11: AM. What a funky place New York really ees.

We set up and ran some tunes down for a few hours Sat. eve. but didn't record till Sun. We did Trouble no More & Cross to Bear & Dreams and they came out really well. The producer is a good cat to work with, He's Eenglish, and everything is working out pretty well. Today we were

From Berry to Linda, New York, New York, August 14, 1969

362

working on Black Hearted
Woman all day but didn't finish
cause we changed it around so it
is more together and were jeist doing
part at a time. Its going to come
out good.

We are staying at a funk
Hotel, its clean though just old,
called the Wellington but they were
heetling us cause some group
split without paying them, so Atlantic
is putting us up at the Holiday Inn
on 5 7th St. and weare checking
out of here & in there in the Morn.
Needless to say it will be much

much better. It won't make
me feel like were staying in
a funky city I'll be able to get it
together better. Leaving our great
little apartment and checking in
a funky Hotel just spaces me out
too bad, you know. Its like being
in an old movie.

Write to the Holiday Inn
on ~~57th St~~ 440 West 57th St.
N.Y. N.Y. to me B.D., O.K.
Bees Leenda.

smooch you Love, B.D.
& leeda

Holiday Inn ® OF VIRGINIA BEACH-VIRGINIA

"BRIDGE TUNNEL"

5725 NORTH HAMPTON ROAD • U. S. RT. #13

VIRGINIA BEACH, VIRGINIA 23455

Thanksgiving Day

Dear Donna,

Well, our tour got off to a really great start, we didn't even play our first date here in Virginia. I'm not feeling too good at all about the whole thing tonight, I guess I'm pretty disappointed and more than a little homesick for you and the baby. I guess I'm tired, too.

Did you have turkey? I sure hope so. They had a giant spread here at the Holiday Inn and it was pretty good.

I'm too sad to write, I'll write more later after something good happens.

All My Love Forever,
D——

Your Host...
from Coast to Coast®

From Duane to Donna, Virginia Beach, Virginia, November 27, 1969

"A LANDMARK OF N.Y.C."

HOTEL CHELSEA
New York

AT SEVENTH AVENUE
WEST TWENTY THIRD STREET
NEW YORK, N. Y. 10011

CABLE ADDRESS • HOCHELSEA • NEW YORK
TELEPHONE CHELSEA 3-3700

Bees Leenda,

Am up early this mornin as we are leavin to go to a gig. I'm sittin here lookin out the window at Red Dog as he has wiped out a Volkswagon on his way out of the parking lot and has traffic hung up for two blocks.

LARGE and SOUND-PROOF ROOMS

From Berry to Linda, New York, New York, February 14, 1970

HOTEL CHELSEA
New York

AT SEVENTH AVENUE
WEST TWENTY THIRD STREET
NEW YORK, N. Y. 10011

CABLE ADDRESS • HOCHELSEA • NEW YORK
TELEPHONE CHELSEA 3-3700

It's pretty funny though,
really.

I sure does miss you
and your Bee Bop. Give
her a hug.

As far as I can see we
should be home Tuesday
sometime. Can't Wait
to be back in the arms of my

HOTEL CHELSEA
New York

AT SEVENTH AVENUE
WEST TWENTY THIRD STREET
NEW YORK, N. Y. 10011

CABLE ADDRESS • HOCHELSEA • NEW YORK
TELEPHONE CHELSEA 3-3700

Bees

Squeeze!

Love, B.D.

LARGE and SOUND-PROOF ROOMS

Sunday

Dearest Spoon,

Thanks for the sweet secret message. Please try and have a little faith, honey, and everything will be alright.

Eric Clapton has asked me to join his band. I really don't know what to do, but don't mention a word of this to anyone at the house, or leave this letter where others might read it and do something foolish. It would mean about $5,000 a week to us, as well as a home in England and a lot of things we'd like to have.

From Duane to Donna, Milwaukee, Wisconsin, September 5, 1970

We've cut a really super album together, and Eric plans a European as well as an American tour, and the receipts would be phenomenal on both. I'll be getting 20% of all of it, so I plan to do both of those tours with him.

I'll write more later when my thought is more stable. I'm really up in the air right now.

All my love to Gragin and everyone there.

Love Always,

Duane

P.S. Shh!

Photo Credits

All photos in the book appear courtesy of Galadrielle Allman, with the following exceptions:

Pages 119 and 134: courtesy of Steven Paley

Pages 151, 166, and 244: courtesy of the Estate of Twiggs Lyndon

Page 203: courtesy of Sidney Smith

Page 232: © A. J. Sullivan

Pages 262, 286, and 313: © Jim Marshall Photography LLC

Page 300: © Jeff Albertson/Corbis

Page 274: courtesy of Jeffrey Mayer

Insert:

Page 3 (top right): courtesy of Castle Heights Military Academy

Pages 4 (top and bottom) and 13 (top): courtesy of Stephen Paley

Pages 5 (top), 8 (bottom), 9 (top), 10 (top), and 11 (middle): courtesy of the Estate of Twiggs Lyndon

Page 5 (bottom): courtesy of Pete Carr

Page 9 (bottom): courtesy of Sally Jo Doud

Page 10 (middle): © Bob Gruen/www.bobgruen.com

Pages 10 (bottom) and 12 (top and bottom): © Jim Marshall
   Photography LLC
Page 11 (bottom): courtesy of the Estate of Tom Doud
Page 13 (middle): courtesy of Sydney Smith
Page 14 (bottom): courtesy of the Estate of James F. Higgins

ABOUT THE AUTHOR

GALADRIELLE ALLMAN is the producer of *Skydog: The Duane Allman Retrospective* (Rounder Records). She lives in Berkeley, California. This is her first book.